Rewriting
the
Self

With a new introduction by the author

Mordechai Rotenberg

Rewriting the Self

Psychotherapy and Midrash

Transaction Publishers
New Brunswick (U.S.A.) and London (U.K.)

Library of Congress Catalog Number: 2003066303
ISBN: 0-7658-0567-7
Printed in the United States of America

Library of Congress Cataloging-in-Publication Data

Rotenberg, Mordechai.
    [Re-biographing and deviance]
    Rewriting the self : psychotherapy and Midrash / Mordechai Rotenberg ; with a new introduction by the author.
        p. cm.
    Originally published: Re-biographing and deviance. New York : Praeger, 1987. With new introd.
    Includes bibliographical references (p.) and index.
    ISBN 0-7658-0567-7 (pbk. : alk. paper)
        1. Psychiatry and religion. 2. Midrash—Psychology. 3. Psychotherapy. I. Title.

RC455.4.R4R68   2004
616.89—dc22
                                                        2003066303

TO MY MOTHER:
WHO PROVIDED THE ROOTS
AND TO MY CHILDREN:
THE LIVING FRUITS

Contents

Introduction to the Transaction Edition   ix
Preface   xiii

1   Introduction: Living through Midrashic Interpretation   1

2   Narrative "Missionarism" in Dialectic Psychotherapy   24

3   The Midrash and "Biographic Rehabilitation"   49

4   Philosophies of History and the Psychology of "Self-Renewal"   72

5   The Oedipal Conflict and the Isaac Solution   93

6   The "Non-Melting Pot"   111

7   The Hermeneutic Dialogue and Interhemispheric Balance   125

8   Linear Conversion versus Cyclistic Teshuvah: An Empirical Differentiation   149

9   The Midrashic Dialogue between Past and Future   172

10   The Temporal Dialogue as "Chutzpah Therapy"   188

Bibliography   203
Index   213

Introduction to the Transaction Edition

In the most famous Jewish book of mysticism, the *Zohar*, it is stated that "everything depends on *mazal* [a force beyond one's control], even the Torah in the Temple" (*Zohar*, Idra Rabba 149).

This popular statement has been widely used by Jewish authors to console themselves or other writers to indicate that even a good, innovative, important book may often fall into the category of unnoticed and unsold. The metaphoric use of "the Torah in the Temple" comes to stress that even such a holy book as the Torah would remain unrevealed and thus unstudied and unpracticed if not for a force that is beyond any human being's control. It therefore symbolizes that the popularity certain books enjoy depends on *mazal*, and is not necessarily a reflection upon their quality.

Today, it appears to me that, from all the books and articles I have published during my "thirty years war" for the advancement and enhancement of dialogic theory, this book on "re-biographing"* enjoyed the widest attention. The implication that disseminating the "re-biographic" concept was part of a "war" intends to stress that, at the time, the phenomenological possibility of a narrative retelling one's life story was not easily acceptable in academic circles.

After publishing the article "The Midrash and Biographic Rehabilitation" in the *Journal for the Scientific Study of Religion* (25: 1, 1986), I was invited to defend my thesis at a colloquium that took place in New Haven. Attendees of this session, representing the departments of history, psychology, and religious studies from Yale and Wesleyan Universities, read my article before the meeting so that we could plunge directly into a question and answer dialogue. Since at the time the positivistic orientation of historiography was still highly predominant, a historian addressed me with the following question: "So, according to your prescribed psychotherapy, you actually encourage people to lie about their past?" Seizing the opportunity to highlight re-biography, I answered with a dramatized apology: "Sorry lady, I forgot that you historians adhere only to the truth; I belong to the liars…" I then added that I do so only because everybody accepts the idea of the retroactive "political rehabilitation" of powerful people who faltered in their past, while the poor, weak, social misfits are asked to carry the "guilt cross" of failure. I stressed further that the idea of "re-biographing" in no way erases past "sins" and misfortunes, but only encourages people who corrected their behavior to reread their past failings from a more self-forgiving angle. By using Sholom

---

* Originally published under the title *Re-biographing and Deviance: Psychotherapeutic Narrativism and the Midrash.*

Aleichem's classic story about the happy orphan who enjoys the pity of his family and neighbors, I implied that by "humorizing" his situation, the state of being a poor orphan was not obliterated, but only ameliorated.

But, as I stated, in spite of my dialogic emphasis, according to which past events may not be erased but only reinterpreted, students of psychotherapy preferred at this "pre-narrative" time to accept even Milton Erickson's "born again" hypnotic invention of a new past (see J. Haley, *Uncommon Therapy*, N.Y.: Norton, 1973) rather than the autobiographic rewritten self, emanating from the Jewish cyclistic notion of re-narrative repentance (*teshuva*).

Several books and doctoral dissertations supervised both by others and myself focused on studying the impact of how the rereading of one's biography or, rather, the recomposing of one's life melody affected his or her ability to function in everyday life.

It is possibly the underlying difference between the Western linear perception of life as a deterministic process of an irreversible "fall" and the Jewish cyclistic idea of repentance (*teshuva*, literally meaning "return") that bestowed some "luck" on the optimistic notion of re-biographing. If, hence, chapter 3 of the book—which now carries the title *Rewriting the Self*—begins by formulating a new radical possibility for rehabilitation, then perhaps this intriguing reversal of time perspective entailed the lucky secret for attracting the attention of researchers.

Indeed, the idea that people may hope to have a good past in their future was used on the one hand by students studying the possibility of rewriting atrocious, humiliating memories from the Holocaust, while on the other hand criminologists have used its utility for rehabilitating ex-convicts.

I shall not overwhelm the reader with detailed research findings, but do state with some satisfaction that, generally, the paradigm of re-biographing, in the sense of descending into one's failing past in order to reread it for the sake of a new ascent into a rehabilitative future, has been advocated by many psychotherapists and criminologists (e.g., see S. Maruna, *Making Good*, Washington D.C.: APA, 2001).

Nonetheless, from a completely different angle, I think that some readers would be interested to learn how the concept of "rewriting one's self" may help to explore delicate issues pertaining to "free will" by using the conception of rewriting one's biography.

Zviya Shimoni, in her doctoral thesis (The Hebrew University of Jerusalem, 1997), found that many children (second generation) of Jewish people who repented (*ba'aley teshuva*) encountered ambivalent feelings about their newly imposed religious lifestyle, mainly because they were not given the free choice to accept or reject the new religious way of life their parents adopted. The implications of this study may therefore be relevant for other children of people who chose a drastic change in their lifestyle.

While the above research directions and clinical applications are briefly mentioned, I find Ayala Yeheskel's study of Holocaust survivors so essential in its contribution to the theory of "rewriting the self" that it justifies a fuller presentation. In her doctoral thesis and later in her book, *Weaving the Story of One's Life: Re-biography of Holocaust Survivors* (Tel Aviv: Hakibbutz Hameuchad, 1999), Yeheskel diverged from the traditional research orientation, which only documents people's sufferings, by examining how the mode of retelling the Holocaust experience was reflected in the survivors' ability to function after their rescue. The discovery that those who were able to weave their humiliating experiences into a life story with which one "can live" succeeded to lead a better and more constructive life as compared to those who couldn't "rewrite" their atrocious experiences into a biography with which "one can live" seems highly revealing. Thus, one woman who felt that it was her mother's will that she, the daughter, should survive "in order to tell," rationalized all her sufferings and humiliations as hurdles that she had to live through in order to fulfill her mother's will.

While this woman was capable of functioning constructively after her survival, one physician, who felt that he behaved like a coward by deserting his family, who sacrificed their lives so that he could complete his medical training, seemed unable to function properly in his everyday life after surviving, although he was able to fulfill his duties as a physician.

Accordingly, it is only because I find Yeheskel's work so highly innovative in its pioneering demonstration—that one's ability to "rewrite one's self" may have a direct impact on one's ability to function in everyday life—that I felt the need to share these findings with the reader.

I would like, however, to stress further that, on a more general level, it is because the "narrative fad" has gained so much popularity in spite of its roots in the shallow existential trend asserting that everybody has a self-realization right to adhere to his postmodern narrative, that the empirical evidence showing how *her-story* or *his-story* affects real *history* might have significant implications for future research on rehabilitating defeated selves.

Mordechai Rotenberg
Jersualem
September 2003

Preface

This book is intended as a third part in a trilogy that seeks to present a dialogistic psychology or a "dialogo therapy" as an alternative framework to the dialectic perspective that predominates in Western social sciences. The book follows Max Weber's sociology of religion, which assumes that behind every psychology there is a theology. Its leading hypothesis is that, although the Oedipal psychology of parricidal growth is grounded in a dialectic theosophy that posits that Christianity could develop only by destroying its Judaic father religion, the foundations of a dialogic psychology of progress must be sought in a theosophy of cyclic continuity like Judaism. Accordingly, this book should present a challenge to both secular and religious authorities because it claims that the neutral medical definition of mental problems that they usually accept, in fact, "conveniently" releases them from having to question the theological bias underlying the treatment methods that they endorse.

Although the presumptuous undertaking of presenting dialogicalism as an alternative approach to psychology is far from being complete, it is hoped that the effort to extend the Judeo-Hasidic contraction paradigm from the interpersonal space sphere developed in my *Dialogue with Deviance* to the intrapersonal sphere of time will open up a new vista for constructive "dialogues." According to Judaism, it is permissible *lefaresh* (to interpret) but not *lifrosh* (to withdraw from the community). The Midrashic dialogue thus refers to a psychology of multiple interpretations and not to a fundamentalist excommunication of the "old" psychology.

Because this volume constitutes a culmination and an amalgamation of many years of research of "living dialogue," naturally many of my ideas were gleaned and crystallized through interaction with friends and colleagues. Unfortunately, I can not list them all here.

I would like, nonetheless, to express my indebtedness to Professor Nathan Rotenstreich for his continuous encouragement to transpose the historiosophical query with which, to my mind, he was preoccupied for many years to the psychosophical arena. I would also like to thank Professor Amos Funkenstein for the advice and suggestions he offered after reading an earlier version of this manuscript. I shall never forget Professor Robert Nisbet's congratulations upon reading my proposal to study the psychological implications inherent in the Jewish conception of progress. While I take full responsibility for the interpretative system offered in the book, I am especially grateful to Professor Norman Lamm, president of Yeshiva University, and to Professor Isidore Twersky, head of the Harvard Center for Jewish Studies, whose enthusiastic comments about my theory of Midrashic narrative psychology strengthened my feeling that my "coming to bless the Jewish Midrash, didn't turn into cursing it." To my doctoral student, Uri Timor, and to Dina Vardi and Sharona Komem, go special thanks: to the former for allowing me to use cases from his research and to the latter for permitting me to cite cases from their clinical practice. I would like to also thank my students David Berlin, Michal Chalifa, Noa Chason, Judith Yaniv, Tamar Atzmon, Ivon Veler, and Nissim Ben-Lulo for collecting the data in the research reported in Chapter 8. Last, but surely not least, I would like to express my gratitude to my wife, Naomi, to Sherry Kisos for typing the manuscript, and to Dr. George Zimmar of Praeger Publishers for helping me turn it into a readable book.

I would like to acknowledge here that an earlier and shorter version of Chapter 3 was published in the *Journal for the Scientific Study of Religion* 25(1): 41–55, 1986, and is reprinted here by permission. The earlier, shorter version of Chapter 7, which was presented in August 1984 at the 31st Annual Meeting of the Institute on Religion in an Age of Science, which took place in Star Island, New Hampshire, and parts of Chapter 6, which were presented at the 1985 meetings in Star Island were published in *Zygon, Journal of Religion and Science* 21(2): 201–217, 1986, and in 21(4): 473-490, 1986, respectively and are also reprinted here by permission.

Finally, this is the proper place to acknowledge with thanks that the research project on which this book is based was supported in part by the Memorial Foundation for Jewish Culture. It is hoped, however, that this book will not be a memorial *tombstone* for Jewish psychology, but rather a *cornerstone* for its self-renewal.

1 Introduction: Living through Midrashic Interpretation

The rapidity with which the "hermeneutic renaissance" recently permeating the philosophy of literature and criticism is also gaining increasing popularity in the social sciences in general and in the "psychotherapies," in particular should not be too surprising.

After all, if hermeneutics is the science of interpretation, then if social psychologists are busy designing experiments to test, for example, attribution theory, that is, how people ascribe traits to others, they are, in essence, studying patterns of interpretations; and if psychotherapists are either "psychoanalyzing" people's pasts, or assigning new "here and now" meanings to people's existentially conflicting life stories, they are, in fact, reinterpreting and renarrating their biographic perceptions or experiences.

This book addresses itself to the psychotherapeutic-actualizing components inherent in the Judeo-Midrashic system of hermeneutics. More specifically, it is the purpose of this book to argue that the Judeo-Midrashic narrative system contains a pluralistic free-choice-based metahermeneutic code that is amenable to a psychotherapeutic perspective for reinterpreting life stories, in the sense that it urges people to select their personally suiting interpretation of life from a multiplicity of available narratives.

Thus, the underlying assumption guiding the thesis of this book is that it is not so much the particular therapeutic technique of interpreting life situations, but the key narrative or the hermeneutic metacode of who may interpret and how one may narrate life that underlies an effective system of hermeneutic psychotherapy. By metahermeneutic codes which operate as Platonic ideas, I have in mind such deeply entrenched belief systems about what makes society and human growth possible as are usually inculcated through the religiocultural environment surrounding people during crucial periods of their life span.

1

Thus, if Gregory Bateson, Milton Erickson, Viktor Frankl, and their students were able to train or teach people how to assign new meanings to paradoxically conflicting situations by "reframing" or recontextualizing these disturbing experiences, it was because they usually were drawing their success stories (as most innovating therapists do) from a very limited "hermeneutic circle" of Western middle-class people who had been already exposed to, or conditioned by, existential "here and now" interpretation codes. In other words, the popular method of "reframing" by changing "here-and-now" situated meanings seems to take for granted the a priori acceptance of the aura that has characterized, for example, California existential spirit since the 1960s.

Since the assignment of meaning in the therapeutic, or in any other interactive, situation is a communicative device that requires a regulative common denominator between the assigner and the assigned, it would be highly questionable whether and when such existential "reframing" or reinterpretations would be accepted, for example, in Oriental and/or fundamentalistic societies. Thus, while an interpretation of death in a suicidal war as an "entrance fee" to paradise might be acceptable (even as a style of actualization) among those exposed to the Iranian-Shiite hermeneutic code, it would most probably be rejected or defined as insanity by those raised by Western codes such as the California existentialist "religion" alluded to above. The position to be developed in this book is that people's problems can usually not be "mended" by a "here-and-now reframing" because these may be rooted in their total identity that often involves their personal biography and collective history.

The impossibility of assigning a free-floating meaning to which one has not been culturally conditioned was best explained by Gregory Bateson (1972) when he equated the process of interpretation and assigned meaning to a telecommunication mechanism.

What differentiates a signal from noise is that the former constitutes an accepted pattern of redundancy that helps the receiver (who recognizes it is a signal only because it is redundant) to understand the meaning of the message. That is to say, that it is only the repetitive regularity in sounding a telecommunicative noise that turns it into a perceptable, meaningful message, so "that the concept of redundancy is at least a partial synonym of meaning" (Bateson, 1972:414). Thus, the assignment of a recontextualized-reframed meaning would be meaningless if it was not internalized via the regulative process of redundancy. From a Weberian sociology of religion perspective, which assumes that social norms are usually secularized patterns of religious ethics, one may argue now that one acquires these redundant regularities of meaning comprising signals in the religious-cultural norm systems to which one has been repetitively exposed. It would thus appear that if you scratch the surface of any norm regulating psychology or psychotherapy, you will find behind it a theology or a theosophy that manifests itself in various secularized norms and forms of ontology.

According to this vein of thought, it might be argued that pluralistic free-choice approaches to psychotherapeutic narratology may be traced to or identified in the ancient Judeo-Midrashic hermeneutic metacode. While it is thus the major goal of the book to demonstrate how people may therapeutically rehabilitate their biography by reinterpreting their failing past according to their future aspirations, in this introductory chapter I shall only show how Midrashic narratology offers a choice between competing interpretations of text and life stories. Since metahermeneutic codes are introduced here as Platonic ideas that shape the interpretation of life and not vice versa, both the Midrashic pluralistic key and its opposite—the fundamentalistic hermeneutic code that will be discussed here—must be understood as exaggerated (pure) ideal types. In presenting the pluralistic and the fundamentalistic hermeneutic systems as two diverging approaches to psychotherapeutic interpretation codes of life stories as two contrasting "ideal types," I somehow follow Theunissen's (1984) comparative encounter between Husserl's transcendentalism and Buber's dialogicalism. While it is beyond the scope of the present introductory chapter to explicate these two ontological points of view, it seems clear that Theunissen's rigid bifurcation between these two frameworks are used mainly as an ideal-typical confrontation tool, because in reality Husserl's and Buber's philosophies do overlap in many respects.

Thus it is only as an ideal type that such fundamentalistic notions as the "original sin" conception of Oedipal guilt for interpreting biographies described below may be contrasted with the multiple open structure of Midrashic narrativism. On the empirical level, there might obviously exist a variety of hermeneutic metacodes that comprise combinations and deviations from the presented ideal types.

I realize, however, that while it might be important to construct exaggerated ideal types in order to sharpen and polarize possible differences, the above traditional safeguarding statement concerning plausible empirical variations that might deviate from the ideal types might turn this introductory chapter into the apologetic document that, because introductions are usually written after the book is completed, was equated so appropriately by Franz Rosenzweig (1977) to the cackling of the hen around the eggs that she has already laid. To minimize the apologetic tone in this introduction to Midrashic "rebiographing," I shall thus drop the academic evasive "cackling" and turn now to explicate briefly the Midrashic idea of pluralistic narration by contrasting it first with what I term the fundamentalistic "original sin" idea of *biographic interpretation*.

THE MIDRASH AS A METACODE FOR PLURALISTIC NARRATIVISM

Shoshana Felman (1983) was essentially correct in presenting Freud's Oedipal theory as a key narrative because he turned this reference narrative into a fundamental, and to his belief a universal, story, according to which everybody's biography should or could be reinterpreted.

While Oedipus is thus introduced as a psychoanalytic key narrative because presumably it merely reads, uncovers, or interprets an already-existing fundamental truth about people's guilt toward their parents, the a priori presence of such guilt feelings might be a true fact, from the present perspective, only among people who have been previously socialized to internalize an "original sin" belief in man's unshakable guilt.

As it will be demonstrated, Freud indeed conceptualized his dialectic patricidal notion of guilt, in original sin terms, but he went on to preach his "psychoanalytic gospels" as a universal truism.

In his hermeneutic study of this concept Ricoeur (1981) showed nonetheless how original sin, in terms of a biological infectious "natural guilt inherited from the first man" (p. 281) that is presumably already present in infants, was an exclusive Christian idea. Ricoeur pointed out that "Augustine is responsible for the classic elaboration of the concept 'original sin' and for its introduction into the dogmatic deposit of the Church on an equal footing with Christology" (p. 278).[1]

The difference then between uncovering the *fundamental* Oedipal guilt in someone who was already exposed to the original sin metahermeneutic code and the *fundamentalistic* imputation of such Oedipal guilt to one who has not internalized such a code, parallels, to say the least, the difference between manipulating people to accept a patricidal blaming interpretation of their past and reinforcing an Oedipal guilt in a person who actually killed his parents. The position this book takes, however, is that psychotherapy need not enforce new fundamentalistic techniques for reframing or reinterpreting, but should help troubled people who are captured in any fundamentalistic belief system to accept a multiple hermeneutic code that will enable them to free themselves from any fundamentalistically internalized code. They will then be able to freely choose their own personally suited life story interpretation.

It is thus from this vantage point remarkable that in recent years there has been an influx of literature (to be mentioned later) that strives to show that Midrashic freedom of choice for reinterpreting life was not limited to those neutral norm-regulating areas that help the Jews to adapt to their everchanging environment, but that Midrashic pluralism, in fact, laid also the foundations for the legal (*Halachic*) machinery. The popular *Midrashic* idea that "the Torah has seventy faces" that is, seventy interpretations, is accordingly extended also to the legal world of *Halacha* (law). In the Jerusalemite

Talmud (*Sanhedrin*, 4:b) it is stated: "Had the Torah been given as one cut [without possibilities for divergent interpretations] we could not stand on our feet. . . . It is necessary that the Torah be capable of forty-nine ways of interpretation of affirming an opinion and forty-nine ways of opposing it."

To be sure, by Midrashic pluralism or by free-choice narratology, especially in terms of its impact on legal (*Halachic*) interpretations, I do not intend to impute an "anarchic" kind of attribution of meaning to the Midrashic system of hermeneutic. While "the opening of text, to a Western mind, presupposes an *a priori* reùnunciation of any 'truth of meaning,'" as Betty Roitman (1986:159) indicated, Midrashic narrative pluralism operates within Rabbi Akiva's unifying conception of "All is determined, and yet, all is open" (*Fathers*, 3:19). Thus, while biblical interpretation calls for inexhaustible semantic inquiries, even contradictory interpretations of the biblical text must be retained because all interpretations are believed to have been dictated or inspired by God.

But what is the phenomenological meaning of the word *Midrash*. The term, which is derived from the Hebrew word *darash* (searched, interpreted) is a verb, that is, a function or activity; a noun, referring to biblical and Talmudical expositions; and an institution, referring to the *Beit Hamidrash* (house or school) where the actual work of studying or interpreting is done. As far back as the Talmudic era (first to sixth centuries), when the oral law became the normative vehicle for regulating the entire spiritual and terrestrial activities of Jews, a continuous need emerged to apply the Torah (the written law) to all conditions of life with its changing circumstances. This was done partly through the continuous process of law making (Halacha) and partly by Midrashic expositions (see Strack, 1969:202) that, according to Zunz (1974:21), "maintains the transmitted word but at the same time changes it."

While experts differentiate between the terms *derush*, *midrash*, and *derasha*, by and large, the *midrash*, or Aggadah, (although these are not quite synonymous terms), referring mainly to the use of symbolic legends, stories, and parables, according to Strack, contain two major forms: the Tannaic or Halachic Midrashim and the Homiletic Midrashim. The former are more closely connected with scripture because of their regulative-legal function, while the latter, which refer mostly to compiled sermons delivered in synagogues and public places during the Sabbath and festivals, allowed a more freely creative concretizing interpretation of scripture because its function was "to bring Heaven nearer to the congregation" (1969:202).

Although as a practical matter, the custom of delivering public Midrashic sermons never ceased, and while the compilation of Midrashim that were believed to be part of the transmitted oral law continued until the eighteenth century, there is great dispute as to how much normatively binding significance should be attributed to various later Midrashim, especially to those that are moral-ethical and not Halachic. However, there seems to be a more gener-

al consensus that the Midrashic method, with its open-ended symbolic parables and with its legal expositions, often allowed for a dialogical "co-existence" of seemingly contradictory interpretation of scripture by relying on
Talmudic dicta such as the one stating that "these and those are God's living
words" (*Gittin*, 6:b). In effect, the Midrashic method with its constitutional
paradox offers a priori divergent and often contradictory interpretations of
laws and events to be used differentially according to temporally changing
circumstances.

Accordingly, poverty may be described (see Kadushin, 1938) in one single
Midrash as God's love; *Midat-Harachamim* (pity, compassion), and as
God's justice, *Midat Hadin* (sternness, punishment) because

> No one can deny the blighting effects of poverty, but it is equally true that
> on occasion, poverty may make for spiritual growth. . . . [and hence] we
> are dealing, then, with things that are logically contradictory but psycho-
> logically, correct, with interpretations of paradoxical character. (Kadushin,
> 1938:196-97)

The Midrashic dialogue (between past and present) facilitates the reorganization of seemingly contrasting conditions or positions, so that by selectively and creatively reinterpreting past events to suit future aspirations,
historical cognitive dissonance may be reduced. Indeed, Kadushin (1938),
who insisted that rabbinic thought's organic nature ensured that each concept may be understood only in terms of its integral relationship to other
concepts that only together constitute a whole, used the Midrashic literature
to demonstrate how its method of continuous concretizing reinterpretation,
in fact, featured and explained Jewish survival with its dynamic mechanism
for periodic "self-renewal" and progress.[2]

> Rabbinic haggadic literature represents an interaction between the life of
> people and the creators of literature. . . . The concepts which gave mean-
> ing to and determined the moment-to-moment experience of the people
> were the subjects of discourses by the Rabbis delivered before the masses.
> (P. 188)

It is, then, this dynamic concretizing process of *derush* that continues to
this very day and that explains how the phenomenological world of the ordinary Jew is constructed through the narrative machinery operating in the
synagogues or in the Beit Hamidrash he visits. Although the meaning and
use of the concept Midrash might now be clear to the reader, I should stress
at the outset that while there is a difference between Midrashic or Aggadic
legends and Talmudic statements per se, I shall use here the word *Midrash*
as a general term referring to both Talmudic legal disputes and to Midrashic
legendary sources, for it is the process of *derush* (searching and debating the

implications emanating from legal and legendary sources) occurring in the Beit Hamidrash that constituted the dynamic survival psychology of Judaism.

MIDRASHIC PLURALISM IN ACTION

To highlight the extent of power inherent in human interpretation, the famous Midrash about the Aknai Oven is used by many students of Judaism as the classic symbol for human rights to interpret God's laws given at Sinai.

In the famous Talmudic story, the question that came up regarding ritual purity (the details of which are insignificant from the present perspective) caused sharp disagreement between the majority of the Talmudical scholars and the powerful authoritative Rabbi Eliezer, who apparently surpassed everybody else in wisdom, legal knowledge, and so on. The Midrash tells us that after a long dispute, which involved several miracles caused by Rabbi Eliezer to prove his point, a heavenly voice (*bat kol*) declared: "Whenever Rabbi Eliezer expresses an opinion, the Law (Halacha) is according to him" (*Baba Mezia*, 59:b). Although his was a minority opinion, the support from Heaven should have settled the matter, but no, in spite of Heaven, continues the Talmudic Midrash, Rabbi Joshua stood up and responded with what can be termed *chutzpah* toward Heaven and proclaimed: "It is not in Heaven!" (Deut., 30:12). These powerful words, "It is not in Heaven!" which are direct citations from the Torah, were used subsequently by writers on Halachic interpretation, not only to symbolize that majority rules, but, more important, to demonstrate that the Torah has been given to humans and that it is thus for them to interpret the law as they understand it in the relativistic terms prevailing during their life times, even if they are at times wrong. The dialogic element, which would in the present terms signify God's volitionary, space-evacuating contraction that urges man to use his "*chutzpah* power," which is effective even in relation to Heaven, is epitomized in the beautiful postscript "punch line" of this Midrash, which tells that once Rabbi Natan met Elijah the prophet (who presumably never died) and asked him what God's response to Rabbi Joshua's daring statement was. According to the Talmudic Midrash, Elijah replied, "God was laughing and saying, "My sons have defeated me; my sons have defeated me," (*Baba Mezia*, 59:b).

God's laughing was then interpreted not only as His permission for man to use *Chutzpah* in interpreting His divine law but also as a sign that this was the wish inherent in God's self-contracting space evacuation for human volitionary actions, in the first place.

To stress that it was not Rabbi Joshua's unique charismatic-authoritative power that counteracted the objective absolute heavenly voice, but that it was the principle of human interpretability that overturned the law against heaven precisely because the law must be human, subjective, and relative, one may cite another Talmudic story in which a legal decision was made against the authoritative objective opinion of none else than the same Rabbi Joshua. The Talmud (*Rosh Hashona*, 25:a) recounts an incident in which the head of the high court (*Sanhedrin*), Rabban Gamliel, and Rabbi Joshua disagreed about the reliability of the available testimony on the basis of which the new calendric year must be set. Since such calculations determine the exact days of the next High Holidays, Rabban Gamliel ordered Rabbi Joshua to appear before him "with his walking stick and his money" on the day that would be the Day of Atonement (*Yom Kippur*) according to Rabbi Joshua's calculation and a regular weekday according to the ruling of the Sanhedrin headed by Rabban Gamliel. The point in this classic story is again, not only that by obeying Rabban Gamliel and so violating "his" Yom Kippur by carrying money, Rabbi Joshua was forced to accept majority rule, but also that while Rabbi Joshua might have been objectively correct in his calculations, a decision was made on the basis of the human interpretation of those who happened to be in office at the time, even if they were wrong.

While thus far these Midrashic stories demonstrate only that the rules governing legal interpretations were not fundamentalistically set according to the a prioristic voice of the written word of Heaven, but left open to the will of humans, the reader might come to think nonetheless that what predominated was a single and not a pluralistic interpretation system.

In other words, one may wonder: If it is indeed the rule that once a legal interpretation that eliminates all other interpretations has been made, where is the dialogic principle of competing yet coexisting interpretations that, I claim, may serve as a model for the people's free-choice-based multiple-interpretation guide for their life stories?[3] True, since we are dealing with legal (Halachic) matters, there must be a decision, and hence, on the face of it, we may not draw much evidence showing how one may choose a reinterpretation for one's biography by demonstrating how the *Midrashic* hermeneutic code affected the *legal halachic* system, because in legal affairs it is not the lay individual who chooses a biographic interpretation but the majority of judges who have to reach a decision in one direction or another.

It is remarkable, however, that Midrashic stories were used by the Talmud to humanize narrativism by urging the judges to minimize fundamentalistic authoritative heavenly interpretations of the law. In fact, the Talmud states very frequently (see Jacobs, 1984:27) that even the legalist is instructed

"Whenever the Halacha is uncertain (*rofefet*) so far as the court is concerned and you do not know what is to be done, go out and see how the community conducts itself and do likewise."

Thus, while Midrashic pluralism would refer mainly to ethical-moral issues, even the hard-nosed legalists cannot be oblivious to the pragmatic needs of the people and to the ethical spontaneous choice-based interpretation system that these needs generate. The metacode for multiple interpretations emerges then out of the continuous dialogue that is to prevail between the legalist and the community, between man's logic and God's voice, between the coercing quality of sternness (*midat hadin*) and the free-choice quality of compassion (*midat harachamim*), between Cabalic-mystic idealism and philosophical logical realism, between the poetic Midrash or Aggadah and the prosaic *Halacha*. As Rabbi Louis Jacobs stated: "Any neat distinction between Halakah and Agadah [the nonlegal side of Judaism] is untenable" (1984:11).

Moreover, the hermeneutic choice element that the dialogue between competing approaches to life is to generate is thus inherent in the very definition of what is to constitute the relationship between the written and the Oral Torah. To elucidate the meaning of the term *Oral Torah*, the Talmud (*Tmura*, 16:b) tells us how Rabbi Yochanan and Resh Lakish studied the Aggadah (i.e., the Midrash, which together with the Talmud comprises the Oral Torah) from a written book although it was strictly forbidden to put the Oral Torah into writing. To justify their behavior, these scholars stated that since it is sometimes permissible to break the law in order to act for God (*Tehilim*, 119), and in view of the increasing difficulty of remembering the entire body of the Oral Torah, it might at times be important to study from written books so the law would not be forgotten.

In other words, if the Oral Torah is meant, by definition, to provide a continuous "oral" interpretation of the written Torah, it is also by definition antifundamentalistic in the sense that it preserves opposing opinions in order to allow a choice between them through the continuous process of dialogue.

The dialogue of Midrashic multiple interpretation may thus operate on the basis of what I termed the Cabalic *Contraction* dynamics (Rotenberg, 1983). Very briefly stated, based on the Cabalic contraction paradigm, man's behavior may be patterned through the principle of "imitatio Dei" by imitating God's volitionary contracting withdrawal into Himself in order to evacuate space for the world or for any opposing "other" opinion or entity.

Accordingly, even in legal matters, the opinion of the "other" minority is never eliminated but is temporarily contracted, as explained by Rabbi Eliezer Berkowitz:

> The minority opinions have been preserved so that if a *Beth Din* (court) ever arises that would find the rejected view of an individual teacher justified, it would have the authority to accept it and to rule accordingly against a previously followed practice established in accordance with the majority.

> The minority view is kept in abeyance . . . till such time valid arguments
> would be found for its acceptance. The teaching of the minority is not sup-
> pressed; it may retain its theoretical validity. (1983:49)

Indeed, in using this contraction paradigm to explain the evolvement of
hermeneutic pluralism inherent in the oral nature of Talmudism, David
Hartman (1985) has recently argued that it is only through God's volitionary self-limitation (contraction) that one may understand the possibility of
moral and intellectual freedom:

> In the Bible, God limits His power in history in order to activate the will to
> moral action; in the Talmud, human independence is expanded to include
> the intellect. God's self-limiting love for human beings is expressed in His
> entrusting the elaboration and expansion of the Torah to rabbinic scholars.
> (P. 32)

Using an insightful observation demonstrating how the "not in heaven"
principle of multiple human interpretation evolved from the declining role of
the prophets, who relied on God's revelation to ascertain the correct (and
possibly more fundamentalistic) understanding of the Torah, Hartman (p.
34) cited the following Talmudic text:

> Rav Judah reported in the name of Samuel: "Three thousand traditional
> laws were forgotten during the period of mourning for Moses. They said to
> Joshua 'Ask': he replied: 'It is not in heaven.' (*Temurah*, 16:a)

Thus, since "prophetic revelation" determining *the* correct interpretation
is no longer available, one has to rely on multiple alternative interpretations. It is, however, the contraction principle, which explains how, paradoxically, the very traditional belief that retroactively all interpretations are
part of God's revelation at Sinai, that makes multiple interpretation imperative. That is to say, that within a contractional framework, the relationship between the notion that the law is a revelation *from* Heaven and the
idea that Torah is *"not in* heaven" is paradoxically complementary and
not, as it is often assumed (e.g., Schimmel, 1971), contradictory.

Thus, if according to the contraction principle, God's volitionary self-
limitation hides any one fundamentalistic "revealing" interpretation, this
state of "hidden-revelation" by definition requires the paradoxical coexistence of contradictory interpretations in whch the "I" interpretation may
not eliminate or synthesize the "thou" interpretation because who is to determine which is the correct "revelation."

The dialogic idea that a "multiple choice" interpretation system is possible only when Heaven may be defeated by earthly justified *chutzpah* toward
Heaven that does not eliminate its heavenly voice or the "other" interpreta-

tion, is epitomized in the much-cited classic Midrash concerning the eternal disagreement between the Talmudic houses of Shammai and Hillel.

Moreover, according to this classic dispute the dialogic multiple herme- neutic code entails also a time element. As is well-known, in this famous case of disagreement between Hillel and Shammai, there was also a voice from Heaven, which in this case was heard to proclaim: "Both these and those are the words of the living God but the *Halacha* (law) is in accordance with the House of Hillel" (*Talmud, Eruvin*, 13:b).

Since it is obviously impossible to accept simultaneously two opposing le- gal decisions, what we have now in this much-cited classic Midrash is the operational guiding bedrock for a pluralistic hermeneutic code that operates according to the contraction principle, not only in space but also in time.

Thus, Shammai's interpretation is not eliminated but "contracted" (kept in abeyance) until the time when his opinion will be valid and appropriate according to new emerging circumstances. Similarly, all opposing ap- proaches are preserved for personal choice in space and time. Indeed, the hermeneutic "multiple choice" code that comprises the basis for the psy- chology of everyday life, begins for the ordinary Jew when he listens, as alluded to earlier, to the *derashot* in the synagogue and when he reads the weekly portion of the Torah. For not only will he find that for every deed, sin, and law described in the Bible, there are opposing interpretations, such as those that will condemn Reuben's incestuous sin and those that will acquit him (Gen., 49), but, immediately upon opening a typical Bible that contains commentary, this Jew would be exposed to as many as forty-five narrations, including mystic-Cabalic interpretations based on *Sod*[4] (secret teachings), which appear on one side of the page, and opposing rational interpretations of *peshat* (straightforward logical teaching), which are on the other.

This is not to say that no one claims that Jewish interpretations are rigid, at least in regard to legal matters. It is however, precisely the coexistence of opinions attributing rigidity to the Jewish hermeneutic system of Halacha, and the predominant opinion, which perceives it as a multiple interpretation code in all matters, that embodies the dialogic tension between opposites pervading Midrashic narrativism. Viewed from a psychophenomenological angle, Midrashic narrativism may thus train people to live in the "schizoid" world of *Kushya* (questions) where the dialogic hypothesis, and not the dia- lectic synthesis, constitutes life (see Rotenberg, 1978; 1983).

Moreover, it is on the basis of such a paradox-based thought system that one could hypothesize that Midrashic narrativism may socialize people to read "double messages" that would lead to choice-oriented growth and not necessarily to psychotic breakdowns, as many Western psychopathologists posit. Thus, while in conflict-based interpretation systems, apparent contra- dictory messages must inevitably lead to unresolvable communicative expe- riences that trap people in a "double bind" (see Bateson, 1972), Midrashic narratology is a priori predicated on paradoxical interpretations. Accordingly, seemingly contradictory texts and communicative messages may always, at least in theory, be reinterpreted in such a way that the logical connection between the apparent contrasting statements is reestablished.

Thus, an apparent paradoxical contradiction between the promise "But there shall be no poor among you" (Deut., 15:4), and the statement: "For the poor shall never cease out of the land" (Deut., 15:11) appearing seven verses later, is reconciled by the Midrash (*Iben Ezra*) in a manner that reinforces the principle of choice. In essence, if Israel hearkens to God, there shall be no poor among you. However, since there is no such thing as a righteous man who never sins (see Rashbam), and since therefore there is always a chance that one may fall into poverty, therefore God commands you: "Thou shalt open thine hand wide unto thy brother" (ibid.). Paradoxically then, since one cannot be perfectly righteous without giving charity, this situation exposes everybody to the danger of poverty; while giving charity eliminates the need for poverty. The world can thus exist only through the dialogical tension between the state of "eternal poverty" and "no poverty," depending on people's choice-based conduct. Put differently, the possibility of virtue (achieved by giving charity) depends on the persistence of vice (the impossibility of being perfectly virtuous).

In fact, Midrashic "double messages" that, I say, epitomize a choice-oriented socialization may often be transmitted through the interpretation of a short biblical passage comprised of only two words. Let me elucidate this important point. In discussing the Midrashic principles guiding the methods for combining and computing letters, Heinemen (1970) stated that since it is believed that originally the letters of the Torah were not divided into words, "according to the Rabbis . . . the narrator is not only permitted but obligated to interpret . . . letter by letter or groups of letters [and hence because] every letter has its own life, it is permitted to combine letters even those far apart into new words" (p. 103).

This principle, which is anchored in the belief that Torah is *from* Heaven but not *in* Heaven, that is, that every letter is holy but it is up to us humans to interpret them, bestows upon man the responsibility to understand the choice element inherent in Midrashic hermeneutics. A classic example is the verse, "And the Lord God said, it is not good that the man should be alone, I will make him a help against him" (Gen., 2:18).

The two self contradictory words, "help against him" (*Ezer Kenegdo*) are explained by the Midrash (*Midrash Rabba*, 17:3) in terms of the said choice-fostering paradox, by using a hermeneutic principle that separates these two words. These words must hence be read "help, against" and the woman will accordingly become man's right-hand "help" if he (her man) deserves it, but if he does not deserve it, she will turn "against him."

Similar to this "women's lib" *Midrash*, which makes man's deserving-ness dependent on his freedom of choice to do good or evil, is the classic Midrash about Israel's future redemption. Accordingly, the two self-contradicting words *beita achishena* (*Isaiah*, 60:22), which mean literally "I shall hasten it" (*achishena*) and "in its due time" (*beita*), were also divided by the *Midrash* (*Shir Hashirim, Rabba*, 8:12) to read: redemption will occur in due time if Israel does not deserve it (*beita*); but if they deserve salvation, I will hasten it (*achishena*). Thus, since God drove man out of Eden after he ate from the tree of knowledge that "condemned him to freedom," the re-entrance to his "paradise" will always be guarded by the double-edged "flaming turning sword" (Gen., 4:24) of free choice between good and evil.

Midrashic hermeneutics thus constitutes not merely a structural-organic thought system in which every concept or idea might a posteriori be related to other concepts, as Kadushin (1938) posited. Rather, it seems to entail a psychological code that may help people to neutralize or resolve a priori possible constraints and "double bind" contrasts that modernity imposes upon life.

From a therapeutic perspective, this would mean that *Midrashic* interpretation would require that (a) therapists may not assume that "language which is spoken by one population is a reflection of the total culture" (Levi-Strauss, 1963:681), because since *Midrashic* socialization contains more than one linguistic structure and more than one phonemic system, a particular word or expression may at one time reflect rational modern thinking and at another time be understood only within the mystic-Cabalic structure from which it originated; and (b) that concomitantly the teacher-therapist may offer his "student-client" a "multiple choice" interpretation for his present or past disturbing experiences. These therapeutic interpretations would include rational and emotional options, similar to the selection of personally fitting interpretations of text available to the Torah-reading Jew.

In the Talmud (*Shabbat*, 31:a), there is a story about Hillel, who was once asked by a prospective convert to teach him only the written law so that he might subsequently live only by the written word. Hillel, who temporarily accepted this condition, began by teaching the convert-to-be the Hebrew alphabet. In the second lesson, however, Hillel deliberately misnamed the letters so that "aleph" (*a*) was "bet" (*b*) and "bet" was "aleph." When the convert-student protested, insisting that it differed from the first lesson, given the day before, Hillel was said to have answered: "If you trusted me when yesterday I taught you the written letters, you have to trust me also today when I teach you the oral Torah," though this might lead to opposing conclusions according to which *a* is *b* and *b* is *a*.[5] Thus, Jewish socialization is a priori antifundamentalistic in its hermeneutic conception.

Indeed, while such opposing schools of interpretation as the "hassidim and Mitnagdim" or the "Perushim and Zadokim" featured Jewish history, it was only in the eighth century, when the Karaite sect declared the acceptance of only the written Torah as its doctrine, that it was excommunicated by the Jewish majority, possibly in accordance with J. S. Mill's dictum that "the principle of freedom [here of interpretation] cannot include the freedom not to be free . . ." (to interpret).

Psychologically speaking then, the strict coercive element of the stern law (*din*) is never eliminated but is rearranged or reorganized and reinterpreted via a dialogue with the element of compassion (*rachamim*) so that in a Cabalistic sense, the letters *nituk* (separation) can always be rearranged to comprise *tikun* (correction). To give the psychologically oriented reader an example of how the temporal "contraction" principle (according to which the law is never eliminated but "contracted") is applied by the Midrashic "multiple choice" interpretation system to even a most extreme case of deviant conduct, let us discuss now in some detail the Talmudic hermeneutic "acrobatics" in relation to what I termed (see Rotenberg and Diamond, 1971) "The Biblical Conception of Psychopathy."

REINTERPRETING THE "STUBBORN AND REBELLIOUS SON" AD ABSURDUM

In the Book of Deuteronomy (21:20) it is written:

> If a man have a stubborn and rebellious son, that will not hearken to the voice of his father, or the voice of his mother, and though they chasten him, will not hearken unto them; then shall his father and his mother lay hold on him, and bring him out unto the elders of his city, and unto the gate of his place; and they say unto the elders of his city: "This our son is stubborn and rebellious, he doth not hearken to our voice; he is a glutton and a drunkard." And all the men of his city shall stone him with stones, that he die; so shalt thou put away the evil from the midst of thee; and all Israel shall hear and fear.

Taking this law literally by reading it fundamentalistically, this law would obviously appear cruel to the modern reader. However, since by using ingeneous "hermeneutic acrobatics," the Talmud (as we shall see below) has "interpreted this law out of existence" as Berkowitz (1983:81) phrased it, many apologetic post-Talmudic commentators dealt only with the qualities of disobedience appearing in the first part of the biblical definition of the "rebellious son." These apologetic interpreters thus tried to demonstrate how the Talmudic restrictions in fact curtailed the unlimited patriarchal "Patria Potestas" authority of the father in ancient times. However, by failing to construe and apprehend the psychological meaning of gluttony and drunkenness, which the Talmudic interpretations treat systematically, these commentators lose sight of both the temporal contraction element and the psychological "multiple choice" code that are implicit in this Talmudic case of hermeneutic exercise.

Let us consider the Talmudic stipulations in order: Talmudic restricting interpretations appeared to be based on two criteria: (1) whether or not overindulgence in eating, drinking, and so on was indicative of an unchangeable form of addiction, and (2) whether the cause of this behavior pattern was endogenous rather than exogenous.

Accordingly, the rabbis of the Talmud (*Sanhedrin*, 71:a) discussed in much detail the conditions under which one will most likely form evil eating and drinking habits. For example: "If he ate raw meat or drank undiluted wine, he does not become a 'stubborn and rebellious son'" because in their view, one cannot become habituated to eating raw meat and drinking undiluted wine. Similarly, his is not liable: "if he drinks wine from the vat before it has matured [because] wine is unattractive until it is forty days old." The Talmud also states: "He is not liable unless he buys meat and wine cheaply and consumes them," the implication being that if he has to pay a high price, he will not be in a position to maintain an addiction. Further: "If he ate in a company celebrating a religious act, he is not liable until he eats in a company of good-for-nothings. If he stole—he is not liable until he steals of his father's and eats it in the domain of strangers, 'which is easily within his reach. . . . Rabbi Jose, the son of Rabbi Judah said: until he steals of his father's and his mother's."

The general hazards and evil involved in drinking wine, as implied in the law of the stubborn son, were pointed out repeatedly by the Talmud. For example: "Look not thou upon the wine . . . for it leads to bloodshed."

Maimonides (1949:157) elaborated on the Talmudical definition by emphasizing the callous, loathsome aspects of overindulgence. He explained that the law

> Refers to the way in which the stubborn and rebellious son gorges. He is executed for the loathsome manner in which he gratifies his appetite, as it is said: "He is a glutton and a drunkard" (Deut. 21:20) The traditional definition of these words is: a glutton is one who eats meat voraciously; a drunkard is one who drinks wine immoderately.

Elsewhere, Maimonides (1885:158,9) stressed the social consequences of behavior specified by the label "stubborn and rebellious son":

> It is well known that it is intemperance in eating, drinking, and sexual intercourse that people mostly rave and indulge in . . . can generally disturb the social order of the country and the economy of life. . . . See how the law commanded to slay a person from whose conduct it is evident that he will go too far in seeking the enjoyment of eating and drinking. I mean the rebellious and stubborn child: he is described as a glutton and a drunkard.

The procedure that was to be followed in warning and disciplining the "rebellious son" according to the Talmud and Maimonides was as follows: First, the parents had to warn and chasten him in front of two witnesses not to continue his evil practices. If he continued his wicked, stubborn behavior and these two witnesses corroborated the parents' accusation, then the culprit was lashed before a tribunal of three judges. If, thereafter, there was no improvement in his behavior, he was tried by a tribunal of twenty-three judges and if all the necessary proofs were produced, he was considered incorrigible and was liable to execution.

Implied in the prescribed procedures was the necessity to prove that the state of drunkenness, stubbornness, and so on was inherent rather than attributable to parents or circumstances.

Thus, Josephus Flavius, (1830, IV:94) the first-century (A.D. 38–100) Jewish historian suggested that the law excludes those cases in which the problem was attributable to lack of parental care. To support the charge of "stubborn and rebellious son," the father must be able to say:

> That when thou wast born we took thee up with gladness, and gave God the greatest thanks to thee, and brought thee up with great care, and spared for nothing that appeared useful for thy preservation, and for thy instruction in what was most excellent.

According to the Talmud and Maimonides, if waywardness occurred in conjunction with the following circumstances, the son was not liable:

> A son can be condemned only if he has two parents.

> If his father desires to have him punished, but not his mother; or the reverse, he is not treated as a "stubborn and rebellious son"; unless they both deserve it.

> Rabbi Judah said: if his mother is not fit for his father he does not become a "stubborn and rebellious son." . . If one of them [his father or his mother] . . . was lame, dumb, blind, or deaf he does not become a "stubborn and rebellious son."

The given reason for this mitigation derives from the assumption that cripples are to be suspected of bitterness and cruelty.

Rabbi Judah also discusses the absurd conclusions entailed in the word *voice*, which appears in the passage requesting that the parents must declare before the elders: "This our son is stubborn and rebellious; he doth not hearken to our voice." Rabbi Judah (ibid.) stated:

> "Doth not hearken to our voice" says the Bible. "Voice" is in singular. Now father and mother may agree in this matter and speak as if with one voice, but in actual fact they each have a voice of their own. But the Bible says: "Our voice"; it can only mean that their voices are alike also in the physical sense. But if their voices must be undistinguishable then it means that the parents have to be alike physically in appearance and height. [Nonetheless, here Rabbi Judah reaches an important conclusion]. All these conditions, of course can never be met. Therefore it never happens, nor will it ever happen.

As Rabbi Judah's hermeneutic acrobatics "interprets this case out of existence" (because it is impossible that parents will physically resemble each

other like twins) the Talmud's conclusive rhetoric punch line is most interesting: "If so, [that it cannot happen] why was it written?" and the Talmud
answers: "to interpret it and be rewarded for its study."

While this law would appear then as a sheer intellectual exercise, the psychological implications of being "rewarded for its study" appear far-
reaching. The theoretical attitudes toward the stubborn and rebellious son
expressed in the Talmud refer consistently to an apparent incorrigible,
hopeless state, inherent in the youth, and not to a condition that is the con-
sequence of adverse circumstances or mistreatment by the parents and that
will lead inevitably to a life of serious crime. To illuminate what I have
termed the "psychopathic" elements constituting the "stubborn son" (see
Rotenberg and Diamond, 1971), the discourse of the first-century philosopher Philo (1930, VII:457) in regard to what can be termed as the "psychopathic" dynamics of "inability to love" appears most instructive:

> And therefore he omitted any mention of love for parents because it is
> learned and taught by instinct and requires no injunction, but did enjoin
> for the sake of those who are in the habit of neglecting their duty. For when
> parents cherish their children with extreme tenderness, providing them with
> good gifts from every quarter and shunning no toil or danger because they
> are fast bound to them by the magnetic forces of affection, there are some
> who do not receive this exceeding tender heartedness in a way that profits
> them. They (the children) pursue eagerly luxury and voluptuousness, they
> applaud the dissolute life, they run to waste both in body and soul, and suf-
> fer no part of either to be kept erect by its proper faculties which they lay
> prostrate and paralyzed without a blush because they have never feared the
> censors they possess in their fathers and mothers but give in to and indulge
> their own lusts.

Thus, as justification for the harshness of prescribing the death penalty
for the stubborn son, Rabbi Jose, the Galilean, is quoted in the Talmud
(*Sanhedrin*, 72:a) as saying:

> Did the Torah decree that the rebellious son shall be brought before Beth
> Din [court] and stoned merely because he ate a tartemar of meat and drank
> of log of Italian wine? But the Torah foresaw his ultimate destiny. For at
> the end, after dissipating his father's wealth, he would still seek to satisfy
> his accustomed gluttonous wants but being unable to do so, go forth at the
> crossroads and rob. Therefore, the Torah said, 'Let him die while yet inno-
> cent and let him not die guilty, for the death of the wicked benefits them-
> selves and the world.'

In summary, the psychological lesson that we may derive from the "stubborn and rebellious son" is that the story epitomizes in essence the dialogic
contraction possibility ad absurdum.

On the one hand, all the possibilities of extreme deviant conduct attributable to circumstantial mitigations are enumerated and discussed in psycho-

logical and legal terms. On the other hand, the criminal-penal death penalty is in theory not eliminated but contracted and restricted ad absurdum so that it may "reward its interpreters" through the ongoing dialogue between the element of sternness (*din*) and the element of compassion (*rachamim*) that it is to maintain.

To give this case a realistic dimension, the dialogical tension offering a narrative choice begins with the question of the very feasibility of the occurrence of such an extreme case. While the Talmud cites Rabbi Judah's conclusion that such an extreme case never happened and never will happen, the counter opinion of Rabbi Jonathan (*Sanhedrin*, 71:a), who stated "I saw him [a 'stubborn son'] and sat on his grave"[6] is also cited by the Talmud.

Further, the temporal element stipulating that if no environmental mitigating circumstances are operative, this youth ought to die because in such a case he would eventually become a highway robber, appears at first sight to represent a linear causal model of determinism. Nonetheless, the mitigating restrictions provide in fact the very rehabilitative contraction dynamics alluded to above.

Thus, in relation to the problems of drunkenness, stealing, and disobedience to parental authority, which characterize intergenerational conflict throughout history, the Talmud points the way to a restricting hermeneutic code that could diminish intergenerational tension because it retroactively "re-biographs" the delinquent's failing past. This mitigation is accomplished by contracting and minimizing past juvenile delinquency through a process of reinterpretation that attributes failure to all possible youthful mistakes that the Talmud enlisted.

In other words, since it is most probably impossible to find a "highway robber" whose parents spoke not only in one educational "voice" but who resembled each other physically, and since it is most unlikely that addicted alcoholics supported their habit during their youth only be stealing money from both of their parents and by drinking only cheap wine (as the Talmud stipulated), what is left is only the reverse implication. Accordingly, it is not only the role model, Resh Lakish, who became a famous Talmudic scholar after being a "highway robber," but theoretically almost all repenting highway robbers and addicts could "re-biograph" their failing past by attributing their juvenile delinquency to circumstantial problems (such as parental disharmony) once they have repented and corrected their conduct. Thus, while one may overly "whitewash" one's "psychopathic" *past* as innocent circumstantial episodes, the threatening *future* of the "highway robber" image, though contracted, is never entirely eliminated so that, in theory, one may still be judged accordingly.

Put differently, this case encompasses in essence all the potential components for the contracting dialogue in time that I shall term *biographic rehabilitation* or simply *re-biographing* through the "multiple choice" code of interpretation.

Thus, it is not the mitigation of the penalty for "highway robbery" that is implicit here, because this act should be, and usually is, penalized in all civilized countries. But it is the neutralization of the deterministic stigmatizing tendency of "once a highway robber—always a highway robber" in the cases of those that ceased to rob that is implied in this Talmudic exercise of "interpreting this possibility out of existence." It is only in the case of "repentance" that one needs to "re-biograph" one's youth and "de-label" the "social death penalty" by reinterpreting past failures as resulting from parental inconsistency in education, from parental cruelty, or by attributing it to any other circumstantial causes.

A BRIEF OVERVIEW OF THE CHAPTER ORGANIZATION

Having introduced the "stubborn and rebellious son" case as an illustration of how a hermeneutic dialogue may be maintained between one's past failing "I" and one's future "thou" over which the threatening stigma of the deterministic "highway robber" label hangs, I would like to present a brief overview of the outline and layout of the book.

Before doing this, one methodological or rather terminological word of caution is in order. As I introduce Midrashic hermeneutic pluralism as a *dialogic* circular system of psychotherapeutic contraction in time by contrasting it with what I term the linear *dialectic* and fundamentalistic approach to therapy, I have to qualify my usage of such terms.

Thus, while the terms *circular* and *linear conceptions of time* are borrowed from the domain of historiography, and the term *fundamentalism* is borrowed from theology and the dialectic terminology from philosophy, there is no intention to present this book as a professional contribution either to philosophy of history or to theology. It is, however, precisely because such terms as *dialecticism* and *fundamentalism* have been used in a popularized way and hence have exerted so frequently divergent and often contradictory phenomenological impacts in the social sciences, that they have to be dealt with within their social scientific contexts. By emphasizing the need to come to terms with such "social scientized" concepts, there is, however, no intention to conceal the somewhat polemic tone of the book, which indeed attempts to present Midrashic narrativism as an alternative model to psychotherapeutic actualization. The chapters can, therefore, be read separately or as one continuous discursive presentation.

Thus, in the second chapter, I demonstrate how orthodox Freudian and neo-Freudian psychotherapeutic narratology essentially constitutes a fundamentalistic interpretation system in which the analyst operates as an "elect" missionary who feels that only he is authorized to manipulate the "convert-analysand" until he accepts the one and only permissible "Oedipal-insight-oriented" interpretation of his past neurosis, which then justifies the interpretation of his past as an unavoidable "original sin guilt."

To give the reader an immediate demonstration of how Midrashic narrativism operates, in the third chapter, the actual possibility of temporal contracting interpretation through a therapeutic intrapersonal process is discussed by presenting the Midrashic model for "rebiographing'" sinners. A non "original sin" based biographic rehabilitation perspective, based on biblical case studies that were interpreted by the Midrash and the Talmud, is presented and I show how "repenters" may reinterpret and contract their failing past and expand their future aspirations by identifying with biblical role models who sinned but were subsequently acquitted by the Midrash.

In the fourth chapter, I will demonstrate how Hegelian dialectic theosophy of history operated as a hermeneutic metacode that affected Freudian Oedipal interpretation.

According to this thesis, social progress and personal growth are possible as part of historical necessity via the negating elimination of Father Laius or the capitalist class system. It will be shown further how, by contrast, Jewish cyclistic philosophy of history essentially entails the components of a psychological self-renewal theory of growth.

In the fifth chapter, an encounter between the Oedipal key narrative for dialectic progress and the Isaac metahermeneutic code for dialogic continuity is presented. It is thus argued that in view of the many available myths concerning intergenerational tension, only the dialectic metacode of progress via father elimination explains why Freud selected the Oedipal story as a key narrative, when in Jewish socialization, solutions to intergenerational tension are patterned on Midrashic interpretations of the biblical story of Isaac's Akeda. In that respect, an analysis of Midrashic interpretations of the *Akeda* paradox shows how continuity is possible in spite of tension; how an intergenerational dialogue may prevail in spite of the sword hanging over Isaac's throat.

In the sixth chapter, the encounter between dialectic and dialogic systems of interpretation will be further extended to such sociological phenomena as immigration patterns and collective settlements, on the one hand, and to cognitive learning styles on the other. It is thus demonstrated how the dialectic notions were used first by early settlers in Palestine to negate the diaspora (*shlilat hagalut*) and how the American dialectic "melting pot" philosophy was subsequently abused in Israel by European "enlightened" Jews as a basis for absorbing immigrants. Similarly, it is demonstrated how the Talmudic learning system, with its dialogic interpretation style, was rejected by European Israelis in favor of a dialectic learning system.

In the seventh chapter, information about how Western imbalanced development of left (rational) and right (emotional) brain hemispheres, which often resulted in psychological disorientation, is being applied to the problem of multiple versus mono interpretation systems of life stories is presented. Based on the Hasidic-Cabalic notion of mutual contraction, my previous theory of dialogue will be extended to demonstrate how the Jewish hermeneutic code entails an interhemispheric balancing model that a priori trains people to interpret reality simultaneously through rational Talmudism and Cabalic mysticism.

In the eighth chapter,the recently popular conversion movements and new religions and cults are discussed in terms of their psychotherapeutic implications by presenting results of an empirical study that differentiated between the linear process of converting in a dialectic fashion from one religion (which is negated) to another new religion-cult, and the cyclistic *teshuvah* process of dialogic returning to one's parental religion.

To close the Midrashic "hermeneutic circle" that focused primarily on the psychotherapeutic time perspective, in chapters nine and ten the discourse about the possibility of a dialogic interpretation model through temporal contraction culminates in a discussion of the phenomenological impact of Midrashic messianic ideologies on the psychology of hope and future orientation.

While the phenomenological construction of future reality is, by definition, utopian, the concrete differential implication emanating from a teleological *reading* of one's predetermined finite future and the free script *writing* of an infinite future are outlined in terms of (a) their concrete usage in clinical cases treated by psychodramatic and "reframing" techniques of therapy; and (b) their impact on therapy in cultures in which oldness connotes physical-organic decay in contrast to their effect on cultures in which oldness denotes spiritual growth.

The problems of interpreting the present, which is the pivotal meeting point between past and future, is treated here only in relation to past and future because the theory of contraction that I developed in my book *Dialogue with Deviance* (1983) deals in essence with how the "Judeo-Hasidic" dialogue operates in the "here and now" sphere of interpersonal space. It is the problem of an intrapersonal dialogue in terms of contraction or expansion of past or future time with which the book is primarily concerned.

In concluding this overview, I allow myself once more to repeat my plea to the reader to perceive the dialogic model inherent in the Midrashic multiple hermeneutic code as an exaggerated ideal type (which probably does not exist as a pure "ideal" type) that does not attempt to eliminate the dialectic approach to therapeutic growth and progress. Indeed, if the Midrashic schema for psychotherapeutic interpretations was conceived as the new "messianic" remedy that is to substitute for all previous models, I would be presenting a dialectic model that violates my own dialogic intentions. It is thus only to facilitate the introduction of an alternative paradigm that might in fact have been already partially and perhaps intuitively disseminated and applied by existentially anchored, nonorthodox approaches to therapy that the polemic tone style of presenting extreme contrasts appeared useful and legitimate. Moreover, the very emphasis on the paradigmatic impact of hermeneutic metacodes presumably inculcated during socialization presupposes the coexistence of what I term dialectic and dialogic metacodes. If, nonetheless, this book will help people to "contract" the fundamentalistic and deterministic impact of a prioristic metabeliefs on their lives while expounding the scope of human narrative choices necessary for living, then it still outweighs any future "academic castigation."

NOTES

1. It is beyond the scope of the present study to follow Kierkegaard's (1980) very complicated discussion concerning the possibility that Adam's "original sin" is a cause of people's subsequent sins, which they presumably inherited, or rather contracted as a biologically infectious "guilt germ" in their mother's womb. Kierkegaard's assumption that hereditary sin as a cause of anxiety may only be understood as a dogmatic presupposition, would, however, parallel my conceptualization of metacode beliefs that may phenomenologically shape one's biographic interpretation.

2. In his ethnographic study describing the functions of the *Shiur* (Talmud classes for people who work during the day time), Heilman (1983) used the concept of "contemporization" to describe a process presumably akin to "concretization." While both concretization and contemporization denote the possibility of reinterpreting the past to fit present needs, the latter refers, according to Heilman's operational definition, mainly to a symbolic reenactment of the past. Accordingly, it should be stressed that Heilman's demonstrative example in which a rabbi explains that the contemporary reading of certain "outdated" portions of the Torah's "In remembrance of the Holy Temple" (p. 91), may represent only specific orthodox sections of Judaism. However, both secular Zionists following interpretations of such leading scholars as Achad Ha'am and religious Zionists who claim to follow the inspirations of Rabbi Kook, interpret the functions of reading and studying the Torah and Talmud in terms of its relevance to the future reconstruction and redemption of Israel.

3. While Abraham Amsel's (1976) discourse about the Jewish attitude to mental disturbances is highly simplistic in its shallow, nonsystematic documentary method, he seems essentially correct in presenting free will and personal responsibility as the master key for understanding Jewish approaches (although there are many) toward deviance.

4. The four letters *P,R,D,S* that comprise the Hebrew word *Pardes*, meaning literally "orchard" but symbolizing also immersion in dangerous theosophic speculations, are traditionally used to signify the four levels of Jewish Biblical commentary: P—*peshat* (straightforward logic interpretations); R—*remez* (implicated interpretations); D—*derash* (legendary homiletic interpretations); and S—*sod* (mystic-cabalistic interpretations). It is of interest to note that in his study of Christian biblical exegesis, Todorov (1982) also discussed four levels of interpretation that might derive from the Jewish *Pardes* conception. Nonetheless Todorov persistently indicated that "the Christian tradition of biblical exegesis . . . consists in restricting the proliferation of meaning, in seeking one meaning that is preferable to the others" (p. 126) and that behind its interpretive strategy "there lies a principle that is no less powerful for being unformulated: a word has, at bottom, only one meaning" (p. 106). Accordingly, if biblical hermeneutics indeed exert paradigmatic influence on therapeutic possibilities, as it is

here assumed, then Christian exegetic doctrines might contain a fundamentalistic trend that might be discovered in certain therapeutic interpretation dicta.

5. The passages in Deuteronomy (17:9–12) stating that "thou shalt come unto the . . . Judge that shall be in those days . . . and according to the Judgement which they shall tell thee, thou . . . shalt not deline . . . to the right hand nor to the left" were interpreted by Rashi as follows: "even if he [the Judge] says that right is left and that left is right." While this interpretation might appear fundamentalistic, in its Midrashic origin it comprises, in fact, the very principle of pluralistic interpretation. Thus, it is not only that it is up to whichever elected judge happened to be in office "in those days" to interpret the law, even if he is mistaken, but, according to the Jerusalemite Talmud (*Horayot*, A:5) and the *Sifri*, Rashi's instructions also entail a possible rejection of the Judge's decision because sometimes "to you it seems that right is left or vice versa but objectively the Judge should be heeded only if he says that right is right."

6. One derives a realistic feeling that this law was taken seriously in admonishing and in "treating" rebellious sons from first-century writers such as the philosopher Philo who discussed the problem of curability in somewhat Lombrozian (with whose name the idea of innate criminality is associated) terms. "Now if the insolence of young men can be thus cured, let them escape the reproach which their former errors deserved . . . but if it happens that these words and instructions conveyed by them [parents] in order to reclaim the man, appear to be useless, then let him therefore be brought forth by these very parents out of the city with a multitude following him, and let him be stoned." [Philo (1930, 7:451), on the other hand, added the phases of imprisonment and degrading]: "And therefore fathers have the right to upbraid their children and admonish them severely and if they do not submit to threats conveyed in words to beat and degrade them and put them in bonds. And further if in the face of this they continue to rebel, and carried away by their incorrigible depravity refuse the yoke, the law permits the parents to extend the punishment to death." Consequently, when Josephus Flavius (16,11:341) condemned King Herod for executing his two sons, he was apparently convinced that they did not show the severe behavioral symptoms of a "stubborn and rebellious son," as he states: "besides being ill-natured in suspecting and speaking to their father . . . they [were in] no way deficient in their conduct." Moreover, referring mainly to the abolishment of the death penalty prescribed for this case, according to some sources, the rebellious sons were flogged by the Jewish courts in postexile times (see *Talmudic Encyclopaedia*, 1951, 3:366) or Falk (1964, 54:81–2).

2 Narrative "Missionarism" in Dialectic Psychotherapy

In the early 1970s, Lionel Trilling (1972:140) made the following observation: "At the present there is a withdrawal of credence from Freudian theory. This development cannot be ascribed to any simple cause, but the contemporary disenchantment with narration as a way of explaining things surely has some bearing upon it." Trilling, who described psychoanalysis as "a science . . . based upon narration, upon telling" (p. 140) that purports, like other social phenomena, to expose the inauthenticity of people's conscious life, was apparently unaware of the possibility that the recent "renaissance" of hermeneutics and narrativity in philosophy, literature, and phenomenological sociology might have precipitated Freud's "second coming" as a pioneering virtuoso in the art of interpretation.

Thus, social philosophers like Habermas (1972) argued, for example, that Freud's psychoanalysis is concerned with the therapeutic applicability of hermeneutics. Nevertheless, more than anybody else it was probably the philosopher Paul Ricoeur who, in his monumental work *Freud and Philosophy* (1970), opened the way both for the psychologists to use Freud's gravestone as a cornerstone of a reconstructive psychology of narrativity and for those following the literary critics to use the same rocky monument to throw "deconstructive" stones at the Oedipal despotic fathers on whose paradigmatic influence they were forced to pattern their work. Ricoeur (p. 8) showed that while the hermeneutic field referred originally *only* to the "theory of rules that preside over . . . the interpretation of a particular text," Freud ventured to decipher dreams, neurotic symptoms, or the unconscious as if they were a text constructed as a language governed by signs and symbols.

The major goal of this chapter is to present Freudian orthodox[1] neonarrativism as a "missionary" system in which a "convert-analysand" is being manipulated to accept one fundamentalistic interpretation of his biography.

24

Nonetheless, before we define our terms and proceed with our discourse, it would seem in order to ask how, or rather who, made it possible to transform hermeneutics from a method of text interpretation to a method of interpreting life? It is usually agreed that it was probably Wilhelm Dilthey, who in the nineteenth century was the first to introduce hermeneutical ideas as a potential method for historical understanding (*Verstehen*). It is, however, more important to stress also, that hermeneutics was used as the bedrock both of Husserl's phenomenology, which meant, according to Heidegger's and Schutz's refinements, that one's "life world" can only be understood as a subjective *inner* experience (*Erlebnis*) and of an "empathic" kind of psychology through which it became a major tool, or "technology" in Schleiermacher's sense, for assigning meaning to the lives *of others*.

More specifically, while Dilthey's historicist hermeneutics was essentially epistemological in the neo-Kantian sense of knowing or rather "self-knowledge," it laid the foundation for two dangerous passages. The first passage is from Dilthey's epistemology of knowing to Heidegger's ontology of being. Thus, hermeneutics, defined as a phenomenological "subjective" experience of being, includes, as H. G. Gadamer (1975) proclaimed, the prejudices of the individual who is now the sole interpreter of his own reality. The second, and more "disastrous" passage is, as Ricoeur (1983) claimed, from a subjective understanding of the particular to an "objective" interpretation or explanation of the general. Within the present context, this later Diltheyan Romantic modality of histoical knowledge or biographical self-knowledge, which contains the methodological temptation to attribute causally "objective" interpretations to the lives of others becomes crucial. This trap of causal attribution, which is embedded in the very historical method of retrospective understanding, must, by definition, presuppose an empathic capacity to transpose oneself into the mental life of others, be it in the nonactive past or in the interactive present. At any rate, from the present perspective, there is a crucial difference if one subjectively misinterprets one's own life or if one misattributes causal interpretations to others' lives.

While it is not essential to determine here (see Rotenberg, 1974, 1975) whether humane benevolence such as the undifferentiated inclination to sympathize with people is equivalent to or, to the contrary, far from being tantamount to, a specified capacity for accurate empathy, the methodological complications emanating from the implied differences between a subjective and an objective interpretation of people's lives place hermeneutics in the midst of contemporary controversies in the social sciences.

As it is central to the thesis to be developed here, I shall return shortly to differentiate between what I term dialectic and dialogic codes in order to interpret which determines "who" may select "which" hermeneutic rules to interpret texts or lives. With this distinction I thus hope to demonstrate that the rationale for imposing "causally objective" life stories on others, that most neo-Freudian psychonarrators and literary critics use is, in fact, guided by Freud's Oedipal myth.

More specifically, it will be shown that the "orthodox" interpretations of Freudian neo-narrativism that I claim operate, as mentioned above, like a "missionarizing" system, use the Oedipal metahermeneutic decoding dogma as a fundamentalistic objective way of interpreting people's life stories in causal terms. By the term, *missionarizing*, which according to the *Encyclopaedia Brittanica* is "used to denote organized efforts for the propagation of a religion," I have in mind both the soft manipulative "spiritual mediating" tactics and the "pure proselytizing" method of "going headlong at it" mentioned by Lifton (1967:269).

My metaphorical use of the term is intended to stress, however, that by using either one of the manipulative methods, the analyst's ultimate goal is, like the missionary's, as noted by Elizabeth Nottingham (1971:186), the dialectic substitution of a "true" conception of life for an "erroneous" interpretation.

> It was the manifest aim of the missionaries that their preaching of the Christian Gospels should bring benefits to their hearers by pointing out to them the "true" road to salvation and replacing the "erroneous" teaching of the indigenous faith.

Now, as alluded to in chapter 1, by the use of the term *metahermeneutic code*, I am not referring to the actual process of interpretation but to the superorganizing principle that provides "prejudice," in Gadamer's terms, or the axiomatic "master key" for decoding texts or lives. Viewed from a life history perspective, we may assume that such metahermeneutic master keys are "prejudiced" axioms for understanding and interpreting life, that people acquire, as indicated earlier, in their respective cultures or religions. Psychological narrative theories may thus be divided between those guided by a closed fundamentalistic, or by an open multiple, code for interpreting life.

Very briefly, representatives of the narrative trend in psychology, whether inspired by, or oblivious to, philosophers' rereading of Freud's interpretations, may be roughly divided between phenomenologically oriented social psychologists who focus on describing or *explaining* behavior and the psychotherapists who concentrate on curing or *retraining* behavior. Thus, Mancuso and Sarbin (1983), for example, observe that people tend to use specific narrative principles in order to organize chaotic sensory inputs, especially those concerned with their "selves," into coherent stories or plots that contain a beginning, middle point, and ending.

Gregen and Gregen (1983) have established, similarly, that there are three rudimentary narrative forms along that people tend to use to generate coherence and direction over time of their life events. These three temporal dimensions are: stability, progression, and regression.

Although Mancuso and Sarbin and Gregen and Gregen imply that people choose these narrative forms freely depending on what Mancuso and Sarbin termed "root metaphors," fairy tales, religious myths, or the mass media to which they have been exposed, they do not spell out the differential circumstances determining whether and how people would freely switch from one code to another if, say, the events comprising their life story constitute an unpleasant plot of failure.

Narrating therapists who do deal with people's failures, especially those with a psychoanalytic orientation, may be divided, however, between those who follow Roy Schafer (1983) and insist that the analyst has to train the analysand to reconstruct his life history according to Freud's Oedipal "sex-aggression" code and those who would follow Spence's (1982) lead in arguing that since the reconstruction of one's past via psychoanalytic narration inevitably distorts historical-biographical truth, narrative truth elicited during the "here and now" of psychoanalysis is preferable.

It should nonetheless be stressed at the outset that while Schafer and Spence are divided in regard to the possibility and significance of establishing a causal correlation between the "here and now" psychoanalytic narration and one's past history, they both seem to accept Freud's one-sided hermeneutic code for interpretation.

Thus, Spence's pragmatic and future-oriented interpretation, according to which the *constructed* interpretation entailing what he termed an "artistic truth" that, like a "here and now" appreciation of a painting, cannot and need not be correlated with any historical facts, appears to be hermeneutically more neutral than a *reconstructive* interpretation that claims to be bound by a *causal* deterministic connection with a specific historical past.

If, however, this present-based interpretation is governed only by Freud's Oedipal hermeneutic code, we still have only one fundamentalistic "missionary" system of therapeutic narration to be imposed by a manipulating yet tyrannic father-analyst on an analysand.

To put it more clearly, let us accept that it might indeed be therapeutically beneficial if an analyst does not interpret a person's current problems as resulting from his past predestined yet unavoidable Oedipal guilt. Nevertheless, the imposition of one psychoanalytical fundamentalistic interpretation indicating that this person's present problems are a function of his *current* murderous Oedipal hatred toward his parents must lead to the one and only dialectic solution of future personal growth—that progress in a Hegelian-Marxist class "replacement" sense is possible only via the symbolic killing of one's parents on the "psychoanalytic trial bench" (about which more will be said later).

It is here that the question of "how many" alternative interpretations are available for selection and "who" may select them to narrate another person's life story acquires its concrete epitomizing significance. Thus, it is probably not accidental that in order to evade the problem of selection of codes, most psychologists prefer the noncommittal general term *narration*, which refers merely to the process of telling a story or accounting for events, to the concept of hermeneutics, which is embedded in the old complex arena concerning the science of interpretation, where biblical exegesis, philology, philosophy, and historiography intersect.

It is by differentiating between the *dialectical* and *dialogical* metahermeneutic principles that seem to guide the psychology of narrativism that we may now return to analyze the above mentioned theoretical expositions of what can be termed *narrative psychology*. To do so, let me begin by defining these two basic narrative categories and then, in order to facilitate a broader analysis of the sociotherapeutic implications emanating from these differentiated interpretation systems, I shall discuss the problem of psychotherapeutic "missionarism" by introducing the concepts of "Karaism" or fundamentalism which, to my mind, underlies the dialectical systems of hermeneutics.

By *hermeneutic dialecticism* I refer to the popularized interpretation of Hegel's synthetic *aufheben* (integrating elevation), which in Marxist-Darwinian terms means that through conflict and negation only one antithetic principle or "fitting class" may predominate through the elimination and replacement of the no-more-"fitting" class thesis or principle. By contrast, if two classes or principles or, from our perspective, two alternative "I and thou" systems of interpretation coexist, we would term the dynamic tension between them *dialogic*. For our present purpose, a good example of the latter is Ina Rossi's (1983) attempt to formulate a reciprocal-complementary approach to sociological research that would preserve both the objective social-structure methodology and the subjective phenomenological principle for studying social phenomena.

Thus Rossi states:

> I understand social praxis as the acting out of the dialectic tension between the subjective and objective principles . . . which does not eliminate one of the two principles but reproduces their tension at a higher level. The performance of such dialectic tension is the key explanatory variable of social dynamics. (P. 320)

While Rossi and most other social scientists use the term *dialectic* to define both the process of "replacement" and the dynamic situation of reciprocal complementing tension—although admittedly the latter "differs from the Marxist notion of the dialectic of opposites" (p. 35), I prefer the term *dialogue* to describe reciprocal tension. I insist on the proposed semantic distinction because, among other advantages, only the term *dialogue* differentiates between replacement situations in which there is no "dialogue" between the "replacer" and the opponent who is to be "replaced," or rather eliminated, and the dynamic situations in which a constant coexisting "dialogue" between seeming opposites may prevail.[2] Although in the present chapter I shall deal only with the psychology of dialectic narrativism, it is with this differentiation (between the dialectic and the dialogic) that we may now examine the question of *who* may "replace" or interpret other people's reality according to the dialectic code for narration.

THE HERMENEUTICS OF DIALECTIC "MISSIONARISM" AND "KARAISM"

To understand the inherent difference between social-psychological, or rather phenomenological, narrativism, according to which people possess a dialogic free will to tell and retell their life stories in different versions as often as they want, and the dialectic narrativity in which one person (analyst) manipulates another person (analysand) to internalize one fundamentalistic interpretation of his biography, one has to trace the genesis of hermeneutics as a guiding philosophy of a multiplicity of disciplines.

Zygmunt Bauman (1978) opened his book *Hermeneutics and Social Science* by introducing the challenge of hermeneutics with the following definitive statement:

> Hermeneutics (from the Greek *hermeneutikos*, 'related to explaining'; . . . clarifying . . . rendering the obscure plain, the unclear clear) was for many centuries a subdiscipline of philology. Since most of the texts considered essential in the Christian world were available in contradictory versions, bearing traces of sloppiness and absentmindedness in an endless chain of anonymous copyists, the question of authenticity, of the true version versus distorted ones—could not but turn into a major concern for scholars. . . . It was in the sixteenth century that hermeneutics emerged from relative obscurity and swiftly moved into the very centre of scholarly argument. It owed its sudden eminence to the Catholic-Protestant debate regarding the authentic text of the Bible . . . and the true meaning of its message. The practical urgency of the matter, . . . propelled hermeneutics into a central position in the humanities. (P. 7)

Originally then, hermeneutics focused its efforts on establishing one authentic true interpretation out of a multiplicity of sloppy and contradictory texts.

In differentiating between the Aristotelian and the biblical exegetic origins of hermeneutics, Ricoeur (1970:24) tackled two of the major problems that concern us here: (1) the possibility of univocal versus plurivocal meaning and (2) the question of who has the authority to interpret. Concerning the first problem, Ricoeur argued that although "being" may only be understood in plurivocal terms because it may not be univocally defined, in the Aristotelian treatise *Peri Hermeneias* ("On Interpretation"), "the task of founding a theory of interpretation, conceived as the understanding of plurivocal meaning, has not yet been accomplished.'' The difficulty of establishing such a plurivocal theory stems, according to Ricoeur, mainly from the fact that, for Aristotle, the hermeneutics of ''saying something about something'' was essentially comprised of declarative propositions predicated on the dialectic logic of opposition, according to which communication is possible only if words have only *one* true or false meaning. Just as he views as a shortcoming the impossibility of Aristotle attributing multiple meanings to ''Being,'' so Ricoeur considers the second hermeneutic tradition as limiting due to the problem of authority: ''What limits the definition of exegetical hermeneutics is, first, its reference to an authority, whether monarchical, collegial, or ecclesiastic, the latter being the case of biblical hermeneutics as practiced within the Christian communities (p. 24).

In the light of Ricoeur's recognition of the limitations imposed by the questions of authority and of the attribution of uni- versus plurivocal meaning, it is surprising that in his enthusiastic treatment of Freud's text ''freed'' hermeneutics, he fails nonetheless to realize that implicit in Freud's psychoanalytic interpretation is a violation of both the limitations he is concerned with. I shall return to a discussion of the gist of Ricoeur's eloquent analysis of Freud's hermeneutics, but from the present perspective, Ricoeur's statement may serve as a challenging lead for our own discourse:

> This notion of text—thus freed from the notion of scripture or writing—is of considerable interest. Freud often makes use of it, particularly when he compares the work of analysis to translating from one language to another; the dream account is an unintelligible text for which the analyst substitutes a more intelligible text. To understand is to make this substitution. The title *Traumdeutung* . . . alludes to this analogy between analysis and exegesis.

It is to this Aristotelian dialectic *substitution* of a ''false'' interpretation by the *one* fundamentalistic ''true'' psychoanalytic interpretation made by the authoritarian analysis that our discussion will turn now by interweaving hermeneutics with the concepts of ''missionarism'' and ''fundamentalism'' or ''Karaism.'' *Hermeneutic missionarism*, as it will be used here, was selected as an appropriate metaphoric term capable of designating the dialectic situation found in both religious Christianity and orthodox psychoanalysis in which one ''authoritative'' person (missionary or analyst) manipulates another person until he is persuaded to accept the one and only fundamentalistic ''true'' interpretation of reality, religion, or biography. Psychoanalytic missionarism operates, then, as a subtle manipulative ''brainwashing'' technique that aims to recover one fundamentalistic true biography, as described by Peter Berger (1963).

> The Chinese ''brainwasher'' conspires with his victim in fabricating a new life-story for the latter, just as does the psychoanalyst with his patient. Of course, in both situations the victim/patient comes to believe that he is ''discovering'' truths about himself that were there long before this conspiracy got under way. (P. 64)

As will be shown below, the term *missionarism* appears now useful for our analysis not only because, as a Christian method, it elucidates *how* the one, and presumably the only, "true" authentic version of a text or reality is disseminated, but also it determines who has the authority to impose that interpretation.

In his classic genealogical study of social morals, Nietzsche (1969) argued that

> the judgement "good" did *not* originate with those to whom "goodness" was shown! Rather it was "the good" themselves . . . the noble, powerful, high-stationed and high-minded, who felt and established themselves in their actions as good that is of the first rank, in contradistinction to all the low, low-minded common and plebian. It was out of this *pathos* of distance that they first seized the right to create values. (P. 25)

Nietzsche thus showed how

> the real etymological significance of the designation for "good" . . . led back to the same *conceptual transformation* that everywhere "noble," aristocratic in the social sense, is the classic concept from which "good" in the sense of a . . . high order, "with a privileged soul" . . . runs parallel with that other in which "common," "plebian," "low" are finally transformed into the concept "bad." The most convincing example of the latter is the German word *schlecht* (bad) itself: which is identical with *schlicht* (plain, simple) . . . [which] originally designated the plain, common man. (P. 27)

By contrast, the German word *gut* (good)—Nietzsche (p. 31) stressed—signifies the man of "godlike race," a meaning "identical with the popular (originally noble) name of the Goth." Here one may add that it is actually unnecessary to regress to the Goths, because the German word *gut* signifies, like the English word *goods*, "property," that is, the master who owns the estate and the goods.

Foucault (quoted in Sheridan, 1982:119) went even further to show that the German word *wirkliche* (meaning literally "real" or "true"), which Nietzsche used to define history (*wirkliche historie*), is in fact also class-biased because etymologically the word *wirk* stems from the same root as *werk* (work), meaning "working" and "effective" and hence "useful."

Thus, Foucault argued that this Protestant ethic-based community of labor "acquired an ethical power of segregation, which permitted to eject, as into another world, all forms of social uselessness" (Sheridan, 1982:25).

After our short detour into the genealogy of the "roots" of social power, let us return now to our major discourse of what I termed "hermeneutic missionarism" only to discover that the possession of power to interpret texts or lives may be but one step removed from the selective possession of power to coin value-biased words.

The genealogical Christian roots of the "missionary-imperialistic"[3] method by which only selected "elect" persons are empowered to interpret and thus control other people's "understanding" (*Verständnis*) of life, is compellingly illuminated in Frank Kermode's (1980) analysis of what he termed Mark's interpretive formula of exclusion. Kermode, for whom interpretation is a discriminatory instrument of social control, stated that

> the power to make interpretations is an indispensable instrument of survival . . . [hence] in all the works of interpretation there are insiders and outsiders, the former having, or professing to have, immediate access to the mystery, the latter randomly scattered across space and time, and excluded from the elect who mistrust or despise their unauthorized divinations. (P. xi)

To demonstrate how the discriminatory process of what I termed "hermeneutic missionarism" was institutionalized by Christianity, Kermode (pp. 28, 29) used Mark's interpretation of Jesus's preaching to a crowd that included the Twelve Apostles by telling-teaching "many things in parables." Kermode stressed that Mark (4:11–12) has it that when, later, the twelve, baffled, asked Jesus to explain the purpose of his parables, he was said to have replied

> that they the elect, know the mystery of the Kingdom and do not need to be addressed in parables, but those outside are addressed only thus "*so that* they may see and not perceive, and hearing they may hear but not understand, *lest* at any time they should turn, and their sins be forgiven them." (P. 29)

Kermode went on to demonstrate that while Matthew's interpretation of Jesus's reply to the Twelve Apostles is presumed to be milder, it bestows, in fact, a causal predestined power upon those who may interpret and understand. Thus "the implication is that the exclusion arises not from the speaker's intention, but from the stupidity of the hearers, so that the blame is theirs" (p. 31).

Kermode, who demonstrated how a general interpretative distortion of the Old Testament was imperative for Christianity because "without the transformation of the Old Testament . . . the entire history of Christianity would have been different" (p. 19), exposed for us the Christian roots of "hermeneutic missionarism," which—I suggest—may be identified in secular hermeneutic methods as psychoanalysis, where, similarly, only "elect-analysts" are permitted to interpret. We may thus understand why only those who were predestined to be Oedipal Kings were able to interpret the riddle proposed by the Sphinx, so "that the history of interpretation may be thought of as a history of exclusions," as Kermode (p. 20) put it.

Another compelling example of how the "elect" establishment might use esoteric language to control the lower-class masses might be derived from George Orwell's classic *1984*. In their analysis of Orwellian linguistic structure, Hodge and Fowler (1979) used Basil Bernstein's distinction between "elaborated and restricted codes" to demonstrate how Orwell's "Newspeak" is to be used as a social control system. Whereas "Oldspeak" is, presumably, like the restricted code, characterized by simple sentence structures and lack of abstract concepts used by the working class, "Newspeak" would be like the elaborate code used, as Bernstein claimed, by the professional middle class to control the lower classes.

Hodge and Fowler claimed, however, that "Newspeak turns out to be a particular kind of restricted code . . . especially designed for the ruling class" (p. 10). Orwell's "restricted-Newspeak" thus resembles Jesus's parabelic language that facilitates a higher level of control due to its mysterious code of riddles and restricted hints, known only to the elect rulers. Indeed, Hodge and Fowler stressed that "when the language of control is backed up by the reality of power, the more massive the deletion . . . the more powerful, mystified, and irrational the control" (p. 18). Thus, as Orwell says, Newspeak exaggerates *ad absurdum* the dialectic process of "missionary" replacement and fundamentalistic imposition of one interpretation of life for another obsolete system:

> The purpose of Newspeak was not only to provide a medium of expression for the world-view and mental habits proper to the devotees . . . but to make other modes of thought impossible. It was intended that when Newspeak had been adopted once and for all . . . Oldspeak [would be] forgotten. (Quoted in Hodge and Fowler, 1979:21)

By introducing the hermeneutics of "Karaism," we now realize that "missionary" hermeneutics, which authorizes elect insiders to interpret the lives of damned outsiders, must inevitably be linked to only one fundamentalistic-causal code of interpretation that the "missionary" analyst imposes on his subject.

The term *Hermeneutic Karaism* was chosen because it designates a fundamentalistic interpretation of Scriptures that was condemned by predominant rabbinic Judaism. Very briefly, the Karaites are a small, originally Jewish sect, dating back to the beginning of the eighth century, that adheres only to the written law (the Bible) and that rejects the rabbinic oral law (the Talmud). Karaism (as derived from the word *mikra*, which may be used synonymously with the term *bible* but which means literally "reading") recognizes the Scriptures as the sole and direct source of all religious and normative behavior. According to some sources (see *Encyclopedia Judaica*), Karaism also carried the idea of "calling" (*likro*), which designates (as known, for example, in the Shi'ite Moslem sect) a propagandistic calling for a fundamentalistic return to the Scripture and the eschewal of all other, mainly rabbinical, traditions. For a discussion of the impact of hermeneutics on life, Karaism appears more suitable than *fundamentalism* per se because, in practice, it did not reject modernity and, more important, it is not imbued with the fanatical aura that characterizes contemporary fundamentalism.[4] This is, however, not to say that the Karaites did not develop various hermeneutic traditions much the same as it is also difficult to establish (see Wieder, 1962) whether freedom of interpretation is allowed in Karaism. It is neither my aim to suggest that the rabbinates always permitted multiple legal or normative interpretations of the Scripture, as the "oral" connotation of Talmudism would imply. It is nonetheless the conceptual difference between a Karaistic notion of sticking to the written and the rabbinic-Midrashic notion that the "Torah has seventy faces," that is, multiple interpretation possibilities, that should interest us here.

Accordingly, it is perhaps not accidental that while the Hebrew word *Rav* (rabbi) connotes strength and authority, the word *rav* also means "plenty" or "many." It may thus be stated that, by and large, rabbinic *Midrashic* tradition of hermeneutic pluralism, which accepted both the written and the oral law, facilitated throughout the ages the interpretation that concretized the Torah according to the changing events and needs of the people (see Kadushin, 1938). Hence, if rabbinic Midrashism practically required the attribution of spiritual meaning to terrestrial activities, while the Karaiti "eye for an eye" is, for example, interpreted literally to this day, we would say that any "fundamentalistic" interpretation of a text, event, biography, or ideological doctrine that is not updated via reinterpretation may be viewed as "Karaistic."

What seems imperative now is to show that in a dialectic kind of hermeneutics, the problem is not only that the "missionary" elect-analyst is authorized to interpret other people's reality but also that this interpreting synthesizer may use only one rational[5] Karaistic (fundamentalistic) interpretation of the other's past failures, which must then be *causally* related to the current state of neurosis. The need for a Karaite cause-and-effect model for interpreting biographies is necessary in order to confirm the analyst's authoritative claim for his rational interpreting ability, which would be shattered if the analysand was free to choose any one of a multiplicity of noncausal and hence nonrational interpretations in reconstructing his life story. It is here that the metahermeneutic code, that is, the main guiding interpretation "switch board," would mark the difference between the phenomenologically oriented psychologist and the deterministic analyst. In the first case, people may freely use their own narrative "key board" in order to choose any suitable interpretation to reconstruct their biographies. In the second case, analysts would be the sole controllers of the hermeneutic "master key" in imposing, as we shall demonstrate, their a priori "Karaistic cause-effect" interpretation via their analytic missionary manipulation techniques. According to Peter Berger (1963), the former, phenomenological construction of reality, which "allows one to perceive one's biography as a movement within and through specific social worlds, . . . makes us little less likely to be trapped by every missionary band we encounter on the way" (p. 65).

THE "ORIGINAL SIN" CAUSE IN DIALECTIC NARRATIVISM

Let me demonstrate now how and why it is imperative for the dialectic missionary-narrator to impose on the "missionarized" other only one, fundamentalistic "Karaite" (which eliminates or replaces all other) interpretation, which must be related to one rational causal code guiding the entire hermeneutic system.

Let us consider Freud's interpretation code as applied, for example, to the following typical dream.

> Here is another innocent dream, dreamt by the same patient. . . . *Her husband asked her "Don't you think we ought to have the piano tuned?" And she replied: "It's not worthwhile, the hammers need reconditioning in any case."* . . . This was a repetition of a real event of the previous day. Her husband had asked this question and she had made some such reply. But what was the explanation of her dreaming it? She told me that the piano was a *disgusting old box*, that it made an *ugly noise*. (1900:186)

Through an association between another occasion when this woman said "it's not worthwhile" and the previous day's analytic session when it only *appeared* to Freud "as though she were saying: 'Please don't look; [at her chest because] it's not worthwhile,'" Freud inferred that the word *box*, in German *kasten* used for the piano, "was a substitute for a chest (*brustkasten*); and the interpretation of the dream led us back to the time of her physical development at puberty, when she had begun to be dissatisfied by her figure" (p. 186).

Freud thus concludes that "we can hardly doubt that it led back to still earlier times, if we take the word *disgusting* into account and *the ugly noise*" (p. 186).

I think that it will not be too biased to suggest that the spontaneous reaction of an unbiased reader to Freud's preposterous dream interpretation must be one of total astonishment unless he is preconditioned by a belief in a causal paradigm of personal growth embedded in what may be generally termed, as indicated above, an "Oedipal-original sin" conception of man's guilt. In other words, without the a priori acceptance of the causal connection between the unavoidable sexual guilt presumably suppressed during the Oedipal period and the subsequent neurosis, Freud's word substitution game would have been, to say the least, inconceivable. This preconditioned belief in a causal paradigm expounding life, I propose, seems to constitute the metahermeneutic code or the "master key" for interpreting behavior. This "master key" seems, paradoxically, to be more deeply entrenched the more it combines rational convictions with irrational beliefs because prejudices may thus be easily disguised by causal explanations.

Indeed in Freud's Oedipal-original sin guilt, metahermeneutic code, the Christian[6] belief in the irrational "original sin" is clearly intertwined with the rational dialectic notion of father replacement that underlies Freud's Oedipal man:

> Original sin and salvation through sacrificial death become [the] bases of the new religion founded by Paul. . . . The way in which the new religion came to terms with the ancient ambivalency in the father-son relationship is noteworthy . . . the Son who has taken the [patricidal] guilt on his shoulders . . . to displace the Father. . . . [he] could not escape. (1967:175)

Let us refer to another example, in which interpretation leading back to the "Oedipal-original sin" cause, is even more unequivocal and blatant. In his analysis of the famous Wolf-man case, Freud explained how he filled the gaps in his patient's memory in order to construct a complete interpretation. Thus, in regard to an infantile incident between the Wolf-man and his nursey-maid, Grusha, Freud wrote

> When he saw the girl on the floor engaged in scrubbing it, and kneeling down, with her buttocks projecting . . . he was faced once again with the posture which his mother had assumed in the copulation scene [which he presumably observed]. She became his mother; he was seized with sexual excitement owing to the activation of this picture and, like his father (whose action he can only have regarded at the time as micturition), he behaved in a masculine way towards her. His micturition on the floor was in reality an attempt at seduction, and the girl replied to it with a threat of castration [teasing and scolding him]. (1971:234)

Here the metahermeneutic code for establishing a causal connection between the neurotic present and past "Oedipal-original sin" guilt is directly used to reinforce Freud's "missionary" interpreting authority. This Oedipal metahermeneutic code, according to which current neurosis presumably originated in early childhood, is indeed used by Freud as a "master key" for interpreting all dreams, as stated in the following generalization: "A succession of meanings or wish-fulfillments may be superimposed on one another, the bottom one being the fulfillment of wish dating from earliest childhood" (1900:219). Thus, without this a priori acceptance of the Oedipal-guilt cause (rooted in early childhood) as a metahermeneutic code, the immediate question that came to one's mind would be somewhat as follows: If an infant can indeed be sexually aroused by the sight of a female's posture, why must this excitement be triggered only through the indirect association with the parents' copulation scene? And, moreover, why must the maid "become his mother" unless one accepts a priori that sexual arousal must always be traced to the Oedipal incestuous cause which must be somehow connected to the castration threat although there is no real indication of the father's threat. Indeed, Otto Rank (1978) was probably the first to question the therapeutic effectiveness of Freud's fundamentalistic application of the causal infantile "coitus witnessing" dogma when he asked:

> What value this has psychologically and therapeutically when the result of
> an analysis of several years may be nothing but the still doubtful fact of
> coitus witnessed in childhood. Even if one could grant such psychological
> efforts a therapeutic value, the systematic application of this method as a
> principle of interpretation in every instance would still be open to question.
> (Pp. 87–88)

Thus, without such a singular fundamentalistic ("Karaite") causal code, it
would seem impossible to construe the basis upon which Freud and such neo-
Freudians as Roy Schafer assume their missionary authority to impose their
dialectic interpretation and diagnosis,[7] which eliminates all other possible interpretations, on their analysands, even by distorting their biographies.

However, if one accepts this code, one could argue that the fact that the
dialectic narrative truth of the Oedipal complex cannot be verified by historical truth, as Spence (1982) has so skillfully demonstrated, is insignificant because of the "fundamental" truth inherent in the "Oedipal-original
sin" guilt dogma that serves as a metacausal code for interpreting *all* "neurotic" dysfunctions.

Indeed, I cannot recall a more compelling detailed analysis than Spence's
criticism, of how the various contributory factors distorting historical truth
are enhanced instead of being diminished by the intimidating manipulation
that the analyst uses, for example, during transference:

> One of the background influences on the way in which the past is put into
> words is the patients sense of whom he is talking to—in more theoretical
> terms, the state of transference. . . . The patients report will be slanted to-
> ward the side of persuasion—he speaks in order to win some kind of re-
> sponse from the analyst. Under these conditions, the truth value of what he
> says may tend to deteriorate. Under the press of a strong transference . . .
> what the patient is saying about the past must be translated into what he is
> demanding in the present. If he needs to be pitied, for example, he might
> exaggerate the misery of his childhood; if he wants to be praised for being
> an exceptional analytic patient, he might generate a crystal-clear memory
> of an infantile event. These reports have nothing much to do with the past.
> (Spence, 1982:94, 95)

Thus, if manipulative pressures for transference distort biographic truth,
and if, conversely, biographic truth is rejected as "resistance," one is forced
to conclude that only by accepting an axiomatic or dogmatic "Karaite"
(fundamentalistic) code like the "Oedipal-original sin" as a primal cause can
such neo-Freudian narrators as Roy Schafer (1983:275) (who uses "transference" and "resisting" as his major narrative structures) state without
hesitancy that "so many highly particularized, even seemingly opposite life
stories get to be retold convincingly as the familiar Oedipal story." (Schafer,
1983:275).

Indeed, the a priori acceptance of Freud's Oedipal code as a primal cause or metahermeneutic guide is not implicit but explicit in Schafer's narrative psychoanalytic credo:

> Freud saw the makings of a story that . . . he organized around what he called the nuclear complex of neurosis, that is, what was *for him* and remains *for us* the most adaptable, trustworthy, inclusive, supportable and helpful story of them all; the Oedipal complex in all its complexity and with all its surprises. (Ibid., p. 276)

It should therefore not be too surprising to discover that Schafer described openly and bluntly how he imposes his "sex-aggression" (original sin) cause-and-effect interpretation on his analysands via his "missionarizing" techniques:

> The analyst's retellings progressively influence the what and the how of the stories told by analysands. . . . The analyst slowly and patiently develops an emphasis on infantile or archaic modes of sexual and aggressive action. . . . Repeatedly the analysands stories . . . go through a series of transformations until finally they can be retold not only as sexual and aggressive modes of action but also as defensive measures. (Pp. 219–224)

Another example of how the Oedipal metacode is imposed, as a "Karaite" (fundamentalistic) key for interpreting behavior on a cross-cultural level is Jacob Arlow's (1985) psychoanalytic treatment of the "personal myth."

Like other psychoanalysts, Arlow believes that many autobiographies take the form of "personal myths" because repressed unconscious fantasies tend to distort memories.

Although Arlow asserts that "in selecting details that conform to a particular theory of pathogenesis, there is always the risk that the therapist may impose his own mythological view of the patients past upon the biography" (p. 4), he does not hesitate to impose the Oedipal myth as a universal metacode suitable for interpreting the Western cases he treated as well as conflicts associated with the non-Western Hindu god-figure Ganesha.

The details of how Arlow uses the Oedipal interpretation as a "Karaite" (fundamentalistic) metacode for establishing one universal truth are tedious and redundant here. It is striking to note, however, that while in the Hindu tradition the substitution of heads symbolizes spiritual growth (because new heads are added), Arlow insists that the meaning of Siva's giving his son Ganesha a new head instead of the head that he cut off by mistake can be understood only in Oedipal castration terms.

In concluding our argumentative discourse purporting to expound how and why the "Oedipal-original sin" code is used in dialectic hermeneutics to impose one "Karaite" interpretation of past failure, we could say now that

Habermas (1972) was probably right when he defined Freud's "depth hermeneutics" as depending on causal explanations of pathology. Habermas's "wishful thinking" in conceiving psychoanalysis as a critical science must have misled him, however, into believing that Freud's method leads to a self-formative or a self-reflective state in which an individual is emancipated and freed from the unconscious repressions that society has imposed upon him.

If, however, we are correct in assuming that in dialectic narrativism the "Oedipal-original sin" is not self-emancipating but an oppressive act of interpretation imposed (missionarized) by the ruling father/analyst, we must ask now how one's unchangeable "original sin," "I" (failing past) enters into a therapeutic dialogue with one's "It" or "Thou" (future aspirations)? In other words, the question is whether in the Freudian hermeneutic scheme, one can shake, change, or reinterpret one's past Oedipal guilt (the cause of one's present failing neurosis) in order to be permitted to pass through the gates leading to an emancipated "new" successful future. In dialectic psychology, two patterns of hermeneutic pathways to the future may be recognized. In both of these conflict-based pathways, the gates to the future may be opened only via the dialectic process of death and birth or rebirth. One is directed, *inward* and one is directed *outward*. That is, in the first, the sequential process of destruction and construction is *intrapersonal* and in the second it is *interpersonal*.

Self-Blaming "Insight" as a Prerequisite for "Rebirth"

To elucidate how progress proceeds via the antithetic conflict-based principle of self-negation or self-destruction, Hegel used two organic analogies. One was that of the phoenix, in which suicidal self-consumption causes a "death-rebirth" kind of self-reproduction, and the second was the fruit-plant metaphor, in which self-annihilating decay breeds life in another, new plant.

In regard to the first case, Hegel (1900) stated

The Phoenix as a type of the life of Nature, eternally preparing for itself its funeral pile, and consuming itself upon it; but so that from its ashes is produced the new renovated, fresh life. . . . It certainly makes war upon itself—consumes its own existence; but in this very destruction it works up that existence into a new form (1900:126,7)

The second, fruit-plant analogy, is used by Hegel to explicate the organic nature of the rise and fall of the nations:

"The life of one nation causes the fruit to ripen. . . . This fruit however, does not fall back on to its own lap. . . . The fruit will bear seeds once more, but seeds of another nation" (1920:50).

What seems to come through loud and clear from Hegel's influential paradigm of growth, is the theme of organic blossoming fitness as a criterion for life and of death as a prerequisite to a revived future.[8]

In his classic study *The Varieties of Religious Experience*, William James (1971) concluded, in regard to the possibilities of inner psychological conversion, that "the completest religions would therefore seem to be those in which the pessimistic elements are best developed. Buddhism and Christianity are the best known to us of these. . . . The man must die to an unreal life before he can be born into the real life" (p. 171).

I think that it does not require a mystical imagination to recognize in James's "death-rebirth" psychological model, Hegel's conflict-based dialecticism embedded in an unshakeable "original sin" guilt from which one cannot break out into the future without a prior self-destructive death. In other words, a *breakthrough* must be preceded by a *breakdown*. This seems indeed to be James's formula: "This is the religious melancholy and 'conviction of sin' that have played so large a part in the history of Protestant Christianity. The man's interior is a battle-ground for what he feels to be two deadly hostile selves, one actual, the other ideal" (p. 176).

Sarbin and Adler (1970,71) have already noticed that the application of the death-rebirth theme might be identified in many psychotherapeutic practices. It would thus be of no special novelty to show how in the psychological literature, the emergence of the new self after the preadolescent inner *Sturm und Drang* (storm and stress) battlefield, is described in Hegel's dialectic terms of revival from the ashes of one's own old self.

Moreover, Sarbin and Adler's (1970-71) reference to cathartic, "illumination" or to reaching a gradual or a sudden state of *insight* (especially in the case termed by James the "sick soul") as marking the entry into the "rebirth" stage might also sound quite reasonable and familiar to the reader.

It seems, however, important to demonstrate here that from a hermeneutic point of view, Freud's Thanatos-based "insight therapy" is, in fact, often used as a tool by which Oedipal narrativism trains the analysand to internalize the "original sin" guilt, as a toll fee for entry into the gates of the future. Again, from this angle, Habermas (1972) might be correct that Freud's "depth-hermeneutic" is a self-reflective process. It seems, however, that this self-reflecting *insight* does not necessarily emancipate the individual from socially imposed repressions but, instead, might operate, at least during its initial stage, as a dialectic self-blaming mechanism of self-destruction.

In other words, insight, from the present perspective, is not necessarily associated with the second dialectic phase of "rebirth," but might, in fact, manifest the first self-negating phase of "death" via the self-blaming story-telling method used by narrative analysts like Schafer (1983) who "slowly and patiently develops an emphasis on infantile or archaic modes of sexual and aggressive action" (p. 223). After all, what happens in practice when the analyst's influence on "the what and how of the stories told by analysands" (p. 219) focuses on "infantile modes of sexual and aggressive action"?

I propose that this analytic relearning to tell one's life story in terms of "infantile modes of sexual-aggressive actions," which may enhance, at least initially, one's self-destructive and self-blaming guilt, is, in fact, acquired through what is known as therapeutic "insight." By introducing "insight-therapy" as a self-reflective method of narration by which one learns to re-interpret one's life story in self-blaming terms of the unavoidable Oedipal guilt, I am obviously not suggesting that the term *insight* as such implies in-ternalization of guilt. Nonetheless, for our purpose, the broadest relevant definition of insight might still be Angyal's (1965) differentiation between the sudden or gradual increment of fragmentary knowledge and the "total resulting knowledge of personally relevant factors" (p. 261). Thus, the cog-nitive sequential process of gaining accumulative insights that establish the causal connection between past unconscious guilt and present neurosis may undoubtedly characterize "talking therapies" for which the inclusive term *insight therapies* may, as Perry London (1969) suggested be appropriate.

In the present context, one should stress, however, that insightful self-awareness in regard to causal relations between biographical facts has noth-ing to do with therapy or cure (see Rieff, 1966), or as Angyal (1965) puts it, "Every therapist knows all too well that there is a world of difference be-tween a patient's gaining an insight and his responding to it" (p. 271).

Insightful acceptance of guilt is, however, a prerequisite for entering the improved future, as Angyal states one page later: "Progress means respond-ing to real guilt with regret; feeling horror rather than self-loathing or indif-ference" (p. 272).

Thus, "insight therapy" refers first of all to the self-negating phase in the dialectic process, during which the analyst forces the analysand to accept his evil nature as a moral philosopher would see it

> The patient may be said to have been forced to face not only his guilt but in addition, the evil within him which is the reason for his guilt. . . . It is an acknowledged part of his Self, no longer alien to that Self. In psychoanalyt-ic terminology, the patient has *insight*. (Fingarette, 1963:159)

To give the reader a concrete and more contemporary illustration of how the analyst manipulates ("missionarizes") the analysand to accept this self-blaming hermeneutic phase in the dialectic psychology of "death-rebirth," let us return now to Schafer's *alt-neu*[9] (old-new) narrative -insight therapy. Schafer (1983:198–202), describes the case of a successful attorney who spe-cialized as a consultant on bankruptcy problems, and who, according to the analytic interpretation, "had unconsciously chosen this realm of work be-cause . . . it represented dealing continuously and only half hopefully with death, the threat of death, and the making of reparative efforts."

According to Schafer, during the initial (nonmissionarized?) history tak-ing, the attorney "portrayed his parents as enemies to one another"; his father, whom he feared but could later dismiss as irrelevant, chronically angry and remote, and his mother, whose behavior he copied in order to be close to her, chronically depressed.

After working through "transference" and breaking initial "resistance," the life story was reinterpreted for the first time somewhat as follows: It was not the mother to whom he felt close by emulating her depressions, but the father, who visited him often in a home of distant relatives to which he was sent for some months during his preschool years. According to his memories, he was looking forward to his father's self-sacrificing visits and subsequent efforts, because he helped him to develop intellectually, culturally, and professionally. These ties with the father, which seemed to be substantiated by his subsequent actual success as a lawyer, were later interpreted (second narrativism) as attempts "to rescue him from the depressive entanglement with his mother."

To fit the metahermeneutic code leading to Oedipal self-blaming, the attorney's life story was, however, reconstructed a third time and here I prefer to let Schafer (1983) speak for himself:

> Working directly within the transference, the analyst was able to go on to develop interpretations of passive homosexual love—of the analysand's wishing to be impregnated by the analyst but having to defend against showing that . . . by . . . maintaining a detached manner. . . . Yet another function of his detached position in the transference and his correlated dismissal of his father's importance to him was to discover and continue to repress his having wished in his early years to be his mother's lover and his father's successful rival. (P. 200)

This "missionarized" Oedipal triconstructed life story was then followed by the attorney's self-blaming guilt for driving his mother to "her death wishes" and by his self-destructive fears of being castrated by his "ever angry oedipal father" as a result of which his legal preoccupation with death, "was a living death that guaranteed survival and gratification" as Schafer (p. 201) phrases it.

In the present context, it is insignificant whether this attorney's behavior or the behavior of anyone else going through any other psychoanalytic narrative insight therapy, resulted in subsequent cure or a successful "rebirth." What seems important from our perspective, however, is that in dialectic therapy, entry into the cured stage of "rebirth" must be preceded by an Oedipal self-blaming phase of "death." Thus, in the West, it would indeed seem most likely that an ex-convict or any ex-mental patient would not be reinstitutionalized, but would also not be eligible to bear the mental health title of "normalcy," or might even be labeled a "psychopath" if he were not willing first to renarrate his life story by confessing his Oedipal "original sin" guilt through the process of "insight therapy."[10] Thus, the road from the *reincarcerating* "outside" to the *reincarnating* "inside" leads through the confession gate of *insight*. While "insight," as a dialectic self-negating internalization of the "original sin" guilt is portrayed here as a prerequisite to a future "rebirth," this does not mean that a restorative millenarian "second coming" entails no future. It suggests only that in a "rebirth" therapy, the future, which is to emerge from the "ashes" of an organic self-destroyed past executed by a Protestant self-blaming "court of insight"[11] (in which failure may serve retroactively as a predestinational proof of damnation), must necessarily begin by returning to a "born-again" point of departure.

By reversing the dialectic from self-destruction to a patricidal father-killing, improved future construction is possible, however, according to Hegel's second organic metaphor of the "fruit-plant," in which the new plant inevitably enhances the decaying process of the plant that bred it. Indeed, independent consciousness is possible, according to Hegel (1979) only by risking the self and destroying the other: "The individual who has not risked his life . . . has not attained to the truth of his recognition as an independent self-consciousness. Similarly, just as he stakes his own life, so each must seek the other's death" (p. 114).

Future Construction Through Oedipal Deconstruction

Ricoeur (1970) differentiated between two diametrically opposed kinds of hermeneutics. At one pole, hermeneutics is understood as a *restoration* of meaning; and at the other pole, hermeneutics is used as a tactic of *suspicion*, a demystification and reduction of illusion and the destruction of the sacred. "Hermeneutic restoration," which according to Ricoeur is grounded in faith, characterizes phenomenology:

> It is a rational faith, for it interprets; but it is a faith because it seeks through interpretation, a second naïveté. Phenomenology is its instrument of hearing, of recollection, of restoration of meaning. "Believe in order to understand, understand in order to believe"—such is its maxim. (P. 28)

Psychoanalysis aligns itself, according to Ricoeur (p. 27), with the hermeneutics of suspicion,[12] in which interpretation begins by doubting and ends by "tearing off masks" and by reducing disguises.

Although one could question whether a psychoanalytic interpretation based on a "Karaite" (fundamentalistic) "faith" in the causal impact of Oedipal guilt should not be classified as hermeneutic restoration, at least in a negative sense, what we have now is a reversed dialectical model of futurism predicated on Hegel's fruit-plant metaphor. That is, if Ricoeur is essentially right, that according to Freud's decomposing archeological model, King Laius's "royal semen," which gave birth to Oedipus, also contains the seeds by which Oedipus may "blossom" only by tearing off the mask or crown of Laius —then the recent flourishing of deconstructive narrativism in literature and anti-psychiatry could be understood as a dialectic "fruit-plant" process of creativity.

It seems ironic, though, that Freud, who was unable to accept, for example, Jung's deconstructive Oedipal rebellion (see Alexander, 1982) against himself, should in fact be the father of Jung's patricidal hermeneutics. Thus, Avineri's (1969) observation that Hegel and Marx apparently believed that the dialectic principle of self-negation may be applied universally but not against themselves, seems to hold true for Freud's dialectics as well. This does not mean, however, that Oedipal deconstruction through the hermeneutic of suspicion that "reduces disguises" and "tears off masks" may not breed new creative blossoming "fruit-plants."

The Oedipal "fruit-plant" that I have in mind is the recent popular school of hermeneutic deconstruction in literary criticism and its branches in antipsychiatry or rather reincarnated "Oedipalism."

In a succinct, eloquently written book, Christopher Norris (1982) stated that "deconstruction works at the same giddy limits, suspending all that we take for granted about language, experience and the 'normal' possibilities of human communication. . . . Deconstruction is the active antithesis of everything that criticism ought to be" (p. xii).

Thus, deconstruction encompasses the reinterpretation of all communicable possibilities as texts and behavior. The systematic presentation of hermeneutic deconstruction as an Oedipal antithesis to structuralism is beyond the professional scope and interests of the current study because it would require more than a passing comment to demonstrate, for example, whether the pioneering French scholar Jacques Derrida laid the foundations for a dialectic, or rather a dialogic, discourse with the texts that he "deconstructed."

What appears plausible, however, is to suggest that French deconstruction seemed to have provided the deconstructive stones for the symbolic killing of various Oedipal "god fathers" controlling certain poetic or political domains.

Accordingly, it is irrelevant for the moment whether Harold Bloom is a full-fledged literary deconstructionist or rather (as it appears) a reconstructionist. What does seem useful for the present analysis is the dialectic Oedipal terminology that Bloom uses to construe the possiblity of poetic creativity.

In every tradition of poetry, Bloom (1973) maintained, there is a strong patriarchic poet whose "influence" the "late coming" poet cannot escape. The guilt-ridden hatred of the "belated" poet toward the father poet that Bloom termed the "anxiety of influence from which we all suffer, whether we are poets or not, has to be located first in its origins, in the morasses of what Freud called the family romance" (p. 56).

Poetic creativity that must, according to Bloom, emerge from "this anxiety of influence"

> always proceeds by a misreading of the prior poet, or act of creative correction that is actually and necessarily a misinterpretation. The history of fruitful poetic influence, which is to say the main tradition of Western poetry since the Renaissance, is a history of anxiety and self-serving caricature, of distortion, of perverse, willful revisionism without which modern poetry as such could not exist. (P. 30)

Bloom then (p. 32) quoted the poet Keats as having said about Milton that "life to him would be death to me," so that Keats's future as an authentic poet seems to have depended on his ability to destroy or obliterate the Milton that permeated, or rather possessed, him.

If thus I "read" Bloom correctly, or rather "misread" him creatively, his theory of poetic revision or misprision entailed the components of a dialectic "fruit-plant" replacement paradigm when he stated (p. 39) that "prophets and advanced analysts alike proclaim discontinuity" or even more so when he declared conclusively: "I arrive therefore at the pragmatic formula: 'Where the precursor was, there the ephebe shall be,' but by the discontinuous mode of emptying the precursor of *his* divinity" (p. 91).

As we are not interested here in the dialectic evolvement possibilities of poetry, let us examine how Hegel's organic "fruit-plant" metaphor is applied to theories of human behavior and to social praxis through interpretative deconstruction.

In a study purporting to demonstrate how the French psychoanalyst Jacques Lacan influenced antipsychiatry and the 1968 student revolt, Turkle (1978:145) argued that it was Lacan's "subversive discourse" that served as an impetus for the revolting students to begin their war against the establishment by "reinventing language": "Like the schizophrenic they have to destroy ordinary language in order to communicate." Indeed, Lacan's "psychoanalysis" is dialectically constructed by first deconstructing Freudian psychoanalytic theories of the "normal self."

> Lacan's reading of psychoanalysis is subversive in the way it undermines the formulations of the self that are implicit in our language, and it puts each speaking subject in an intimate relationship with the fragmented self experienced by the schizophrenic. Thus the notion of the decentered subject is a crucial link between Lacan and the anti-psychiatric movement, which refuses to view madness as something completely alien to "normals." (Turkle, 1978:146)

The "link" between Lacan's "anxiety of influence" and dialectic movements of antipsychiatry and anticapitalistic establishment is most immanent not only on the demolishing level but also on the "rebirth" or rather "reburst" level of a new (anti) psychiatry that emerged from the decaying "fruit-plant" that bred it. A most vivid example is Deleuze's and Guattari's (1972) "schizoanalysis." Influenced by Lacan's "subversive hermeneutic psychiatry," Deleuze and Guattari maintain that capitalistic societies use the Oedipal code for the internalization of society's superego as a means of repressing boundless desires. The schizophrenic, who refuses to be Oedipalized and whose fragmented thinking has not been coded by the Oedipal prison of language and thought, may then serve as a mentor or model for "schizoanalysis." The construction of schizoanalytic hermeneutics, which is a decoding method geared to uncover the connections within our fragmented self, is possible, however, only after we have destroyed the ordinary language of the "normal" Oedipalized false "whole-self."

Thus, the construction of anti-Oedipus Jr. is possible only by dialectically destroying Laius, or Oedipus Sr., as Deleuze and Guattari dramatically declare, "Destroy, destroy. The task of schizoanalysis goes by way of destruction—a whole scouring of the unconscious, a complete curettage. Destroy Oedipus, the illusion of the ego, the puppet of the superego, guilt,[13] the law of castration" (p. 311)

In summary, while, paradoxically, Deleuze's and Guattari's anti-"Oedipal rebellion" in fact verifies the "Oedipal theory," the hermeneutic possibility of a dialectic "death-birth" replacement was demonstrated above.

Ironically, though, therapeutic cure should be possible, according to both "straight psychiatry" and "antipsychiatry" by destroying and "replacing" the therapist. This logical antimissionary conclusion is usually avoided, however, by psychiatrists—"fitting survivors"—through the dialectic musical chairs technique by which one may use the gimmick of "transference" to redirect destruction back to any "neurotic" or "psychotic" parental figure.

The present dialogic perspective assumes, however, a "coexistence" of both possibilities: progress through destruction or continuity. The paradigmatic roots of progress through dialogic continuity and the differential conditions that facilitate its possible application will be expounded later. To contrast what I termed the "Karaite" (fundamentalistic) "missionary" interpretation of biographies with a pluralistic hermeneutic system, a demonstration of how Midrashic hermeneutics may be used to reinterpret life stories seems in order.

NOTES

1. My emphasis on "orthodox" narrativism is intended to indicate that I am aware of the fact that such nonorthodox psychoanalytic interpreters as Heince Kohut, and Winnicott are more "dialogic" in their therapeutic practice. It seems, however, that Kohut (1984), the most popular "dialogic" psychoanalyst, relinquished neither Freud's "early-life" Oedipal doctrine of causality nor his manipulative, imposing method when he stated in his last book that: "the self-psychologically informed psychoanalyst . . . identifies causal sequences, he shows the patient that his feelings and reactions are explained by his experiences in early life" (p. 25).

2. In applying Greek notions of bipolar "dialected relations" to contemporary psychology, Rychlak (1979:57) asserted that if "we agree on one or two of our opponents' points, we say 'sure' you are right there. But, . . . you are dead wrong on the other points. . . . This area of agreement . . . which . . . was called the *synopsis* by the Greeks; today we call it the *synthesis*." As Rychlak's synthesis refers only to the "area of agreement," we still would not know how to term the area of disagreement if we wished, for instance, to differentiate between a continuous coexisting dialogue on a point of disagreement and a Hegelian-Marxian elimination of one set of opinions.

3. As I have indicated elsewhere (1986), Christian missionarism from the West was usually associated with imperialistic ambitions that facilitated various forms of international social control. This "missionary imperialistic" tradition, whether in its old cruel-coercive form practiced by the inquisition and the crusaders or in its contemporary, more subtle, manipulative methodology, is condemned, for example, by such Eastern Christian sects as the Japanese Makuya (see Teshima, 1981) who profess a more dialogic coexistence of multiple religions.

4. The typical association with contemporary fanatic fundamentalism would seem to be with Iranian "Chumeinism." It is nonetheless precisely because "Chumeinism," like some Christian fundamentalistic sects, is known more for its political views than for its strict interpretation of text, that for the present context, *Karaism* (associated with a relatively unknown sect), seems preferable, as the word *Kara* means literally "reading."

5. Although rationalism and fundamentalistic-dogmatic hermeneutics allowing only one interpretation of text appear as a contradiction in terms, I hope to show that Freud succeeded in superimposing a "rational" cause-and-effect scheme on his fundamentalistic Oedipalism.

6. It should be noted here that Ricoeur's (1981:276) assertion that "speculation on original sin finds itself bound to the Adamic speculation of late Judaism," is quite misleading. It might, in fact, be stated safely that such Talmudic (*Shabbat*, 146:a) declarations that the very act of "Israel's standing at Mount Sinai, purified them from filth" (sins, defaults, etc.), served in fact as an underlying motif for rejecting the notion of original sin.

7. Indeed, Sarbin et al. (1960) and others have adduced ample evidence demonstrating how psychological training in psychopathological diagnosis accustoms clinicians to making reckless stereotypic interpretations of people's behavior.

8. In his recent efforts to convince us that Freud was actually misinterpreted into American biologism, but that he "clearly wanted us to accept psychoanalysis as a humanistic undertaking," Bettelheim (1984) presents the following typical quotation from Freud's autobiography: "After a lifelong detour over the natural sciences, medicine and psychotherapy, my interest returned to those cultural problems which had once captivated the youth who had barely awakened to deeper thought" (p. 48). Besides being a straightforward testimony to Freud's "lifelong" organic biologism, from which he "returned to those cultural problems which had once captivated" him in his youth, the reader is referred to Sulloway's (1983) monumental *Freud, Biologist of the Mind* to learn how Freud's Darwinian biologism predominated his dialectic model of sin.

9. This German term was used by Theodore Herzl to designate the new-old or renewed status of the land of Israel.

10. The very important difference between using "neutralization" techniques (see Matza, 1964) to shake responsibility and the retrospective reinterpretation of failure in constructive terms to release self-blaming guilt is discussed in Chapter 8.

11. The term *court of insight* is a paraphrase of the inner "court of conscience" that the Protestant individualistic doctrine institutionalized to substitute for the Catholic church-based social and religious control system from which it separated. Michael Lerner (1986), who has done extensive group therapy in California to counteract the vicious circle of internalizing guilt-failure among American working

classes, feels that the individualistic Protestant working ethic in fact deepens the self-blaming failure syndrome because it teaches the individual to interpret or accept his own failure as a sign of predestined damnation.

12. Elsewhere Ricoeur (1983) portrayed the relationship between the hermeneutics of restoration and suspicion as a conflict between two forces, whereby the restorative Romantic genre with its nostalgia for the past is being constantly challenged and negated by critical elements such as the *Aufklärung* philosophy of the "Enlightenment."

13. Jonathan Culler (1981) noticed that Freud's distortions of the original Oedipal myth is taken as a general tension although the actual proof of Oedipus' guilt is never presented. The myth never reveals whether Laius was murdered by one person or by a group. The Oedipal guilt thesis is hence constructed on a chain of assumptions that there was one murder and that this murderer was Oedipus, who then felt guilty.

3 The Midrash and "Biographic Rehabilitation"

What is the rehabilitative effectiveness of the statement: "I hope to have a good past"? Having been reared to think in Western, historically based terms, we would probably dismiss such a declaration as senseless because we were taught to believe that our past is a closed book. Accordingly, we train our ex-criminals or ex-mental patients to redeem themselves either in a present based on "here and now" existential salvation or in a "not yet here and not yet now" futuristic "clean leaf" rehabilitation by asking them to erase or accept their unchangeable failing past. By advocating such rehabilitation formulas, however, we rarely come to full terms with the problem of whether and how people are really capable of trading or integrating their old, failing, "Mr. Hyde" self with a new, reborn, "clean leaf, Dr. Jekyl" self.

In essence, the question here is why must Western people "hide" their past, failing, "Mr. Hyde" self? Why shouldn't one be able to correct one's past in order either to bridge the cognitive gap that separates the amnestic death of one's failing past from one's existential "here and now" rebirth, or to minimize the "cognitive dissonance" brought about by the "psychoanalytic confrontation" between one's conscious guiltful past and one's neurotic present.

The possibility of correcting the past for the sake of psychological continuity and cognitive congruity depends naturally on the nature of our beliefs concerning the "is" and "ought" objectivity inherent in the methodology of writing collective history or individual biographies. The unchallenged "closed book" consensus about the impossibility of correcting one's failing past, which even such an optimistic futurist psychotherapist as Viktor Frankl (1982:132) defined as a closed "memory book" in which nothing can be altered or erased, is however, seriously shattered by social scientists who discuss the possibility of reinterpreting one's successful past as actual failure, thus making the past a new deviant identity imputed to one in the present. Social reinterpretations serve people's needs to have a consistent biographical image of the "new" deviant identity. In discussing "biographical reconstruction" of deviant identities, Lofland (1969) noted that

> one of the most broadly and deeply held of human beliefs in recent Western societies is that an actor must have some consistent and special history that explains the current social object that he is seen as being. . . . The *present evil* of current characters must be related to *past evil* that can be discovered in biography. (P. 150)

Conversely, "biographical rehabilitation" would seem possible when we come to deal with the case of "political rehabilitation." In this case, one's hope "to have a good past" may all of a sudden sound more reasonable because one's subsequent rehabilitation, unsatisfied by a "here and now" or "from now on" "clean leaf" credit grants a new rereading of one's past through new "inverting goggles"[1] that retrospectively present a relatively positive and harmonious image of one's total personality (including one's past) in one's own and one's society's eyes.

The purpose of this chapter is to demonstrate how, in contrast to the psychoanalytic confrontation with past failures, the Jewish Midrash provides a framework for reinterpreting and correcting one's failing past through what can be termed "biographic rehabilitation" or simply: "re-biographing."

Let me state at the outset, however, that since our study has been guided by the assumption that specific methods for treating individual histories follow directly from unique philosophies of collective history, I hypothesize here that it is not the historical "closed book" objectivity but the underlying "original sin" kind of approach to past failures that rules out the "corrective rehabilitation" of one's biography. Later I shall come back to defend this proposition but let me first introduce the Midrash as a framework or as a philosophy of history in which, I say, the components of "biographic rehabilitation" or "re-biographing" are available.

THE MIDRASHIC NARRATIVE AS DIALOGUE IN TIME ·

As explicated in Chapter 1, the Midrashic dialogue between past, present, and future facilitates, as Kadushin (1938) demonstrated, the concretization and reorganization of seemingly contrasted conditions or positions in such a way that by selectively and creatively reinterpreting past events to suit future aspirations, historical cognitive dissonance may be reduced.

Indeed, Emile Fackenheim (1972) argued that only the "midrashic framework" can explain how Jews were trained to resolve the dissonance produced by confrontations between their present reality and their past, thus enabling each generation to relive anew (i.e., concretizing or synchronizing) such "root experiences" as the Exodus from Egypt with its miraculous revelation of God. In this framework, every Jew, including the lowly maidservants, experienced the miraculous revelation because presumably every Jew was present at Mount Sinai. Thus, the fluid, concretizing nature of the Midrashic dialogue between principles established in the past and changing accommodations needed in a present to build a future made it possible not to discard or synthesize "ancient" laws but to reinterpret or rearrange them to fit present conditions. As Heineman (1970) said, "To the extent that we mold the present on the basis of the past, we alter the form of the past according to the present" (p. 36).

Our interest here in "Midrashic re-biographing" begins from the observation that while such philosophers of history as Gershom Scholem (1941, 1972) may have succeeded in refuting the Hegelian-Toynbeean *fossilized* conception of Judaism by demonstrating how Jewish mystic-messianism periodically revived and motivated Jews to construct their *future*, the psychological problem of how Jews treated their failing *past* was heretofore largely ignored.

That is, while Scholem (1941) indeed acknowledged the continuity between the Midrashic hermeneutic method and mystic cabalism, since "Aggadic productivity has been a continuous element of Kabbalistic literature" (p. 31), he has been rightly credited for showing only how the mystical-messianic drive emanating from cabalism explains the future-oriented self-renewal of Judaism, but not dealing as such with the Midrashic system (in which Hasidic-cabalism is admittedly rooted) as a "psycho-historical" method for harmonizing the past with futuristic renewal.

The problem of how Jews treated their past psychologically is, however, crucial for understanding the alleged periodic revival of Judaism and, concurrently, the possibility of personal self-renewal, because studies (see Yaker, 1972) have shown, for example, that Western schizophrenics suffer from ruptured linear time conception reflected in their inability to relate their present to past and future.

Moreover, in concluding his study about federal witnesses whose past life and identity had to be buried and erased in order to protect them from potential revengers, Fred Montanino (1984) stated that

> the witnesses' protection experience tells us that . . . we construct reality from the world around us, and past life and interaction are essential parts of this construction. . . . The protected witness experience teaches us further that . . . we cannot escape responsibility for our own past performance, nor can we easily assume a rightful place in collective social life without some recognition of it. We cannot totally divorce ourselves from others who have been part of our social life without losing the part from which we seek to divorce them. (P. 523)

Thus, the dialectic divorce from past identity, be it criminal or "schizophrenic," advocated by the "new leaf" rehabilitation formula seems to pose questions when examined through such extreme cases as Protected Federal Witnesses or degraded political personalities seeking rehabilitation.

Since we are interested primarily in how the Midrash provides the "psycho-sophic" framework for reinterpreting past failures, it would seem useful to limit our analysis to studying only how Midrashic reinterpretation retrospectively acquits individual deeds and collective events described in the Bible as sins.

RE-BIOGRAPHING THE SINFUL PAST

One can best understand how the possibility of "biographic rehabilitation follows from the Midrash by examining Midrashic cases of "re-biographing" in the light of the meaning of the concept *teshuva* (repentance).

Rabbi J. B. Soloveitchick (see Peli, 1980), one of the leading contemporary authorities on Jewish law and philosophy, makes a distinction between repenting by blotting out one's sinful past and the process of rectifiying it. In the first case, past evil or folly is forgiven and/or erased like a debt. In the second case, it is cognitively and emotionally elevated and transformed into personal assets via the process of reinterpretation. Soloveitchick (see Peli, 1980) admitted that the first case, in which "a man . . . who repents erases with one blow, his whole past" (p. 272) requires what we would term a kind of "schizophrenic or amnesic" disconnection from the past and is very difficult, unhealthy, and hence rare:

> I have seen penitents do just that, and the consequences? They became different and estranged from their families and friends, who appeared to them to belong to another eon, a different world, a period when they were entrenched in sin which has now been erased from their consciousness. All feelings and experiences connected with that period were dead to them. (P. 272)

Soloveitchick, therefore, seems to rank the second form of *teshuvah* on a much higher level of spiritual achievement. But how is the elevation of sin possible, especially if one considers this "pygmalionic" relabeling process not only from the repenter's perspective but also from society's point of view?

One of the most quoted socializing statements about the possibility of *teshuva*, which is cited in the name of Resh Lakish, who prior to becoming a major Talmudic sage, was allegedly a famous "gangster," asserts "that repentance (*teshuva*) is so great that premeditated sins are accounted for as though they were merits" (Talmud, *Yoma*, 86:b). Specifically, the Talmud seeks to institutionalize a social-cultural norm by which repenters will not merely be given a "from now on" "new leaf" chance, but will be granted full "biographic rehabilitation" by being permitted to correct, reinterpret, or assign new meaning to their past failing history. Otherwise, it would be impossible that sins premeditated and committed in the *past* could retroactively be "accounted for as merits." Indeed, this "rehabilitative biographic rereading" is precisely what the Midrash does in the following examples of Biblical sinners.

For example, Jacob's "holy cheating" of his father Isaac when stating "I am Esau thy first born" (Gen. 27:1) is reread by separating the words "I am" and "Esau [is] thy first born." The words "I am" are then transferred to the "I am the Lord thy God" appearing in the Ten Commandments that Jacob presumably had in mind when he said "I am" to reaffirm his loyalty to God (see Midrash *Rabba*, 65:18). Similarly, Rachel's "stealing" of her father Laban's images (Gen. 31:32) is reinterpreted by asserting that she took the images "for the sake of Heaven" in order to prevent her father from idol worshipping (Midrash *Rabba,* 71:5). Reuben (Gen. 30:14), picked up mandrakes during "the days of wheat harvest" because during the harvest, the field owners gave up on everything left in the field anyhow and so he did not steal them (Gen. 72:2). And, finally, with Joseph, we have a classic case of retrospective interpretation: namely, the reconsideration of a seemingly detrimental, callous act as an eventually useful event for humanity. What first appeared as the "sinful" selling of Joseph is reinterpreted by Joseph himself when he assures his brothers retroactively: "Ye thought evil against me: but God meant it unto good . . . to save much people alive" (Gen. 50:20).

To be sure, by "biographic rereading," I am referring to the "philologically creative" (see Heinemen, 1970) rearrangement in time and space of seemingly contrasted texts that follows from an organic conception of rabbinic thought (see Kadushin, 1938) or rather from the "paradox" philosophy of *tikun* (correction) on which I elaborated elsewhere (see Rotenberg, 1983). The reader is hence cautioned to understand that the Midrashic rereading of one's sinning past is possible only if it indeed restores (i.e., corrects or rearranges) the organic harmony with one's subsequent repenting past. Thus, step number one in the required sequence of "re-biographing" begins with repentance in a specific present as a prerequisite for re-biographing the past as step number two.

Accordingly (as step no. 1), Joseph first subjected his brothers to the most severe test of repentance, namely, their ability to resist the same temptation to sell or turn in a brother (their "original sin" toward Joseph) even though circumstances seemed to demand it when presumably only Benjamin sinned by stealing Joseph's cup: "but the man in whose hand the cup is found, he shall be my servant, and as for you, get you up in place unto your father" (Gen. 44:17). Hence, it was only after Joseph's brothers withstood the criteria of "absolute repentance" (which refers, according to Maimonides [*Teshuva,* 2:1], to cases in which one has the opportunity to commit a previous sin but does not) that Joseph used retrospective reinterpretation (as step no. 2) to rehabilitate his brother's sin by asserting, "God meant unto good to save much people alive."

Thus, the possibility of retroactive "philological rearrangement" or re-reading of the text describing a sin, which follows from the notion that "the Torah has seventy faces so that its infinite meaning . . . served only as a general framework for a multiplicity of individual readings" (see Scholem, 1974:172) must not contradict the seemingly opposite idea that the Torah is to constitute an organic "living structure from which not even one letter can be excised without seriously harming the entire body" (ibid., 171). Hence, "re-biographing" may be understood as an a posteriori imaginative method of creative reconstruction.

As this subtle pragmatic art of hermeneutic "re-biographing" is very tedious and intricate, I shall present here only selected[2] cases that illuminate how the Midrash "rehabilitates"[3] past sins of repented biblical figures through a rereading of the text describing their sin.

The Incestuous Sin of Reuben

After accounting for the death of Rachel, the Bible states: "And it came to pass, when Israel dwelt in that land, that Reuben went and lay with Bilha his father's concubine: and Israel heard it. Now the sons of Jacob were twelve" (Gen. 35:22,23).

Here the Bible describes Reuben's sin in very explicit terms. And, indeed, Jacob who "heard it" did not forget it when in his subsequent blessing of the tribes he says:

> Reuben, thou art my first born, my might, and the beginning of my strength, the excellency of dignity and the excellency of power: Unstable as water, thou shalt not excel; because thou wentest up to thy father's bed; then defiledst thou it; he went up to my couch. (Gen. 49:3,4)

However, in the Talmud (*Shabbat*, 55:b) we find the very clear-cut rehabilitative statement: "Rabbi Shmuel the son of Nachman said in Rabbi Jonathan's name: anyone who says that Reuben sinned is nothing but mistaken for it is written 'now the sons of Jacob were twelve' which teaches us that they were all equal. Then how do I interpret that Reuben went and lay with Bilha his father's concubine? This teaches that he transported his father's couch and the Writ imputes [blame] to him as though he had lain with her."

Based on this rereading of the verses, the Talmud then offers an explanation for this "transportation of beds" that actually transforms Reuben's act into a righteous deed of honoring his mother Leah: "He stood up against the humiliation of his mother by saying: If my mother's sister was a rival to my mother, shall the bondsmaid of my mother's sister be a rival to my mother? He thus arose and transposed the beds" (ibid.).

To be sure, this "righteous transportation of beds" refers, according to the Midrash, to the fact that when Jacob put the bed of Bilha (Rachel's maid) in his tent after the death of Rachel, whose bed was always next to Jacob, Reuben stood up to defend his mother's honor by substituting Bilha's bed for Leah's.

To present a harmonious image of Reuben's biography, the Midrash is careful, however, to interconnect the reversive rereading of Reuben's sin with his general full repentance in regard to other sins, such as his advice to sell his brother Joseph (see *Bereshit Rabba*, 84:19). Hence, the pragmatic principle of permitting us to see a new consistent personality gestalt in regard to selected biblical figures may be understood as a principle for re-biographing only when an eventual state of *teshuva* becomes the necessary condition for offering new positive circumstantial interpretations to earlier (past) sins.

Using the same opening declaration (cited above in regard to Reuben) that warns against conceiving of various biblical personalities as sinners, the Talmud rehabilitates a great number of them through elaborate techniques, of which I shall present only one example (for each case) of text rereading used for reversing the sins of kings David, Solomon, and Menashe.

King David's Adulterous Sin

In the Bible (Sam. II:3,4) we read: "And David sent and inquired after the woman and one said, is not this Bathsheba, the daughter of Eliam, the wife of Uriah the Hittite? And David sent messengers and took her; and she came in unto him, and he lay with her. . . ." While the Biblical description appears quite straightforward in recounting King David's sin as adultery, the Talmud (*Shabbat*, 56:a) states again:

> Rabbi Samuel the son of Nachman said in the name of Jonathan: whoever maintains that David sinned is nothing but mistaken; for it is written "And David behaved himself wisely, in all his ways and the Lord was with him" (Sam. I, 18:14). Is it possible that sin came to his hand, yet the Divine Presence was with him?

The Talmud then reconciles this seeming contradiction by offering a rereading of another biblical verse. Thus, the Talmud (ibid.) asks: "Then how do I interpret [the verse] wherefore has thou despised the word of the Lord to do evil in his sight?" (Sam., II, 12:9). The Talmud then concludes that "David only wished or intended to do evil [adultery] but actually didn't" by utilizing the following technique.

> Rab observed: Rabbi, who is descended from David, seeks to defend him and [expounds] reverses [the verse] in David's favour. [Thus], the "evil" [mentioned] here is unlike every other "evil" [mentioned] elsewhere in the Torah. For of every other evil in the Torah it is written "and he did" whereas here it is written "to do" [this means] that he desired to do, but did not.

One may notice that in presenting this "philologically creative" yet intricate rereading technique, the Talmud does not hesitate to admit that Rabbi's "nepotism" ("who is descended from David"), contributed to the reversal of the verses' meaning in King David's favor. Yet, here again, the very subtle distinction between the mere intention or desire *to do* evil and the evils that were actually committed is an exemplifying link in the rehabilitation of King David's biography. Nonetheless, while the attribution of intention to do evil appears as a mitigating reinterpretation of past sinning, the Midrashic re-biographing of King David epitomizes, in fact, the infinite possibilities inherent in this hermeneutic multiple choice system. Namely, that the *mens rea* kind of "intention" to sin is, according to a much cited Talmudic dictum (*Yoma*, 29:a), worse than actual sinning. To reconcile this apparent problem, we find, however, the following text cited in the Talmud (*Shabbat*, 56:a):

> "Thou hast smitten Uriah the Hittite with the sword." Thou shouldst have had him tried by the Sanhedrin but didst not. "And hast taken his wife to be thy wife" thou hast marriage rights in her. For . . . everyone who went out in the wars of the house of David wrote a bill of divorcement for his wife.

The point to be stressed here is that the above passage reflects the Talmudic *ahistoric* principle that postulates that the Talmud and Midrashim were delivered on Mount Sinai and accordingly "there is no early and no late in the Torah" (*Pesachim*, 6:b), because otherwise it would have been impossible to assume that the Talmudic stipulation that soldiers deposit a tentative divorce form before going into battle (to avoid unresolved widowhood) was already known and activated during King David's time. Thus, according to this well-known Midrashic stipulation, there was no sinning and no intention to sin. One may thus choose the mitigating interpretation that attributes mere intention, or the *ahistoric* "divorce" narrative.

As in most other cases, the Talmud and the Midrash thus use David's subsequent full repentance as a pivotal point to begin to reverse,[4] via various hermeneutic methods, the meaning of David's earlier sins, in order to make it possible to present him retrospectively as a positive and harmonious role model, in order to encourage prospective repenters. Indeed, in one Midrash (*Shocher Tov, Tehilim*, 51) we find the following citation: "That is what David said of God . . . if you accept me, all criminals will make up with you, and everybody will look at me and I shall testify that you accept the repenters."

King Solomon's Sins

In referring to various sins attributed to King Solomon, such as building places for idol worshipping, mainly for his gentile wives, we find in the Bible the following summarizing statement: "And Solomon did evil in the sight of the Lord, and went not fully after the Lord, as did David his father" (I, Kings, 11:6).

It is interesting to note here that in recounting King Solomon's history, the Book of Chronicles describes him as a righteous king and fails to mention his gentile wives and the high places for idol worshipping that he presumably had built for them (see Japhet, 1977)[5]. While this method of "correcting" biblical history was quite typical of the author of Chronicles, the Talmud seems more anxious to offer a rereading of Solomon's sinful biography.

At any rate, the Talmud (*Shabbat*, 56:b) initiates its rereading of Solomon's biography with an unequivocal summarizing rehabilitative statement: "Whoever maintains that Solomon sinned is nothing but mistaken." Then, relying on another verse (I, Kings, 11:4), which states that "his heart was not perfect with the Lord his God, as was the heart of David his father," the Talmud cleanses Solomon of his alleged sins by stating that "it was [merely] not as the heart of David his father, but neither did he sin."

After this full rehabilitation in regard to the actual commission of sins, the Talmud further explains the passage, stating that "his wives turned away his heart to go after other gods, but he did not go." And, finally, the Talmud (ibid.) admits that the verse: "And Solomon did that which was evil in the sight of the Lord" (I, Kings, 11:6) means that since "he should have restrained his wives, but he did not, the Writ regards him as though he sinned." Thus, in spite of the complete rehabilitation granted to Solomon by the Chronicles' author, and in spite of the Talmud's general statements, which, in fact, fully acquit Solomon of all accusations, the Talmud admits that while, practically speaking, Solomon did not sin, his failure to restrain his wives is considered a sin.

The corrected or "mitigated" form of imputed sinning concurs with the temporal principle of *teshuva*, which stipulates that the eventual state of repentance permits and possibly even requires a retroactive "ascent through descent" (see Rotenberg, 1983) or "redemption through sin" (see Scholem, 1972), or a dialogue betwen one's "re-biographed" sinful "I" (one's past) and one's "thou" (subsequent *teshuva*), which then allows the representation of a positive and harmonious role-model image of the given biblical personality.

The Extreme Case of King Menashe's Sinning

The classic case of King Menashe's sinning, which concludes our list of Talmudic and *Midrashic* "re-biographed" role models, will be discussed here briefly not so much because it represents another example of retroactive rereading of sins, but because it stretches *ad absurdum* the very possibility of retrospective rehabilitation of one's biography through the *teshuva* process. The Bible provides a long list of accusations against King Menashe, the worst of which was the unforgiveable one of seducing others to sin. According to II Kings (21:1–16):

> Menashe was twelve years old when he began to reign fifty and five years in Jerusalem. And his mother's name was Hephzibah. And he did that which was evil in the sight of the Lord, after the abomination of the heathen, whom the Lord cast out before the Children of Israel. For he built up again the high places which Hezekiah his father had destroyed; and he reared up altars for Ba'al and made a grove, as did Ahab King of Israel; and worshiped all the host of heaven, and served them. And he built altars in the house of the Lord, of which the Lord said, In Jerusalem will I put my name. . . . And he made his son pass through the fire and observed times, and used enchantments, and dealt with familiar spirits and wizards: he wrought much wickedness in the sight of the Lord, to provoke him to anger . . . and Menashe seduced them to do more evil than did the nations whom the Lord destroyed before the Children of Israel. . . . Moreover, Menashe shed innocent blood . . . besides his sin wherewith he made Judah to sin.

Thus, King Menashe seemingly committed every possible sin under the sun: he erected an idol in the Holy Temple in Jerusalem; shed blood till "he had filled Jerusalem from one end to the other" (ibid.); made his son pass through the fire of the Molech; consulted spirits and wizards; and, worst of all, seduced others to sin and thus should have fallen under the rare Talmudic category of "impenitents," for whom even the gates of the world to come are presumably closed. And yet, the Talmud grants Menashe an unequivocal rehabilitation that epitomizes the unlimited possibility of *teshuva*. Thus, among the various Talmudic and Midrashic opinions that dispute whether Menashe repented or not or whether he was forgiven or not, we find the following instructive declaration concerning the infinite possibility of *teshuva* (Talmud, *Sanhedrin*, 103:a):

> Rabbi Jonathan said: He who asserts that Menashe has no portion in the world to come weakens the hands of the penitent sinners: For a tanna [a specific type of Talmudist] recited before Rabbi Jonathan: Menashe was penitent for thirty-three years, as it is written: "Menashe was twelve years old when he began to reign, and reigned fifty and five years in Jerusalem, and he made a grove as did Ahab King of Israel." How long did Ahab reign? Twenty-two years. How long did Menashe reign? Fifty-five years. Subtract these from twenty-two which leaves thirty-three."

The above cited Talmudic "re-biographic" exercise, through its complicated technique of rereading the sequence of historical events presented in the Bible, seeks to rehabilitate Menashe as a repenter by assuming that through the equation of Menashe's grove to Ahab's, the biblical verse implies that their sinning and hence their punishment (loss of reign) should be equal. Consequently, since Menashe reigned thirty-three years more than Ahab, the Talmud concludes that during those years, he repented. Indeed, even without the above cited rereading acrobatics, we read further in the Talmud (ibid.):

> Rabbi Jonathan said on the authority of Rabbi Simeon the son of Yohai: What is meant by "And he prayed unto him, and an opening was made for him" (Chron., II, 33:13). Should not "and was entreated of him" rather have been written? This teaches, that the Holy One, Blessed be He, made him a kind of opening in the Heavens, in order to accept him with repentance, on account of the Attribute of Justice.

According to the "Attribute of Justice" (*Midat Hadin*, referring to God's sternness), Menashe's repentance should actually not have been accepted, as he caused others to sin. Yet, we have in Menashe's classic case a most extreme example of how much the Talmud was willing to stretch its "re-biographic" rereading technique of the biblical historical text in order to demonstrate that Jewish *prospective* self-renewal (here extending to the world to come) is infinitely possible through the *retrospective* attribution of repentance or denial of sin.

The foregoing analysis of the strict, intricate biographic rereading techniques used by the Talmud and the Midrash calls for a reexamination of "biographic rehabilitation" in the light of traditional historiographic methods, because in both cases historical documents preserved from the past are *read* in order to interpret certain events in which people were involved. But before doing so, led me introduce briefly one example that illustrates how a biblical collective sin was rehabilitated by the Midrash via the use of a parable, and not through a philological rereading technique.

The "Golden Calf" Collective Sin

The accusations imputed in the Bible (Exod., 32:7,8) to the Golden Calf sin are straightforward:

> And the Lord said unto Moses, go get thee down; for thy people which thou broughtest out of the Land of Egypt have corrupted themselves. They have turned aside quickly out of the way which I commanded them: they have made them a molten calf, and have worshipped it, and have sacrificed thereunto, and said. These be the Gods of Israel which brought thee up and out of the Land of Egypt.

The Talmud (*Avoda Zara*, 4:2) nonetheless reverses the intention of making the golden calf so that by interpreting this premeditated collective sin as a necessary phase in the "ascent through descent" process of repentance it comes to praise the Israelites instead of condemning them: "The Israelites made the [golden] calf only in order to place a good argument in the mouth of the penitents"; which implies that repentance may overcome the most grievous sin. By connecting the Golden Calf sin to Moses' breaking of the Tablets,[6] the *Midrash Rabba* (*Ki-tisa*, 43:1) offers the rehabilitative parable that likens Moses' breaking of the Tablets to a minister (or king) who sent his messenger with a marriage contract to legalize his marriage to his bride. But when the messenger found the minister's prospective wife with another man, he tore up the marriage contract in order to rule out the possibility of her committing an adulterous sin, since only the power of the marriage contract could have made her a legally married woman.

This parable suggests that since the Golden Calf sin was committed before Israel received God's contract or covenant (the Tablets), there was no *idolatry,* as there was no *adultery* in the parable, because Moses broke the "contract" (i.e., the Tablets) that would have legalized Israel's commitment to God. After this tedious presentation of the Midrashic-Talmudic rereading method, let us now return to examine "biographic rehabilitation" as a legitimate method of individual and collective history.

BIOGRAPHIC REHABILITATION AND STORY TELLING

If we would accept now (at least tentatively) that the ideological tradition, which may explain both periodic Jewish revival and the possibility of "biographic rehabilitation," could indeed be identified in the Midrashic method of historiography or rather in its *a*historic methodology, then, what we essentially have now is a rehabilitative "story-telling" method. In differentiating between real living and "recounting" life, Sartre (1980) "recounted" the following experience:

> When I was in Hamburg, with that Erna girl whom I didn't trust and who was afraid of me, I led a peculiar sort of life. But I was inside it, I didn't think about it. And then one evening, in a little cafe at St. Pauli, she left me to go to the lavatory. I was left on my own, there was a gramophone playing Blue Skies. I started telling myself what had happened since I had landed, I said to myself: "On the third evening, as I was coming into a dancehall called the Blue Grotto, I noticed a tall woman who was half-seas over. And that woman is the one I am waiting for at this moment, listening to Blue Skies, and who is going to come back and sit down on my right and put her arms around my neck." Then I had a violent feeling that I was having an adventure. But Erna came back, she sat down beside me, she put her arms around my neck, and I hated her without knowing why. I understand now: it was because I had to begin living again, that the impression of having an adventure had just vanished. (P. 61)

In conjunction with the "Erna story," Sartre advised us that "for the most commonplace event to become an adventure, you must—and this is all that is necessary—start recounting it [because] a man is always a teller of tales, he sees everything that happens to him through them and he tries to live his life as if he were recounting it."

What Sartre suggests, in fact, is that while it may be natural and useful to live by recounting life as an adventurous story, if we want to have a healthy image of ourselves, so that the dialogue between one's past, present, and future, will constitute a consistent harmony, this recounting is, practically speaking, a distortion of real life. Indeed Sartre pointed out that

> when you tell about life, everything changes; only it's a change nobody notices: the proof of that is that people talk about true stories. As if there could

possibly be such things as true stories; events take place one way and we recount them the opposite way. (P. 62)

Thus, "biographic rehabilitation" may appear to be an attractive cure for "ex-failures" because it helps to restore the cognitive congruity and continuity between one's past and one's future-oriented present, but as it is, practically, a distortion of life, it is unrelated to the historical objectivity that underlies most psychodynamic rehabilitation formulas, which must maintain a "closed book" conception of the past.

But here we come back to defend "re-biographing" by putting into question the very possibility of writing "objective" history in the first place.

BIOGRAPHIC REHABILITATION AND HISTORICAL OBJECTIVITY

Let us begin our "crusade" against "historical objectivity" by alerting the reader to the subtle yet significant distinction made by philosophers of history between historical facts and historical interpretations. While Nietzsche is often quoted as having said that "there are no facts, only interpretations," we would have to admit that as lay people we often tend to accept historical events described in "authoritative" textbooks as given, objective, scientific facts, whereas the historians themselves must differentiate between the *objective* historical documents or events and their own *subjective* descriptions or interpretation of these documented events.

Nathan Rotenstreich (1955) noted for example, that whenever historians study such a document as the American Declaration of Independence, the physical written document constitutes an objective historical given, out of which the historian seeks to gain understanding about the nature of the relationship that prevailed at the time between England and its colonies, the American revolution, and so on. However, since documents, as well as other physical remnants of the past, are, like customs and memories, preserved and even studied *selectively,* one may always expect historical interpretations to change either when new documents are discovered or when one historian interprets the same document in a different way than his fellow historians. This selection process, which moves, like the psychoanalytical method, from the documents available in the present to interpret the unavailable past, is twofold to begin with because a certain period or event is selected in the first place as an illuminative explanatory case study while other eras or events are ignored. In other words, while a multiplicity of historical events proceeds sequentially from the past to the present, the present, through the inevitable process of selective interpretations, determines from which past it evolved, that is, which events had causal molding impacts on the present, as Rotenstreich (1955:2) indicated.

Thus, the historical objective events proceed unilaterally and irreversibly from the past to the present and into the future, while subjective historical interpretations maintain a bilateral yet selective dialogue between future and past through the pivotal meeting point provided by the present.

Even more extreme in conceiving history as an inevitably biased and even contradictory method of presenting past events as objective facts is Claude Levi-Strauss (1966) who claimed that

> history is . . . never history but history for. It is partial in the sense of being biased even when it claims not to be, for it inevitably remains partial—that is, incomplete. . . . When one proposes to write a history of the French Revolution one knows (or ought to know) that it cannot, simultaneously and under the same heading, be that of Jacobin and that of the aristocrat. . . . One must therefore choose between two alternatives . . . or alternatively one must recognize them all as equally real: but only to discover that the French Revolution as commonly conceived never took place. (Pp. 257-58)

The biased fallacy inherent in the historical method is, according to Levi-Strauss, due to the inevitably arbitrary choice of coding units that may be significant for one code but not for the other.

> It is thus not only fallacious but contradictory to conceive of the historical process as a continuous development, beginning with prehistory coded in tens or hundreds of millenia, then adopting the scale of millenia when it gets to the 3rd and 4th millenium, and continuing as history in centuries interlarded, at the pleasure of each author, with slices of annual history within the century, day to day history within the year or even hourly history within a day. (P. 260)

Now, if we take the above cited charges at least as precautions against the danger of being victimized by the inevitably subjective "closed book" interpretation of our distant or immediate failing past, we must reconsider the credentials of "re-biographing" as a rehabilitation method through first understanding the real purposes and utility of writing history in the first place.

BIOGRAPHIC REHABILITATION AND USEFUL HISTORY

I once heard a commissioner of prisons, in a talk to inmates, coin the following advisory slogan: "Don't serve time, let time serve you!"

This statement, which may be rephrased as "If you learn from history, it won't have to repeat itself!" suggests that the ultimate purpose of studying history (i.e., past times), biased or unbiased, is to learn from it and not to be *imprisoned* in it.

Indeed, even Levi-Strauss (1966) argues that "the historian's relative choice, with respect to each domain of history he gives up, is always confined to the choice between history which teaches us more and explains less and history which explains more and teaches less" (p. 262).

It is remarkable that while in connection to the "Erna story," Sartre rejected the idea of distorting life even when it fulfills people's needs for adventurous experiences, he obviously included this utilitarian selective approach to the past in his (1960) concept of "totalization." According to the dynamic totalization process, the projected goals to be achieved in the future require a rigorous selection so that only those elements of the past that have direct bearing on the new *project* will be permitted to enter the future.

In examining the "advantages and disadvantages of History for Life," Nietzsche (1980) went to the extreme in cautioning us against some of the dangers history poses to life by differentiating between monumental, antiquarian, and critical history. It is unnecessary for us to discuss the uses and dangers of each of these categories. What interests us here is Nietzsche's brilliant prophetic foresight that with the modern "demand that history be a science . . . life is no longer the sole ruler and master of knowledge of the past" (p. 23).

Hence, the dangers inherent in "modern scientific" methods of collecting nonselective information about the past surpass, by far, all previous "biased" historical methods, because the new historical science operates in the name of the bold motto "let there be truth, and may life perish" (*fiat veritas pereat vita*).

The "scientific-objective" method of collecting endless information about the past may be disadvantageous to life either because "knowledge taken in excess without hunger, even contrary to need, no longer acts as a transforming motive impelling to action," as Nietzsche (p. 24) put it, or because the unlimited ability to collect information about people's past, via modern computers, for example, may at best be used to *control* people's *lives* but *not* to *generate* them.

Now, if the art of generating life and inspiring progress and rehabilitative self-renewal requires not the schizophrenic "death-rebirth" disconnection from one's failing past, but rather one's subjective reinterpreting dialogue prerequisite "here and now" repentance state and which reharmonizes rehabilitation" not as distortion of the past but as a legitimate heir of the historical method.

That is, if historical interpretations, as distinguished from historical events, are by definition selective and subjective and by purpose instructive and constructive, then the "new-leaf" rehabilitative approach to the future, with its "closed book" conception of the past, cannot stem from historical objectivity, but rather from an unchangeable "original sin" kind of conception of people's past.

By suggesting that "closed book" methods of treating people's pasts derive from an "original sin" conception of people's pasts, I do not intend here to provide conclusive evidence proving how the "original sin" doctrine is causally related to all rehabilitative methods that do not permit "re-biographing," (though Freud [1967] himself traced his theory, as indicated in Chapter 1, about the inescapable universal Oedipal guilt that is allegedly buried in people's pasts to the unchangeable totemic "original sin" syndrome).[7] But I do claim that the "closed book" approaches to people's past failures must be rooted in an "original sin" *hermetic* (or closed) conception of the past and not in the historical method, which is by definition *hermeneutic* (or open to reinterpretation). By differentiating between *hermetic* and *hermeneutic* approaches to people's past failures, I am referring mainly to the cultural-social attitude to people's failing pasts that emanates from one or another orientation to the past, because it is usually the society's and not the individual's isolated stigmatizing or self de-stigmatizing beliefs that comprise the main factors of people's rehabilitative prospects. Hence, criminal recidivism and psychotic relapsing, rather than reformed conduct, are consonant with an "original sin" culture.

Moreover, by implying that the psychodynamic approach to past failure is *hermetic* while the Midrashic is *hermeneutic*, I do not attempt to demonstrate how hermetic conception of the past usually characterizes the traditional methods used to study history or biographies. Rather, I argue, as demonstrated in Chapter 1, that while "orthodox" psychoanalytic interpretations of biographies are highly subjective, they impose (as argued in Chapter 2) the only one "Karaite" (fundamentalistic) "Oedipal-original sin" interpretation of the past by which people may internalize only a hermetic and negative conception of their guiltful past. Thus, while both the *hermetic* and the *hermeneutic* approaches to the past are subjective, it is only a Midrashic kind of multiple choice system, that enables the positive "re-biographing" of past failures.

Accordingly, it is certainly and fortunately possible that, in spite of the predominance of an "original sin" kind of belief in particular societies, individual "rehabilitators" engage (sometimes inadvertently) in "re-biographing" while offering "new light" interpretations for past failures. But it is the cultural, religious ideologies that create and institutionalize social attitudes toward the possibility of "biographic rehabilitation," and it is these ideologies that we should seek to identify.

To use an example from the Hasidic culture, the famous story about Rabbi Levy Yitzhak of Berditchev's reaction upon seeing a man greasing the wheels of his wagon while wearing his prayer shawl and phylacteries might be illuminative. It is, after all, only the Hasidic norm allowing the favorite account or "reframing" of failures that would make Rabbi Levy Yitzchak's exclamation: "Behold the devoutness of your people; even when they grease the wheels of a wagon, they are mindful of your name" (Buber, 1978:222) socially legitimate and personally meaningful.

SOCIAL REINFORCEMENT OF BIOGRAPHIC RECOUNTING AND TEMPORAL "CONTRACTION"

If the retroactive method of interpreting collective historical events is by definition subjective and by purpose instructive, then why consider the "recounting" of an individual's biography distortive rather than constructive? Thus, "ascent through descent re-biographing," which proceeds from the prerequisite "here and now" repentance state and which reharmonizes one's past failure with one's future hopes by teaching one to retell or recount "his-story" is not a distortion of this individual's "history." Rather, it can be viewed as legitimate historical rehabilitation method in which those failing parts in a person's history are *contracted* while the reinterpreted reconstructed parts are expanded to create a more congruent life story dialogue between the future-oriented present new "I" and the past "thou."

In fact, some psychoanalysts are proud to present their method as a life story recounting technique in which parts of a person's biography are contracted while others are expanded. As indicated earlier, unfortunately, in this recounting method, the analyst always sees to it that the patient is taught how to reconstruct his analysand's autobiography only according to the "Oedipal-original sin" history of man so that the analysand will gradually internalize a self-blaming autobiography.

According to Roy Schafer's (1983) "narrative psychoanalysis," for example, people's natural tendency to retell and change their life stories is indeed utilized so that when "the analyst retells these stories . . . certain features are accentuated while others are placed in parenthesis" (p. 219).

To cite once again the case of how deviant identities are reconstructed in Western societies, Lofland (1969) suggested that while such contraction and expansion techniques

> are most clearly played out . . . by those involved in the "professions" of psychology and psychiatry, their work is, however, merely a more elaborate and detailed version . . . of a well-nigh universal practice. Acts in his [the deviant's] past that were once viewed in a certain way are reinterpreted. Other acts, which had gone unnoticed or had seemed irrelevant, are brought forth and considered central, for they help others to understand that the Actor was that way all along. (P. 150)

As we are thus able to understand how and why newspapers responding to the public's need to have a consistent (negative) image of a newly recruited deviant person, will dramatize the "evil" items in this person's biography, we can understand why it would be necessary, for true rehabilitation, to reconstitute one's positive image by playing down the failing parts in one's biography.

To be sure, my emphasis on the possibility of rehabilitation through a favorable "re-biographic" process should in no way rule out the occasional need for an "ascent through descent" kind of negative "re-biographing." That is, we should not lose sight of the point that it is only after the "repenting" effect has taken place as step number one that "re-biographing" might be effective as step number two. To minimize the "psychopathization" of life stories, it might often be necessary to first teach individuals to read their past from the angle of failure and delinquency, and only after the "repenting" change has occurred, to help them reread the same past events from a broader and more constructive perspective as the Hasidic "ascent through descent" model would suggest (see Rotenberg, 1983). This imperative antifundamentalistic "free choice" approach to "re-biographing" seems compatible with the Midrashic philosophy since alongside almost every Midrash acquitting a biblical sinner one might find other Midrashim that find him guilty.

On the other hand, this dialogical *intra*personal process, by which one may contract or expand one's failing past, may have minimal rehabilitative effects if it is not legitimized, that is, socially reinforced through a concomitant "social contraction" process of *inter*personal dialogue in space (see Rotenberg, 1983). If one is either enslaved by a culture with an "antiquarian" conception of history that obliterates any "craving for novelty" and self-renewal because it "mummifies" the dead past instead of generating future life (Nietzsche, 1980:21), or if one is imprisoned in an "original sin" based society that permits no retrospective relabeling of sinners (see Rotenberg, 1978), then society's reaction to the individual's private biographic recounting may even worsen, because "once a thief, always a thief!" predominates.[8] There is a story about an ambitious Indian tribe member who, one morning, told his wife with pride that in the night he had dreamed that he became the new chief. The Indian was, however, very disappointed that no one else had had the same dream. Thus there is no point in labeling oneself a chief if the Indian collectivity does not do the same.

In demonstrating how the biblical appeal to the Israelites was always to *remember* the past but not to study it historically, Yerushalmi (1982) argued that "memory is always pragmatic and selective" (p. 10). Thus, if on the one hand, "Israel is told . . . that it must be a kingdom of priests and a holy people" and on the other hand it is constantly reminded "with a hammering insistence: [to] remember that you were a slave in Egypt" as Yerushalmi stressed, then we have in fact a social relabeling model that legitimizes both the selective and pragmatic expansion and contraction of the past and the construction of the future through society's normative recounting of how "slaves can become priests." Indeed, Yerushalmi pointed out that "the rabbis seem to play with Time as though with an accordian, expanding and collapsing it at will" (ibid., p. 17).

Thus, if it seems educationally necessary according to the "accordian" contraction metaphor to highlight and expand one period or event and collapse or contract the other, the rabbinical hermeneutic story-telling method would proceed accordingly and provide full cultural legitimation for the recounting of the specific event or biography by which a "slave may become a priest." To be sure, it is not that adultery would receive a "Shabbateist-Frankist"[9] legitimation[10] in the recounting of the story of King David and Batsheba, since these Jewish false messiahs prescribed salvation through actual sinning. It is only that after real repentance, a circumstantial rereading would be offered to facilitate a retrospective review of the total role-modeling personality (see Dinnur, 1969), with whom prospective repenters may then identify.

Thus, the cabalic reorganizing correction (*tikun*) of paradoxically related (seemingly contrasted) elements in space (see Rotenberg, 1983) becomes in "re-biographing" a reorganizing *tikun*[11] (correction) in time.

It is, accordingly, this dynamic "recounting" dialogue between one's reinterpreted past failing "thous" and one's present repented "I" which receives its reinforcing legitimation from the social-cultural relabeling norm, that seems to have made it possible for many of the contemporary *baale teshuva* (repenters) to experience the spiral "ascent through descent" process of progressive "self-renewal" that we detected in our studies (see Chapter 8). To be sure, it is not that past failures must be reinterpreted as achievements, but that they may be recounted and socially accepted as meaningful and even "adventurous" life stories. For example, we often observe how in certain cultural groups people enjoy telling and even dramatizing their personal miseries and how they succeed to elicit reinforcing sympathy from their "attentive" audiences.

It is thus the predominating Midrashic culture of the repenters (*baale teshuva*) colleges that guaranteed that the dream of becoming a "chief" would be accompanied by the relabeling collectivity. We thus noted in our studies time and again that there was no place like the *baale teshuva* community, where even ex-prisoners could re-biograph their failing pasts as "ascent through descent" adventures necessary for making the "chief" repentance switch in order to become their own new "chiefs" and masters of their future.

Thus, after observing the dynamic power inherent in Midrashic psychology, one wonders whether Hegel (1948) and Kant (1960) inadvertently or advertently ignored this "Midrashic self-renewing system" in Judaism when they explained Jewish survival as a mere "barren legalistic" ("fossilized") system that does not qualify as an ethical-moral religion (see Rotenstreich, 1984) because of its presumed passive obedience to the "Halachic" (legal) frozen norms that were a priori formulated and externally enforced.

Conversely, to learn about the probable ineffectiveness of conventional rehabilitation formulas advocating a "new leaf" approach to the future, which conceives of the past as a *hermetic* "closed book," one may do best by considering, as indicated in the beginning of the chapter, cases of unresolved "political rehabilitation." In a famous case of a political assassination, Abba Achi-Meir, the head of what was labeled a "fascist" right-wing group of terrorists that fought the British government ruling Palestine, was blamed in 1933 for participating in or supporting the assassination of a left-wing Zionist leader named Arlozorov. Although Achi-Meir was acquitted of most accusations and served only a two-year prison term for leading an illegal terrorist group, he suffered till the last day of his life because his own political reference group never granted him, retroactively, a biographic rehabilitation. In the introduction to Achi-Meir's postmortem (1968) book *The Trial*, Y. Nedava wrote:

> Knesset member Shufman . . . quoted from a write-up which appeared in the "Davar" newspaper the day after Abba Achi-Meir's death where it said that during the days of the "Arlozorov assassination" in 1933 the third accused person [Achi-Meir] enjoyed the benefit of doubt together with the two other accused. Ever since he abstained from political activity . . . the court released Abba Achi-Meir before the end of the trial due to lack of evidence proving that he instigated the Arlozorov assassination. Abba Achi-Meir suffered till his last day because the discovery of total truth concerning the Arlozorov assassination was not revealed.

It is thus only from political figures, about whom people write and who are capable of expressing themselves in writing, that we may learn that granting a "new leaf" check for the future without rehabilitating the past, at least in the eyes of one's own reference group, may be ineffective even in cases where there is no clear evidence concerning the failing past.

One should thus suspect that it is only due to the expressive inability of the "silent majority" of the"psychoanalyzed community" who experienced actual failure that we don't know more about the ineffectiveness of a therapy in which the *hermeneutics* of the present is based on a *hermetic past*.

In conclusion, the thesis presented here seeks to raise the following question: If, indeed, historical interpretations are by definition subjective not only for those collectivities that presumably "eliminate" politically nondesireable events or personalities from their encyclopaedias (as the "Orwellian" warning would attribute for example to Communist Russia) but also for those that claim to write an unbiased history of their society, as Levi-Strauss suggested, then why not put "biographic rehabilitation" to good humane use instead of forcing "ex-failing" individuals to carry the "original sin" guilt-cross that their societies succeed in shedding?[12]

After demonstrating how Midrashic "re-biographing" operates and discussing its broader implications for rehabilitation and actualizing psychotherapy, a general discourse about the paradigmatic philosophy of history, or rather *a*historic philosophy emanating from the Midrash, is in order. By keeping in mind the assumption that possibilities of personal self-renewal should be understood as individual cases of collective renewal, the next chapter will attempt to show how Jewish cyclistic philosophy of history, as derived from the Midrashic ahistoric philosophy, molded the Jewish metacode of multiple interpretation and dialogic continuity in time.

NOTES

1. Our metaphoric use of the "inverting goggles," which stresses that people may be taught to perceive their world in a new light, refers to Stratton's (1897) classic study that demonstrated that by looking through special lenses, one's perceptional-visual field can be so inverted that, not only is the world seen perceptually upside down but everything perceived on the left or right is actually on the opposite side.

2. Here is the place to express my gratitude to Shalom Rosenberg who referred me to Margaliyot's (1949) important study of biblical sinners who were acquitted by the Talmud and the Midrash and to Avigdor Shinan who, in "guiding my way into the world of the Midrash," so to speak, helped me to find it. It should be stressed, however, that while most cases used here appear in Margaliyot's collection, our focus on the psychohistorical meaning emanating from the Midrashic rereading techniques goes far beyond Margaliyot's descriptive orientation.

3. It should be stressed here that along with almost every Midrash acquitting a biblical sinner one might find other Midrashim that find him guilty. It is, however, precisely this possibility to identify selectively with a personally suiting Midrash that, concurring with the principle of free will, facilitates this reorganizing dialogue between seemingly contrasted positions in time and space.

4. While I do not want to overburden the reader with a multiplicity of Midrashic rereading examples, the following instance of how the Midrash reverses the meaning of the text, might be in order. In Chronicles I (22:8), it is said that the word of the Lord came to King David, telling him, "thou shalt not build an house unto my name, because thou hast shed much blood upon the earth." While here, again, some commentators explain that God told David that not he but his son Solomon would build the Temple in Jerusalem because he has sinned by shedding unnecessary blood, the Midrash *Yalkut Shimoni* (*Sann.* b, 7:145) states that the shedding of blood refers to the many sacrifices David brought in the glory of God and the only reason for not letting David build the Temple was that it would be, because of King David's merits, indestructable and, because of Israel's anticipated crimes, the time for constructing an eternal Temple had not yet come.

5. While Japhet (1977) was able to show by drawing heavily on Julius Welhausen (see Boschwitz, 1982) how the Book of Chronicles paved the way for subsequent traditions of rereading and rewriting biblical history, her thesis focused, however, mainly on demonstrating how the Book of Chronicles developed a theodicy that showed that every calamity described in the Bible is causally related to a sin proceeding it.

6. A good example of how "biographic rehabilitation" of biblical figures continues to characterize public sermons to this day is the following: In the Jewish "rain prayer" said on the autumn holiday Simchas Torah, Moses is praised for his righteousness in conjunction with what came to be known as the grave sin he committed when he hit the stone from which water came out in the desert, instead of talking to it

as God had commanded him to do. To reconcile this apparent paradox, I once heard a rabbi explain in his Midrashic sermon that Moses' righteousness lay in the fact that Moses was willing to accept the consequent punishment for violating God's word but did not want to bring shame upon Israel by demonstrating publicly that while even a stone listens to God's command, Israel does not hearken to it in spite of all the miracles that God had performed in Egypt and in the desert. When I later asked the rabbi for the source of that Midrash, he admitted that it was his own interpretation (see Krol, 1978).

7. Although discourses such as Weiss-Rosmarins' (1972) have provided sufficient evidence that the "original sin" notion predominates in Christianity but not in Judaism, we are concerned here with its phenomenological (rather than its theological) impact on Freudian thought. The psychological interpretation of the "original sin" as the unshakable Oedipal guilt permeates most of Freud's writings on culture and man. Thus in *Totem and Taboo* (1900, 13:154) he says: "There can be no doubt that in the Christian myth the original sin was against God, the Father. . . . The sin was murder. The law of Talion, which is so deeply rooted in human feelings, lays it down that a murder can only be expiated by guilt."

8. Under the Israeli law of *Takanat-Hashavim* (Criminal Registration and Repenters Stipulation), since 1981 it is in fact possible that under specified circumstances an ex-convict might be allowed to declare that he has no criminal record(!). This law, which in this matter is like the British law, thus constitutes one of the most liberal cases of legalized "biographic rehabilitation."

9. The Shabbateists and following them the Frankists comprised Jewish "false" messianic movements that were rejected in the late seventeenth century by rabbinic Judaism primarily because they interpreted such Cabalic notions as "ascent through descent" into doctrines preaching salvation through actual sinning.

10. The unanswerable question that presents itself in this context time and again is the danger that re-biographing might inadvertently support denials of such mass atrocities as the Holocaust. It is, however, precisely because historiography is selective that a *Zakhor* (remembering) approach is needed to counteract and prevent the periodic danger of historicistic denials of the Holocaust in the name of "objective science."

11. While "new" therapeutic techniques that "renamed" Frankl's (1965) "paradoxical intention" method "reframing" or "reinterpretations" (e.g., Watzlawick, Weakland, and Fisch, 1982) offer to reorganize paradoxical situations and thus concur with the Cabalic *tikun* (corrective) philosophy, they fail to account for two basic problems relating to time and space. First, they fail to reharmonize one's cognitive dissonance with one's possible failing and guiltful past. Second, they evade resolving the "democratic" problem resulting from the mother's plea to her child, "I want you to want to study" (ibid., p. 81). In contrast, the Talmudic (*Yevamot*, 106:a) principle, of "he must be forced till he says I want" suggests that creativity through the Cabalic paradox-based reorganizing "tikun" is possible through a "coexistence-dialogue" between the forcing of the "Jewish mother" and the subsequently virtuous child pianist eventually stating "I want to play the piano."

12. The position advanced here is not as extreme as that of Foucault, who used Nietzsche's genealogy of morals to demonstrate how historians, like other scholars' "will to knowledge," "arouse from their reciprocal hatred, their fanatical . . . competition . . . that slowly forged the weapons of reason" (quoted in Sheridan, 1982:118) so that "in appearance . . . historical . . . consciousness is neutral. . . . But if it examines itself . . . all knowledge rests upon injustices" (ibid., p. 119). Accordingly, the historiographic method is neither objective nor scientific. It does not rest on "neutral historical consciousness," but arises from scholars' "reciprocal hatred . . . competition that . . . forged the weapons of reason." Consequently, one should reject the psychoanalytic method of using "historical objectivity" only "against" individuals seeking salvation from past failures.

4 Philosophies of History and the Psychology of "Self-Renewal"

The previous chapter has demonstrated how the Talmud and the Midrash developed a system of rereading and reinterpreting the Scriptures so that many of the personalities who were described in the Bible as sinners were acquitted by Jewish sages in later generations. As indicated, the possibility of rewriting the biographies of publicly declared criminals or sinners by retroactively correcting their history could be equated to what has become known in our contemporary language as "political rehabilitation." It was demonstrated further that such a philosophy, which allows under certain conditions for the correction of personal and collective history, stands in diametric opposition to what the Talmud calls (*Shabbat*, 145:b) an "objective" "original sin"-based history of people that cannot be shed or changed.

Indeed, Nietzsche (1980) stated that unlike the happy unhistorical animal, Western man "cannot learn to forget but always remains attached to the past: however far and fast he runs, the chain runs with him" (p. 8). From a cross-cultural perspective, we would, however, have to discredit Nietzsche's generalization as an "original sin"-anchored bias if it could be proved that non-Western people internalize corrected views of their past failures. In such cases, they would feel able to *change* their past instead of being *chained* to it.

True, it is inconceivable that in our modern world, for example, people would be taught to forget their age and thus remain happy and ageless. Nevertheless, just as it is hypothetically possible that scientists could produce pharmacological means of rejuvenating body cells, a discovery that would affect not only one's physiological but also one's psychological well-being, certain philosophies of history might provide the means for rereading, correcting, and thus rehabilitating, one's past.

It appears then that we cannot properly treat the problem of man's relation to his lifetime without asking whether we attribute the same degree of

72

significance to the category "man and history" as we do to that of "man and culture or society." The question is whether it is imperative to assess how an individual acts upon and reacts to history, or rather to his *beliefs* in pervasive philosophies of his own or of his society's history and progress. In more poignant terms, one may ask whether it is useful to investigate how an individual's motivations to act and interact are shaped in his social space (which social scientists conceive as a "must") while ignoring him as a product and producer of his own "historical time." After all, motivations (in terms of one's readiness to act) are essentially future orientations that are molded largely by beliefs derived from past experiences. Accordingly, if human behavior is essentially composed of motivation patterns that are directed toward the future and shaped by beliefs about experiences accumulated from the past, then our conception of progress in time would seem to play at least as decisive a role in determining the nature of our performance as would our physical-cultural environment on our behavior.

A quick survey of the relevant literature reveals, however, that while social scientists have made endless and diverse attempts to explore possibilities of "sociocultural" impacts on man's behavior, they have paid little attention to the possible phenomenological effects that various philosophies of history may have on individual conduct per se and on the concomitant psychological theories purporting to explicate them.

While in this sense, behavioral and psychodynamic theories conflict about whether one's physical or one's kinship environment play a more crucial role in shaping one's conduct, they both ignore the possible phenomenological impact that certain ideas about historical progression may have on an individual's course of action.

By phenomenological effects of philosophies of history on human behavior, I am referring to the ways in which various *ideas* about the course of history (not actual history) "show themselves" (see Heidegger, 1962) or are experienced subjectively by human actors and thereby shape their behavior. My insistence that it is the social scientists' business to study the relationship between philosophical ideas about history and man's time-oriented behavior is based on the assumption that while it appears impossible to demonstrate how archetypal collective memories or behavioral patterns are subconsciously transmitted from generation to generation, it would be possible to show how *beliefs* in "archetypal heritages" are manifested in individual or group behavior. A Jewish *enfant sauvage* left as a baby in the forest will neither speak Hebrew nor remember Abraham's journey from Ur to Canaan, as Yerushalmi (1982) argued, but he will probably find interest in the Hebrew language and in the land of Israel (Canaan) if in one way or another he came to *believe* that this land was promised to his forefather Abraham. Thus, his conceptions *about* past time may determine his future activities *in* time.

To elucidate how the time span of our subjective experiences in space may be influenced by beliefs about their historical place in time, one may elaborate on Husserl's (1964) compelling analogy of the melody. While it is true, as Husserl indicated, that our subjective consciousness of a melody[1] may persist long after physical instruments have ceased to produce that melody, it is also true that only our historical cultural conditioning will determine the time span of our subjective consciousness of that melody. In other words, it is usually our sociocultural conditioning (in terms of the beliefs of what is "in" or beautiful due to its historical role in our cultural heritage) to enjoy Eastern or European classical or folk music that determines the time length of our awareness of a melody.

Thus, space and time meet because it is the nature of our belief in historical progression, stalemate, or regression absorbed in our social and cultural space, which will probably also shape the degree to which some specific past memories will, like certain melodies, persist and affect our present perceptions and future expectations, while others may fade. The purpose of the present chapter is thus to explore the impact of certain philosophies of history on individual and group psychology. More specifically, it will be demonstrated that while a major part of Freudian psychology is entrapped in the dominant Christian past-determined philosophy of history, and that the future-oriented psychology emanating from Jewish messianism largely ignores the past, broader Jewish Midrashic methods for reinterpreting the past can be used to build the foundation of a cognitively consistent psychology of dialogue between past, present, and future.

From the present analogical perspective, it is assumed then that specific philosophies of history may operate like a melody. One's conditioning to listen to a past-, present-, or future-determining "melody" will affect the psychology of one's time-oriented life perspective. The Hegelian-Christian "melody" would thus train people to listen only to their past, Jewish messianism would condition them to listen only to the future, and the Midrashic "melody" would presumably teach them to improvise upon melodies of their past so that they will harmonize with the tunes of their future.

To be sure, by "harmonizing" past, present, and future tunes, I do not refer to a *hermetic*-synthesized story or "melody." Rather, by temporal harmony I have in mind the hypothetical open-ended "unfinished symphony" of one's story, which is constantly open for new *hermeneutic* revisions that add consonance rather than dissonance to one's identity.

The focal assumption of the present chapter is thus that future-oriented self-renewal is possible only through a reinterpretative temporal dialogue that reestablishes cognitive consistency between one's failing or sinful past and one's aspiring future. The impact of philosophies of history on individual psychology will hence be examined not merely in terms of the extent to which one philosophy or another allows one to mold one's future, but also in terms of how each permits the reshaping of one's past. In essence then, what the present study seeks to identify is the "historiosophical" codes that implicitly guide hermeneutic (or narrative) psychology. More specifically, the working assumptions underlying the present thesis are, as alluded to earlier, that beneath every psychology there is a theology, or rather a theosophy, and, consequently, that different theosophies (of history) may be identified as metacodes guiding the hermeneutic systems of specific psychological theories of man. This chapter, therefore, endeavors to explore the differential impacts of theosophical "codes" on "narrative trends in psychology," rather than to study how hermeneutic procedures may be or are being used by psychotherapeutic methods.

TYRANNY, DEMOCRACY, AND PHILOSOPHY OF HISTORY

In order to consider the general effect of various philosophies of history on individual conduct, or rather on psychological modes of its interpretation, let us first examine the proposition that various philosophies of history shape collective behavior and action strategies alleged to promote social progress.

In his critical attack on Marxism, Martin Buber (1958) differentiated between apocalyptic and prophetic eschatology. While both kinds of eschatology refer to man's anticipation of an improved future, Buber asserted that according to the apocalyptic belief, the future was already determined in the past and therefore people are, to use Popper's (1960) phrase: "swept into it" as pawns or instruments for its realization. Prophetic eschatology, on the other hand, views each person as an active-voluntary shaper of a future redemption whose dimensions cannot be foreseen. According to Buber, apocalyptic eschatology, which is traceable to ancient Persia, was developed both by St. Augustinian Christianity[2] and the Hegelian-Marxist philosophy, whereas prophetic eschatology originated in ancient Israel. The point to be stressed is that the former legitimizes progress through war and conflict that is carried out by despotic tyrants (e.g., Marxists) since they "only fulfill" predetermined decrees of historical necessity and evolution.

Gershom Scholem (1972), in his study of the messianic idea in Judaism, made a similar distinction between restorative and utopian ideas of messianism. The restorative type of future salvation rooted in the Christian millenarian idea of Christ's second coming refers, according to Scholem, to a Chilliastic reconstruction of a past that has already existed. In utopian messianism, which originated with the Jewish prophets, future redemption referred to the reconstruction of a past plus an ideal future, the kind of which has never existed before.

Taking Buber's and Scholem's distinctions together, phenomenological construction of one's future reality, according to one belief or the other, may have concrete consequential outcomes as suggested by the case of Marxist conflict-anchored despotism implicit in Buber's argument. Indeed,

Robert Nisbet (1979) has demonstrated that, in general, Western ideas of progress and strategies for social change have been dominated for the past two and a half millenia by this conflict-based notion of progress. Thus, from St. Augustine's interpretation of the declining Roman Empire and Hegelian-Marxian dialectic conceptions of the progression of the spirit, modern philosophers of history and evolution such as Spengler, Toynbee, Darwin, and Spencer continued to conceive of the possibility of progress solely in historicistic-linear terms in which the accumulative spirit progresses through *conflict* from one declining nation to a new culture because of the impossibility of national and cultural self-renewal. To be sure, it was this conflict-anchored notion of progress that Hegel reformulated in his famous three-phase organic conception of historical development. According to Hegel's dialectic theory, or rather theosophy, of history, the distinction between the linear progression of the spirit and the inevitable cyclistic decline of nations is due to the biological-organic fact that the nations themselves are doomed to go through three organic cycles or phases: birth (genesis), blossom (maturity), and decay (decline). Social change must thus be conceived in terms of an unavoidable conflict erupting between one declining, no longer fit, nation and its heirs, the organically new young nation of the "fittest." This movement of organic progression via self-annihilation constituted the core metaphor of Hegel's (1964) dialecticism:

> The bud disappears when the blossom breaks through, and we might say that the former is refuted by the latter; in the same way, when the fruit comes, the blossom may be explained by a false form of the plants existence, for the fruit appears as its true nature in place of the blossom. These stages are not merely differentiated, they supplant one another as being incompatible with one another . . . but one is as necessary as the other. (P. 68)

I have just used the somewhat ambiguous terms *cyclistic*, *linear*, and *dialectic* conceptions of social change and historical progress. Before going any further let me attempt to clarify that while the idea of development and change through recurrent conflicting cycles comes essentially from the Greek ahistorical philosophy, it was Giambattista Vico (1668–1744) who incorporated the cosmic notion of cycles into the domain of history by positing what was already implicit in the Jewish Jubileean idea, that recurring cosmic patterns comprise human history.[3] Inspired by St. Augustine's classic analogy of the eternal struggle between the City of Man and the City of God, the organic metaphor of cyclistic change through genesis, blossom, and decay became an archetype for the Christian conflict-based model of struggle, change, and progress, although the Christianized West eliminated the Greek notion of recurrence.

Later, we shall differentiate between organic cyclicism and the cyclistic idea of cosmic rejuvenation used by archaic man, who periodically annulled his own past in order to be recreated anew with each cosmic season. To minimize confusion between cyclic and linear ideas of history, although it is customary to speak of Hegel's dialectic conception of linear progression in cyclistic (organic) terms due to its nonrecurrent nature, it would be helpful to refer to Hegel's linearism as *phases* and not as cycles. Thus Hegelian philosophy distinguished the organic declining *phases* of genesis, maturity, and decay of nations from the *linear* progression of the free, accumulative spirit.

Hegel's dialectic idea of progress added the dimension of self-negation and conflicting oppositions,[4] by which the maturity of one nation (thesis) incorporates its own self-destructive "seeds" (anti-thesis), and after arriving at its inevitable conclusion, is followed by the *synthetic* elevation (*aufheben*) of the spirit to the next nation. Thus, in describing how the accumulative (linear) world spirit progresses from one decaying nation to the other, Hegel (1920) used the organic metaphor to state that

> the particular national spirit (*Volksgeist*) is merely an individual in the course of world history (*Weltgeschichte*). The life of one nation causes one fruit to ripen. . . . This fruit however, does not fall back on its own lap. . . . The fruit will bear seeds once more, but seeds of another nation. (P. 50)

According to the Hegelian philosophy of history, the organic inevitability of self-renewal and the consequent necessity of historical development justifies progress through war and conflict. Hence, Hegel (1900) argued that "war was the indispensable preliminary to the security of Protestants," (p. 541) and, as noted by Buber (1958:10), Marx (1949), who "remained truer to Hegel's belief in historical determinism than Hegel himself", claimed similarly, that "the communists openly declare that their ends can be attained only by the forcible overthrow of all existing social conditions" (p. 48).

The ideological roots of the notion that war between a younger nation and an older one only hastens the natural organic process of self-destruction by which the young and fittest survive may be Hegel's (1900) organic conception of progress. According to these ideas, the dialectic immanent in history only exemplifies the universal principle of opposition or self-negative pervading all reality, since "interest is present only where there is opposition" (p. 128). Indeed, in using the analogy of the phoenix, which eternally prepares the funeral pile upon which it consumes itself, Hegel (p. 127) stated that the outlived nation "certainly makes war upon itself—consumes its own existence" because "national death appears to imply destruction through its own agency" (p. 129).

If a nation seemingly survives in spite of wars and the anticipated process of natural self-destruction, conflict is, in fact, still imminent because its existence should be conceived of as, to use Toynbee's famous term, a "fossilized," unjustified persistence or, in Hegel's own view, "an existence without intellect or vitality, having no need of its institutions . . . a political nullity and tedium" (ibid.).

Before proceeding to discuss how the possible impact of one or another philosophy of history on collective behavior might also be relevant for assessing psychological theories of individual histories, let us restate that our phenomenological perspective assumes that philosophies of history do not merely *reflect* but also *affect* collective and individual conduct. Hence rather than being pawns led by the hand of historical necessity, we might, in fact, be entrapped in the conceptual "pawnshops" of history's philosophers because it is our belief in their ideas that determines whether we may make history or history makes us.

FOSSILIZED OEDIPALISM AND PSYCHOLOGICAL GROWTH

What follows from the foregoing discussion is that, according to the biological-organismic metaphor of social change and historical necessity, growth is a purely natural process that proceeds through war and conflict, because progress of one organism is possible only through its active participation in the inevitable self-destruction process of another, decaying organism.

Thus, if Western thought has been dominated for the past twenty-five-hundred years by the unchallenged conflict-based organismic metaphor of social change, then, as Nisbet (1979) claimed, the idea that the production and development of the "progressing fittest" is possible only through their active participating aid in the annihilation of the "regressing fossils," and may, in fact, underlie and legitimize patricidal and even genocidal theories of psychological and social development.

While the idea that some psychological theories are embedded in patricidal of filicidal conceptions is no novelty (see especially Sheleff, 1981), the theory that their origin may be traced to particular philosophies of history might have far-reaching significance.

The most obvious collective patricidal or genocidal example that comes to mind is the Hegelian attitude toward the antidialectic periodic revival of Jewish nationality. Hegel (1900) viewed the emergence of Christianity out of the self-destructive "dechosenness" and denationalization of Judaism as a natural dialectic process of linear progression by which Christianity' became the synthetic (*aufheben*) progressive movement of the free spirit, an elevated form of a Judaism that had outlived itself.

> The Chosen Family and its possession of Canaan, was taken from the Jewish people. . . . It was left for the Romans to annul its individuality. The Temple of Zion is destroyed; the God-serving nation is scattered to the winds. . . . All that remains to be done, is that this fundamental idea should be expanded to an objective universal sense, and be taken as the concrete existence of man—as the completion of his nature. (P. 412-13)

Consistent with his idea about the progression of the spirit via the antithetic process of self-opposition, Hegel (1900) asserted that the expansion or elevation of the spirit of Judaism is immanent in Christianity, which elevated man to the level of God: "For spirit makes itself its own [polar] opposite . . . that antithetic form of spirit is the son of God. . . . Man himself therefore is comprehended in the idea of God. . . . The unity of man [as an elevated entity] with God is posited in the Christian Religion" (p. 414).

While according to Bertrand Russell (1960), Hegel's absolutism bred war[6] and despotism, Hegel, in his conceptualization of the dialectic progress of the spirit from nation to nation, was not *preaching* the practice of national genocide but only *teaching* the theory of how social fossils are doomed to disappear through the natural process of socio-self-destruction. Bauer (1843), a nineteenth-century Hegelian, took this one step further and objected to emancipation for the Jews precisely because they presumably outlived their mission in the dialectic progress of historical necessity. Moreover, Toynbee (1934) the notorious twentieth-century historian, objected to national revival of Judaism due to the danger immanent in the archaic resurrection of fossils:

> Archaism . . . is most perilous of all when it is taken up by members of a community that is a fossil relic of a dead civilization, since the past to which the archaists have it in their power to cast back may be . . . sharply at variance with present realities. (VIII:301)
>
> Zionist Jews are a fragment of a fossil of alien origin. (VI:64)

For our current limited purpose, however, it is less central (although not less important) to establish whether such dialectic conceptions of organic progress have directly or indirectly contributed to Nazi-like genocides of "fossils" than to determine the extent to which the conflict-based notion of dialectic progress through patricide has permeated modern psychological theories of growth, education, and personality development.

To be sure, what is at stake here is not merely the moral (or amoral) issue of constructing the young via the destruction of the old, but also the total possibility of a self-renewing future-oriented psychology. It is thus important to stress that while the conflict-based, past-oriented, and, hence, predetermined conception of history and future progress was vigorously challenged by such philosophers of Jewish history as Graetz (1975), Rosenzweig (1970), Krochmal (1961), Buber (1958), Scholem (1972), Rotenstreich (1972) and Kochan (1977) who insisted that the Jewish messianic-utopian conception of the future facilitated periodical, "cyclistic" Jewish self-renewal on a sociohistorical level, the potential impact of restorative-apocalyptic versus utopian or prophetic conceptions of the future on contemporary theories of *psychological change* and *psychotherapy* was heretofore never mentioned.

While Freud's early libidinal theory of sublimation resembles the Jewish psychological self-renewal conception of impulse (*yetzer-hara*), his more influential Oedipal conception of man follows directly from a Toynbeean-Hegelian anti-self-renewal and past-determined "fossil" conception of progress via conflict and self-destruction. Thus, in *Moses and Monotheism* (1967, written during Freud's later years), the cultural progression from dying Judaism to Christianity through the inevitable killing of the Mosaic father religion is predicated on a thesis that Freud forwarded persistently, despite all contrary historical evidence (see especially, Yehuda, 1946), that the Jews killed Moses, their father-leader-figure. This dialectic progress via father-killing (patricide) becomes then the universal basis of the psychologically inevitable Oedipal conflict, according to which the growth of a child is possible only through the symbolic killing of the father. Psychoanalysis, then, constitutes one's confrontation with one's unchangeable guilt-laden "original sin" of totemic patricide. In Freud's (1967) own words:

> Paul, a Roman Jew from Tarsus, seized upon this feeling of guilt. . . . This he called original sin: it was a crime against God. . . . In reality this crime . . . has been the murder of the Father. . . . Paul, by developing the Jewish religion further became its destroyer. . . . Christianity marked a progress in history. . . . From now on, the Jewish religion was, so to speak, a fossil. . . . It can scarcely be chance that the violent death of another great man [Moses] should become the starting point for the creation of a new religion by Paul. . . . The way in which the new religion came to terms with the ancient ambivalence in the father-son relationship is noteworthy. . . . The fate of having to displace the father it [the Oedipal son] could not escape. . . . Only a part of the Jewish people accepted the new doctrine. Those who refused to do so will not admit that they killed God whereas we do and are cleansed from the guilt of it. (Pp. 109, 111, 113, 176)

Thus, St. Augustine's progress via the conflict-based struggle between the City of God and the City of Man, which then became a Marxian class struggle, is followed by Freudian father-son conflict. Psychoanalysis, is hence not future-oriented but a confession and a "cleansing-admission" process of unfolding one's past unavoidable patricide: "original sin."

I have mentioned Freud's Oedipal father-son conflict and Freud's psychoanalysis[7] in one breath, but one must be careful to separate these two sequential phases when viewing them in Hegelian terms. While moving from the youth (genesis) phase toward the blossoming maturity phase is possible only by "killing" the fossilized Oedipal father ("killing" him symbolically on the psychoanalytic trial bench), this phase, which culminates in the second phase: self-consciousness, already incorporated the seeds of the third, finite declining phase of self-annihilation: awareness of the past-determined unshakeable "original sin" guilt of patricide. Hence, Freud stated (1900a) that "it is the fate of all of us to direct our . . . first hatred and our first murderous wish against our father'' (4:262). Consequently, psychoanalysis, beginning in the second phase (Hegel's maturing consciousness), cannot be conceived of as a future-oriented self-renewal process, but rather as a past-anchored unraveling process that "brings to light the guilt of Oedipus" (ibid.), because this psychology is embedded in the Hegelian apocalyptic finite and linear conception of historical necessity, in which the future entails the gradual process of decay. Indeed, Ricoeur (1970), who took pains to show that there may be some implicit teleological components in Freud's philosophy of man, asserted that Freud's psychoanalysis is essentially a past-oriented archeology: "Freud expressly stated that the discipline he founded is not a synthesis but an analysis, i.e., a process of breaking down into elements and of tracing back to origins" (p. 460). Ricoeur demonstrated, however, that Freud is even less future-oriented then Hegel.

Thus, unlike some cognitive, goal-oriented psychological perspectives, even synthetic-teleological (i.e., predetermined) self-renewal is quite impossible according to Freudian-influenced psychotherapeutic methods of decomposing or re-excavating one's past history in order to become conscious of how one's past guilt is causally connected with one's present neuroses. In other words, while according to a Hegelian telic psychotherapy, yesterday's slave could progress determinately toward the predetermined new synthetic end of becoming today's master, Freud's archeological psychoanalysis is regressive. In Ricoeur's (1970) view: "the Hegelian dialectic . . . constitutes a progressive synthetic movement, which contrasts with the analytic character of psychoanalysis and the regressive . . . character of its economic interpretation" (p. 463). While with this, Hegel's sociohistorical concept of the *synthetic* possibility of progress does not pertain to any future because it always ends, according to Collingwood (1980:120), with a particular present day (the maturity phase), psychoanalysis is only *antithetic* and hence an anti-self-renewing method that moves only from the present to the past and back to the present. This has been at the bottom of Freud's most influential method of causal dream analysis with which Fromm and Jung struggled unsuccessfully. Thus, Jung (1933)[8] stated, for example:

> This brings me back to the Freudian view . . . that for the purpose of therapy it is necessary for the patient to become conscious of the causal factors in his disturbances. . . . I simply contest the notion that all neuroses . . . arise without exception from some crucial experience of childhood. . . . The dreams I have cited unmistakably present the aetiological factors in the neurosis; but it is clear that they also offer a prognosis or anticipation of the future. (P. 6)

If this thesis about the impact of the conflict-based Hegelian philosophy of history on Freudian Oedipal psychology (whether it allows for a synthetic progress or not) is essentially correct, the most crucial question to which we should address ourselves now is whether Jewish philosophy of historical self-renewal (e.g., the Midrash or messianism) contains the components of a futuristic self-renewing psychology of man. More poignantly, does a people's belief in their periodic *national* self-renewal necessarily produce a concomitant psychology of individual self-rejuvenation? And, is the resultant ability and motivation to mold one's future directly influenced by ideas about one's history?

FINITE VERSUS INFINITE FUTURISM AND THE PSYCHOLOGY OF SELF-RENEWAL

As we attempt to generate our theoretical framework by assessing the possible impact of philosophies of history in hermeneutic psychology, the investigation of the possibility of a futurist self-renewing psychology of man must begin by distinguishing between cosmic versus historic cyclism and finite versus infinite time orientation. Contrasting archaic man, who lives in cosmic-cyclistic time of eternal renewal, with modern historic man, Mircea Eliade (1974) stated in his classic *Myth of the Eternal Return* that

> the man of archaic civilizations can be proud of his mode of existence, which allows him to be free and to create. He is free . . . to annul his own history through periodic abolition of time. . . . This freedom . . . cannot be claimed by man who wills to be historical. . . . Christianity incontestably proves to be the religion of the fallen man . . . to which history and progress are a fall. . . . (Pp. 157-162)

According to Eliade, there is a crucial difference between Christian finite historicism and archaic cyclical time and its periodic regeneration of history:

> For Christianity, time is real. . . . A straight line traces the course of humanity from initial Fall to Final Redemption . . . and it is not an event subject to repetition, which can be reproduced several times. . . . Consequently the destiny of all mankind, together with the individual destiny . . . are both likewise played out once, once for all, in concrete and irreplaceable time. . . . It is this linear conception of time and history. (P. 143)

From a psychological perspective of biographic renewal, there is, however, a great difference between Midrashic reinterpretation of past failures and archaic cosmological cyclism, which abolishes past sins and failures altogether:

> In certain societies the ceremonies of . . . the material expulsion . . . of demons and diseases; the expulsion of the scapegoat in human or animal form . . . is sufficiently clear: . . . we witness . . . the abolition of the past year and of past time. And this is the meaning of ritual purifications . . . an annulling of the sins and faults of the individual and of those of the community as a whole. . . . Regeneration, . . . is a new birth. (P. 54)

Thus, cosmic cyclism based on the out-of-time principle of eternal return and on the seasonal abolition of personal history,[9] differs radically from non-recurrent progression of linear historicism operating through phases within time.

The question, however, remains as to whether a psychology of self-renewal is possible only outside of the framework of time and hence renders renewal a nonaccumulative growth process, an eternal return to a point of departure, or whether, within historical time, one may be recreated in the present in order to construct a progressive future without having to erase one's past.

In order to construe the possibility of cyclistic or spiral progressive self-renewal within time, we shall now introduce the concept of infinity (*ein sof*).

While the Christain historistic-linear conception of progress is essentially grounded in an apocalyptic, *finite*[10] Judgment Day conception of time that has as its beginning point the "original sin," leading (through the Fall) to the end point of Doomsday, Jewish conceptions of space and time are largely dominated by the idea of *infinity*.[11]

One can best understand how the concept of "infinity" (which received its epitomized central meaning in Jewish Cabalic mystic philosophy)[12] was used to explicate the possibility of Jewish self-renewal within historical time by considering how Jewish "emancipated" [13] philosophies of history (mainly since the eighteenth century) defended Jewish survival as a historical nation in spite of their "outlived mission" in the dialectical process of historical necessity. After the emancipation, "for the first time it is not history that must prove its utility to Judaism, but Judaism that must prove its validity to history by . . . justifying itself historically," as Yerushalmi (1982:84) phrased it.

It was, in essence, only such a concept as historical infinity that could reconcile "Hegelian" linear progression with self-renewal. Rotenstreich (1976) showed how Krochmal (known as the "Renak"), whose historical view drew from the seemingly contradictory notions of Vico's historical cyclism and Hegel's linear (three-phased) historical dialecticism, also depended on the infinite concept of the "absolute spirit," which he claimed characterizes only the Jewish nation, to reconcile Jewish periodic self-renewal. Unlike Hegel's single-lined *infinitism* limited to the spirit moving from one decaying nation to the other, Krochmal's "absolute spirit" explains both a physical and a spiritual ability for infinite self-renewal among the Jewish people.

Thus, Krochmal attempted to reconcile Hegelian historicism with Jewish ahistorical infinitism, making it possible to conceive of a self-renewal psychology that would not require the abolition of one's past in order to return to a point of departure. As Rotenstreich indicated: "Krochmal tries to bring together two different connotations of infinity: on the one hand, infinity is synonymous with eternity . . . beyond any reference to time; on the other hand, infinity is synonymous with the unlimited duration[14] in time" (p. 190). Rotenstreich further demonstrated how the nineteenth-century Jewish philosopher Franz Rosenzweig, who perceived Judaism in essentially eternal, ahistorical terms, seems to have utilized the cyclical notion of infinite short-range recurrences in order to preserve the idea of historical time. Individual self-renewal is accordingly possible through one's participation in the calendaric circular recurrence of the Sabbath and the Festivals, which separate holy time from historical time, hence giving "time off" for self-renewal by marking the end of creation on the one hand and the beginning of rejuvenating recreation on the other.

Both Krochmal and Rosenzweig attempted to reconcile Jewish self-renewal with history by utilizing, though in different ways, the concept of infinity. As summarized by Rotenstreich: "Whereas Krochmal attempted to present in his Hegelian thrust, a primordial synthesis between eternity and time, Rosenzweig attempts to present a primordial synthesis between timelessness and time" (p. 199).

This may be viewed, in psychological terms, as follows: According to a Christian kind of finite time orientation, a self-renewal psychotherapy is possible either via a schizophrenic disconnection from one's declining past "original sin" guilt through an amnestic "death-rebirth" process of a "second coming" or through a neurotic subtraction of one's unredeemable past failures (minuses) from one's present achievements or future aspirations (pluses). In dialectic terms, the first case could be conceptualized as a synthesis if the "second coming" self is conceived of as a telic end that emerged out of the ashes of the decaying "first coming" self. In this sense, the "death-rebirth" cure resembles the archaic man's annulling of his past with its nonprogressive return to a point of departure. The second case could be perceived as an antithesis, because here the archeological process of psychotherapy or analysis constantly negates or rather decomposes the natural proclivity for progression ("It is your past unresolved passion for your mother, not your love for your future bride"). Thus, in both cases, progress is hampered by the unbridgeable cognitive and emotional dissonance between one's past guilt and failures and one's future aspirations.

How then does the Jewish conception of infinity within time facilitate a self-renewal that does not require an annulling of the past and that minimizes dissonance between one's past, present, and future? According to a popular joke, an Israeli representative to an international conference on future economic prospects was once told that while other countries have to struggle endlessly with the unforeseen problems of rising inflation, Israel (in view of chronic bankruptcy and its outrageous self-devastating inflation) is at least capable of seeing the *End* . . . (of "it" or rather of itself . . .).

Is it then, due, simply to the Jewish refusal to see its *end*? Is future-oriented optimism only a naive negation of, or a psychological reaction-formation to, its actual fossilized outlived conditions? Or does Judaism's infinite notion of time and history indeed contain the components of a pragmatic psychology of self-renewal?

INFINITE CYCLICISM AND MIDRASHIC RE-BIOGRAPHING

In the treatise distinguishing between Jewish history and Jewish memory, Yerushalmi (1982:10) demonstrated convincingly, as indicated earlier, that while Israel was never told that it must become a nation of historians, there is a consistent biblical appeal to remember the past" (Deut., 32:7). "Remember what Amalek did to you" (Deut., 25:17). "Beware lest you forget the Lord who brought you forth out of the Land of Egypt" (Deut., 6:10). If memory becomes crucial to Jewish faith and to its existence and survival, it obviously cannot encompass a psychology that teaches self-renewal through periodic abolition of the past.

The memory dictum is by nature selective and by purpose pragmatic, so that the *how* and the *why* of what occurred rather than the *what* itself will serve as impetus and guideline for future actions. The memory paradigm may, in fact, constitute the basis for a dynamic psychological dialogue between past and future because remembering does not necessarily connote a *confrontation* with an objective past but rather a subjective *interpretation* of it. But, consistent with our working assumption that it is the specific theosophy of history that guides the specific psychology of hermeneutic therapy, we must identify the particular ideology or philosophy that we claim facilitated this "psychohistorical" dialogue between past and future with its psychologically dynamic nature.

Yerushalmi has suggested that memory was kept alive through ritual and recital. But couldn't rituals and recitals, even if perpetuated through living institutions, become dogmatic, stagnant, and imprisoned in a haunting or nostalgic past if not infused with suitable contemporizing reviving tools? Gershom Scholem, in his struggle against the nineteenth-century apologetic *Wissenschaft des Judentum*, which viewed Jewish irrational mysticism as a "roadblock" toward progress, suggested in his pluralistic[15] conception of Judaism, that it was precisely the subterranean, esoteric, irrational forces and mystical traditions that provided the "building blocks" of Jewish futurist vitality and survival (see Biale, 1982).

In his purely future-oriented exploration of how messianic-Cabalic mystical texts supplied the secret fuel of hope that helped the self-renewing Jewish wagon to ascend from the dark years of diaspora and persecution, Scholem (1941, 1972) did not explain how the cognitive dissonance-reducing dialogue between an individual's *past* failures and his *future* aspirations was maintained or rather reestablished.

Buber was even more obscure with regard to the possibility of an intrapsychic temporal dialogue in which the I (one's past) is to enter into dialogue with his "It" or "thou" (his future) in order to reestablish the temporal cognitive consistency needed for a healthy future-oriented personality. Buber not only ignored the need for an *intra*personal "I-thou" dialogue in time, but, in fact, he never explicated how his *inter*personal "I-thou" dialogue could be maintained in space when conflict emerges, because he essentially believed that a genuine "I-thou" dialogue is a present-based mysterious gift of grace that may or may not occur in the interhuman sphere between interacting partners (see Schwartz's introduction to Rosenzweig, 1970). Implicit in Buber's distinction between the apocalyptic and the prophetic eschatologies and especially in Scholem's differentiation between restorative and utopian messianism, are, however, as mentioned earlier, the components of an intrapersonal psychological dialogue in time.

I propose here that from this perspective, the "I-thou" or "I-it" dialogue may be formulated in dynamic temporal terms so that it will be possible to transpose one's failing "I" (past failure) into the future through a dialogical process by which the future ceases to be an alien "it" in order to become a "thou" that may eventually accept the new future "I." Through the *intra*personal dialogue in time, one would be able then to transpose one's "I," now stuck in one's failing past, into a future positive new "I" capable of relating to a "thou."

The possibility of an intrapersonal temporal dialogue in which the past "I" with its failures may be utilized to construct the future "I" without a schizophrenic "death-birth" return to a point of departure is supported by the infinite[16] conception of time and space available in the reinterpretive method of the Midrash. As outlined in the previous chapter, the Midrashic philosophy of history, or rather a historic philosophy, facilitated social renewal by concretizing and reinterpreting biblical stories and Talmudic principles according to changing needs of the present in order to build a future (see Kadushin, 1938).

Within the present interest in the impact of philosophies of history on the possibility of self-renewal, the case of *teshuva* (repentance) would exemplify the Midrashic possibility of reinterpreting one's past, and "prophetic" or "utopian" messianism would elucidate the possibility of constructing a future surpassing the past. The possibility of psychotherapeutic futurism will be discussed in the final part of this book. However, to facilitate a schematic outline concerning the relationships between philosophy of collective history and the psychology of personal renewal, I should mention that the principle of "cumulative-chutzpah" which I developed in my book *Dialogue with Deviance* (1983) parallels Scholem's category of "Utopian messianism." I have thus indicated that while a Bandurian (1969) modeling or copying model of a growth might follow Scholem's "restorative" futurist conception, the Hasidic "ascent through descent" paradigm in which the son is urged to use his "chutzpah" power to "emulate" and correct Heaven and surpass his father, concurs with Scholem's "Utopian" approach to the future growth, according to which one's future consists of a reconstructed past plus a future that has never existed before.

We may now better understand the phenomenological-ontological possibility inherent in the famous dictum related by Resh Lakish, the most famous *baal teshuva*: "repentance (*teshuva*) is so great that premeditated sins are accounted for as though they were merits." Through the *teshuva* process (Talmud, *Yoma*, 86:b), crimes premeditated and committed in the past may not only be erased like a debt so that through the "death" of this past one may return to a point of departure in order to be "restored" or be "born again," but they may be cognitively transformed in one's own eyes and in the eyes of one's destigmatizing reference group, so that they are "elevated" as Rabbi Soloveitchick (see Peli, 1980) put it, to reach, in a spiral fashion, heights to which righteous people cannot ever aspire. As another often cited Talmudic saying states: "In a place [on the rung] where *Baalei Teshuva* [repenters] stand, the perfect righteous may not stand" (Talmud, *Berachot*, 34:b).

The following case of a famous *Baal Teshuva* will help to illustrate the viability of reestablishing a cognitively consistent dialogue between past and future through biographic rehabilitation.

The Case of Baruch Abu-Hazera

We have said that the Talmudic stipulation that past premeditated crimes of a repenter (*baal teshuva*) may retroactively be accounted for as merits, so that he may stand on a higher rung than the perfectly righteous, could be effective only if re-biographing is reinforced by a socially favorable relabeling process. Like the Indian tribe member who dreamed that he became "chief," one's private self-re-biographing would carry little weight if he was the only one so classifying himself and his social group or the official institutions of his society, that is, the other tribe members did not have the same "dream" to confirm this biographic rehabilitation.

Baruch Abu-Hazera, an ex-deputy mayor, the son of *the* most revered Jewish North-African holy man in Israel, was sentenced in 1980 to a five-year prison term on various charges of embezzlement. He was pardoned by the country's president even before he had completed the regular two-thirds of his sentence, and, in accordance with the death wish of his father, was appointed the succeeding new "righteous" holy man in the Abu-Hazera dynasty. Baruch, who exchanged his modern outfit for the traditional "Galabia" (robe) sits now at his late father's home and daily receives hundreds of pilgrims who either seek a remedy for *health* or a blessing for *wealth*.

According to "Rabbi" Baruch's own testimony, about seven hundred people visit him daily, as opposed to the eighty who visited his father, because he had received from his father a blessing that he was to be four times more successful than his father was. While new charges have recently been brought against him, due to a past, unsettled extramarital affair, in spite of, or perhaps because of, the derogatory publicity, more and more people come to ask for his help, and when he visited Haifa, 12,000 people came to welcome him upon arrival.

The point to be stressed in the Abu-Hazera case is not that charisma celebrated another victory among deviant salvation seekers, but that, according to Baruch's and his society's responses to reporters (see *Ma'ariv*, 18 January 1985), Baruch himself, and the thousands of ordinary citizens who believe in him, do not erase his past but accept him as a holy repenter (*baal teshuva*) who may stand, as the Talmud stipulates, on a higher rung than the perfectly righteous. While there are still voices attempting to assign the "once a thief always a thief" label to Baruch, the very fact that he is already accepted by a great majority of his cultural group as a righteous person may serve as an illustrative testimony to the very possibility of "emulative" self-renewal.

It may thus be expected that as time elapses, Abu-Hazera's past will be reinterpreted and put into a new perspective by drawing on the same role-modeling process applied by the Midrashic and Talmudic treatment of the biblical King David that was described in Chapter 3. It should thus be kept in mind that the principle applied in Midrashic re-biographing of biblical role models is that retroactive contraction (midgetization) of past sins and failures (individual and/or collective) by expanding present and future virtues is used only if subsequent successful repentance justifies an "ascent through descent" (see Rotenberg, 1983) kind of biographic rereading. To use Max Scheller's beautiful analogy, hermeneutic contraction of past failure may be likened to the man who, after climbing up a mountain, looks backward and sees his imagined small image at the bottom of the hill. The above cited illustrative case study of a convicted prisoner would be understood accordingly as representing a cultural principle underlying the possibility of social re-biographing and not as the empirical status of re-biographing in specific cultures. The key concept for a self-renewal psychology is hence the temporal dialogue of re-biographing, which aims to reduce cognitive dissonance and schizophrenic rupture between past, present, and future.

We may now schematize (see Table 1) the relationship between the Midrashic philosophy of history and the dialogic possibility of "emulative" personal growth by comparing it to the "restorative" category of dialectic progress.

Table 1
The "Progress-Growth Scheme

Category	Dialectic	Dialogic
Past-Failure	"Original sin fall"	"Descent for ascent"
Future conception	Finite-apocalyptic	Infinite-volitionary
Messianic salvation	Restorative	Utopian
Basis for interrelationships	Conflicting "battle"	Paradoxical reorganization
Progress	Synthetic replacement (I *or* thou)	Hypothetic continuity ("I *and* thou")
Treatment of past	Archeological confrontation	Contracting reinterpretation
Treatment of future	Copying-rebirth	Emulative-surpassing

In summary, this chapter discussed the impact of two philosophies of history on hermeneutic possibilities in psychology:

1. The Hegelian-Freudian past-oriented perspective of growth through conflict with father (via Oedipal killing) or with self (via "death-rebirth").

2. The Midrashic re-biographic method of spiral self-renewal, in which the past is used through a spiral "ascent through descent" process of *teshuva*[17] to construct a future that surpasses past and present.

Between these two polar therapeutic time perspectives stands the archaic-cyclic mode that denies the past and disregards the future but facilitates periodic creation (or re-creation) and renewal through cosmic repetition and return to a point of departure. The cyclic-cosmic actualization mode has features in common with the existential "here and now" therapy because, essentially, the latter also denies past and future, although it does not link self-realization to cosmic renewal. The philosophical time perspective underlying this present-based mode of hedonistic and possibly nihilistic actualization will be discussed briefly in Chapter 9, which examines the possibilities of writing and narrating one's script for the future.

In the next chapter, an encounter between two key narratives, the Oedipal legend and the Midrashic Isaac, will be presented. These key narratives, which will be discussed in terms of their paradigmatic impact on psychotherapeutic-actualization possibilities, are conceived as symbolic metacodes epitomizing specific philosophies of history because it is the socialization power inherent in such "master" stories that determines the nature of growth and continuity in time.

NOTES

1. Ulric Neisser (1982:147) has shown that the "tone" or "tenor" of a witness might not only reflect a distorted memory but even mislead judges, as happened in John Dean's testimony in the Watergate trial when Dean's testimony was accepted even though "comparison with the transcript shows that hardly a word of Dean's account is true."

2. While the apocalyptic predetermined view of the future has indeed predominated Christian thought, it is important to note that in spite of constant attempts to eliminate them Jewish history was never free from apocalyptic trends (see Scholem, 1972).

3. The Jewish Jubileean idea of cyclicism, which according to biblical hermeneutics affects many spheres of social life in time and space (e.g., the freeing of slaves and the abolishing of debts), will be developed elsewhere. Here it suffices to mention that according to ancient Jewish mystical sources such as *Sefer Hatemuna* (which was already known in the thirteenth century), the world develops as a living organism that undergoes periodic cosmic cycles (*shemitot*) of ascent through descent (see Scholem, 1979).

4. Here it is proper to stress that while the dialectic thinking that facilitated differentiation between knower and what is known was already popular among the ancient Greeks, it was probably Hegel who developed the dialectical method, as Gadamer (1976) put it, by "radicalizing a position until it becomes self-contradictory and, . . . by extending the dialectic of the Ancients and transforming it into a sublimation of contradiction into ever higher syntheses" (p. 31).

5. Cullman (1951), a Christian theologian, conveniently arranges history as a linear progression in time that has as its midpoint the death and resurrection of Christ. "Since the people of Israel as a whole do not fulfill the mission assigned to them" (p. 116), their history is envisaged as a downward or backward progressive reduction process (from the many to the one) and from the center, reached in Christ, redemptive history moves upward or forward "in progressive advance to the many" (p. 117).

6. Philosopher Bertrand Russell (1960:15) maintained that Hegel's Platonian political absolutism did not only inspire totalitarian communism and fascist Nazism because "to Hegel . . . the Prussian State was the best existing at the time when he wrote, that war is good" but according to Russell, Hegel's entire theory of dialectic progress, which was surprisingly accepted in the West, is groundless especially when it dealt with historic temporality.

Thus, Russell wrote

> Oddly enough, for some reason which Hegel never divulged, the temporal process of history repeats the logical development of dialectic . . . to the history that Hegel happened to know. Different nations, at different times have embodied the stages of the idea that the dialectic had reached at those times. Of China, Hegel knew only that it *was*, therefore China illustrated the category of mere Being. Of India he knew only that Buddhists believed in Nirvana, therefore India illustrated the category of Nothing. The Greeks and Romans got rather further along the list of categories, but all the late stages have been left to the Germans. (Pp. 15, 16)

Russell's conclusive remarks concerning Hegel's dialectic racist historicism were hence unequivocal:

To any one who still cherishes the hope that man is a more or less rational animal, the success of this farrago of nonsense must be astonishing. In his own day, his system was accepted by almost all academically educated Germans, which is perhaps explicable by the fact that it flattered German self-esteem. What is more surprising is its success outside Germany. . . . Most curious of all was his effect on Marx. (P. 16)

7. The credit for interpreting Freud's Oedipal theory as a cultural revolt against his Jewish father religion, characteristic of many nineteenth-century "emancipated" Jews, must go to Marthe Robert (1976), or rather to Franz Kafka (1958:337) whose classic statement that psychoanalysis described the Jewish intellectual whose "hind legs were bogged down in their father's Judaism and their front legs could find no new ground" probably inspired Robert. However, since Robert did not identify specific Hegelian influences on Freud's thinking, he failed also to differentiate (in Freud's theory) between the first Hegelian dialectic developmental phase of genesis via conflict and destruction of the old Oedipal-father and the second maturing phase during which one becomes conscious via the archeological-psychoanalytic process of his unavoidable self-destruction and past-determined "original sin" guilt.

8. Jung, whose ventures into the psychology of Eastern mysticism had undoubtedly alerted him to the possibility of cyclistic (incarnational) self-renewal, was essentially imprisoned in the past-oriented "etiological" theory of the predetermined unchangeable nature of the neurotic "shadow." Stewart (1969), however, describes how the Malayan Senoi people teach their children to transform the common dreams of fearful falling into future-oriented, controllable and joyful dreams of flying. Moreover, it is worth pointing out here that the Hebrew word for dream (*Chalom*) and the verb *Lehachlim* (to recuperate from illness) are derived from the same root. This type of connection may not be made between the German word *traum* (dream) and the original Greek word *trauma* (traumata), however, since they are not associated etymologically despite the connotative resemblance that Freudian theory assigned them.

9. While it seems inconceivable for modern man to abolish or periodically annul his own history, one should be reminded that, in fact, man's perception of time became possible only via his observation of the cosmic cyclistic movements by which day turned into night and winter into summer, as was already indicated in the twelfth century by Maimonides (1977).

10. It should be stressed that while the Augustinian conception of time was quite flexible in its rejection of a specific prognosticable finite millenarian period of a second coming and Joachim de Fiores' heretic notion of the third age assumed an indefinite reign of the Spirit of Love and Joy, Christian theology never eliminated the finite Last Judgement conception of history (see Manuel, 1967).

11. The Hebrew word *Olam*, which is derived from the same root as the words *ne'elam* (hidden, unknown) and *taaluma* (mystery), refers to both the infinite geophysical world and to the infinite time (*Leolam*) that future entails. In psychological terms, one could take this contrast a step further by saying that the insistence on one's need for clear "ego boundaries" connotes a finite personality conception in contrast to the mystic longing for an infinite, egoless merging with the cosmos.

12. One might say that Maimonides (1135–1204), who is undoubtedly the most eminent representative of the Jewish rational school of philosophy, also expressed an infinite conception of time as he assimilated the messianic future in the present so that there is no drastic transition between present and future redemption. He thus reaffirmed

the Talmudic view that "the sole difference between the present and the messianic days is delivery from servitude to foreign powers" (Talmud, *Sanhedrin*, 91:b). Even more interesting for the present purpose is Maimonides' antideterministic (infinite) attitude concerning the individual's life expectancy. This radical opinion, expressed as early as the twelfth century, lends historical support to a Jewish psychology of self-renewal (see Weil, 1979).

13. I put "emancipated" in quotation marks to stress what has been often claimed: that as a condition for their emancipation, Jewish scholars (especially those associated with the *Wissenschaft des Judentums*, which was established to defend Judaism as a historical entity) essentially had to accept the dialectic philosophy of history coming out of the German idealistic school of Enlightenment.

14. Bergson's (1978) concept of *duree* parallels and possibly also draws upon the Jewish notion of *infinity*, which postulates daily cosmic renewal (*"Mechadesh bechol yom maasey bereshit"*) (Talmud, *Chagiga*, 12:2). In formulating his theory of "creative development," Bergson pointed toward the possibility of infinite creativity in space acquired through infinite given possibilities in time. This conceptualization becomes quite evident in his refutation of Leibnitz's theological "pre-established harmony," when he states: "If there is nothing unforseeable, if there is no act of renewal and no act of creativity in the cosmos, time becomes obsolete" (p. 46).

15. Here I dare to suggest that if Scholem's conception of Judaism was indeed pluralistic in that he portrayed a coexisting complementary role for the rational-philosophical and the irrational-mystical trends in Judaism, he could not have represented a dialectic view of history as Rotenstreich (1959:120), Biale (1982:4), and others suggested, but rather a "dialogic" (coexistent) view of time and space. According to a strict Hegelian dialectic view, Jewish mysticism and Hasidism would have to emerge out of the ashes of rational philosophical Judaism as a higher synthesized form of Judaism.

16. The psychological implications of the idea that on the one hand, the Torah constitutes an organic "living structure from which not even one letter can be excised without seriously harming the entire body" (see Scholem, 1974:171) and that on the other hand "the Tora has seventy faces so that its infinite meaning . . . served only as a general framework for a multiplicity of individual readings" (ibid., p. 172) surpasses the limited possibility of reinterpreting one's past, introduced here. This hermeneutic-homiletic tradition, which reached its *apex* in the Hasidic-Cabalic mystical traditions, in fact facilitated a pluralistic infinite interpretation of Jewish law, which we would classify here as dialogic because it allowed the coexistence of seemingly contradictory approaches and practices (such as irrational mysticism and rational Talmudism) as long as the organic structure of the Halachic law was not altered, as Scholem, Kadushin, and others have stressed.

17. The term *teshuva* is, as pointed out in previous chapters, derived from the infinite circular concept *shiva* or *sovev* meaning "turning" or "revolving." Soloveitchick (Peli, 1980:98), who presents a circular or rather a spiral theory of *teshuva*, noticed that the term *teshuva* is used in the Bible only to connote a circular coming back or a completing of circular movement. To support this idea, he quoted from Samuel: "Samuel judged Israel . . . and he went from year to year in circuit . . . and his return (*u-teshuvato*) was to Ramah for there was his home" (Samuel 1, 7:15-17).

5 The Oedipal Conflict and the Isaac Solution

Is the popular genealogical "root searching" for cultural and personal identity a regressive or a progressive process? Is progress possible only after a negating "root canal" killing or extraction of the older generation's living nerves, or is growing and branching impossible if the tree's roots are dead?

To scrutinize theories of social progress and personal development grounded in Hegelian-Darwinian dialectic thinking with the above queries, our dilemma may be rephrased somewhat as follows:

Is social and personal development contingent on the *elimination* of the "no more fitting" old ruling class or Oedipal father, or may progress be still possible if the "obsolete" *thesis* (old class or father), which allegedly stands in conflict with *antithesis* (new class or son), continues to coexist with the new class or generation?

By using the hyphenated label, Hegelian-Darwinian dialectics, I suggest that the belief in the inevitable teleological process of evolution through a Darwinian kind of "survival of the fittest," is, in fact, the same as saying in Hegelian, or rather Marxian, terms that social progress proceeds through the unavoidable process of historical *necessity* by which the young antithetic class of the fittest negates thesis, that is, the old, no more fitting, class.

Hence, since a Hegelian Marx as the Darwin of the social sciences (see Avineri, 1969) may in fact legitimize the developmental practices that are founded on destruction of the weak and the old, the analysis below will refer not only to a Marxist literal annihilation of the predecessing nonfitting class by the succeeding class of the fittest but also to an offspring's symbolic Oedipal killing of his parents on what I shall term the "psychoanalytic trial bench." By comparing the two key narratives, the dialectic Oedipus and the dialogic Isaac, it will be argued in this chapter that it is only by referring to

93

the Hegelian-Darwinian theories as his hermeneutic metacodes that one may understand why Freud selected the Oedipal story from all the available legends to interpret and guide the course of socialization.

Before going any further in introducing our discourse, let me concede once again that the Darwinian interpretation of Hegelian-Marxian dialecticism offered here may indeed present a simplistic formulation of development and human relations. It appears, however, that it is precisely the predominance of the Hegelian "simplistic" popularized conception of "dialectic" progress (the *aufheben* process) by which the necessary unbridgeable conflicting negation of thesis by antithesis must presumably desolve into a higher synthesized *new* entity, that seemed to have cause considerable rigidity and confusion in modern sociological and psychological thinking.

In this sense, what is being scrutinized here is the phenomenological impact of Hegelian dialecticism on theories of growth and socializaiton, rather than Hegel's dialectic formulations per se.

It is therefore important to distinguish again between the two models of dialecticism used in traditional literature. Accordingly, the presentation of dialecticism as a static synthesizing entity that occurs as a result of a process of negation by which antithesis eliminates or integrates (swallows) its opposing thesis with which it conflicts should obviously be distinguished from what is known in the literature as *dynamic* dialecticism.

Thus, Sartre's (1960) concept of "totality" would generally concur with the Hegelian finite, or rather static, synthetic dialecticism in which the antithetic entity destroys or substitutes thesis in a Marxist "class struggle" sense. By contrast, Sartre's conception of "totalization" would constitute the dynamic kind of dialectic praxis in which the dialectic tension between infinite opposing elements constantly reshapes reality.

As proposed in previous chapters, in the present context we reserve the concept of *dialecticism* to the first synthetic case of the finite static totality in which one opposing element "replaces" the other—while the infinite dynamic process, in which the "I" and the "thou" coexist and social praxis proceeds not via the elimination of one of the seemingly conflicting principles but through the constant reproduction of the tension between them on higher levels, is referred to as *dialogic*.

If, accordingly, rational consciousness must "substitute" irrational subconsciousness, or behavior governed by the pleasure principle must be "replaced" by behavior controlled *only* by the reality principle, we would say that this therapeutic perspective is *dialectic*. If, however, mental health is fostered via a dynamic balancing tension between these "conflicting" forces, we would term this orientation *dialogic*.

To explore the possibility of progress through a coexisting continuity between the old and the new, it would thus appear useful to differentiate between *dialectical* and *dialogical* modes of development. To contradistinguish from dialectic progress, in which thesis and anti-thesis are swallowed into a new elevated synthetic entity, "dialogic progress" would generally refer to the possibility of growth in which an "I" may emulate and even surpasses the "thou" with whom he or she interacts and through whom he or she develops, without having to destroy him or her (see Bergman, 1974).

A good example of how a conceptual distinction between dialectical and dialogical solution process may help to disentangle a very confounded theoretical theme dealing with progress is the dispute that evolved around the nature, dynamics, and impact of the Oedipal versus the Akeda or Isaac conflict.

JOSHUA VERSUS OEDIPUS AND JUDAS ISCARIOT

Let us begin by examining once more one of Freud's (1900) most quoted argumentative statements, intended to substantiate the universality of the Oedipal complex:

> If Oedipus Rex *moves* modern audience no less than it did the contemporary Greek one, . . . there must be something which makes a voice within us ready to recognize the compelling force of destiny in the Oedipus fate of all of us. A factor of this kind is involved in the story of King Oedipus. His destiny *moves* [italics mine] us only because it might have been ours—because the oracle laid the same curse upon us before our birth as upon him. It is the fate of all of us, perhaps, to direct our first sexual impulse towards our mother and our first hatred and our first murderous wish against our father. (P. 262)

I think that it will not be entirely incorrect to say that with such statements as the one above, Freud pushed from the top of his speculative ivory tower or rather iceberg the "Oedipal snowball" that still keeps generations of psychologists, anthropologists, educators, and writers rolling in heated pro and con arguments as to whether the "Oedipal conflict" or its opposing trend (parent hostility toward offspring), sometimes called "Isaac conflict," or rather the combined Oedipus-Isaac complex, is indeed a universal phenomenon or not.

It is, however, not the irresponsibility of asserting without proving that the Oedipal myth is universal because it "moves" us all, as Freud declares twice (see my italics) in his short statement (since if indeed Sophocles didn't move us sufficiently, apparently Freud did), but it appears that the short-sighted heated pro and con theorizing that emanated from Freud's postulate seems to melt the very "Oedipal snowball" on which these theories are rolling because it focuses on the nature of the intergenerational *tension* instead of assessing how a prescribed *solution* to such natural tensions enhances or hampers growth and progress.

In other words, arguments against the universality of the Oedipal complex seem to miss the point because they focus on the direction of intergenerational tension that may indeed be universal instead of studying the scope and nature of variability in trends and patterns of its solution, which are more likely to be culturally determined.

Hence, the question of whether the patricidal (the killing of one's father) or the filicidal (the killing of one's child) trend is a more predominant feature in intergenerational tensions seems of limited use not only because such trends are usually culturally bound (as are, naturally, most patterns of interpersonal relationships) but because they might be functionally interdependent in the sense that growth and progress might often be possible not in spite of but as a *result* of some tension between patricidal and filicidal trends. In other words, personal growth might often depend on the degree of one's access to a struggle with strong parental figures. Accordingly it might be significant to acknowledge the existence of parent-child abuse (Bakan, 1972) and adult hostility to youth (see Sheleff, 1981) or other forms of youth suppression possibly resulting from the threat of competition and dispossession as Stern (1948), Vernon (1972), Shoham (1977), and others argued. However, since children usually outlive their parents and even progress beyond their preceding generation, we still do not know from such filicidal studies whether progress of the young is hampered or rather enhanced by such filicidal pressures. That is, we do not know whether "filicidal pressures" in fact elicit the sufficient patricidal reactions necessary for children's growth.

Thus, it is only when the Oedipal versus the so-called Laius, Akeda, or Isaac complexes are assessed together in terms of their interdependences and association with specific cultural patterns of growth and progress that the careful reading of various myths becomes meaningful and useful.

It seems, indeed, that having had the ambition to construct a theory of growth and development, Freud himself was already clever enough to present the Oedipal complex *only* as a patricidal *reaction* to Laius's initial filicidal attempt to kill Oedipus. As is well known, Freud later arbitrarily termed this "Laius complex" the "castration complex"[1] although it appears nowhere in the Greek plays or mythologies.

Moreover, while it is thus only by assessing the interrelationship between the filicidal and patricidal pressures that one can understand parent-child conflict, as Wellisch (1954) has rightly contended, it is nonetheless only from the progress (solution) perspective that one may establish how in various cultures, patricidal and filicidal trends contribute either to dialectic versus dialogic patterns of progress or to regression or stalemate.

Accordingly, if filicidal suppression of autonomy exerted by a Prussian-type father results in a patricidal authoritarian Nazi personality in a Christian country like Germany, as Fromm (1960) and others have strived to demonstrate, it is still questionable whether similar filicidal pressures would produce the same authoritarian personality in other cultures.

Leon Sheleff (1981), for example, has rightly criticized arbitrarily apply-ing Freud's Oedipal model to explain the identification with, or revolution-ary reaction against, a tyrannic and oppressive father, in the case of a non-Western Chinese leader such as Mao Tse-tung. However, from Sheleff's own conclusion (on the basis of Mao's biographical studies) about the per-vasiveness of parental cruelty in non-Western China, we still don't know what kind of growth model emerged in China as a result of Mao's commu-nist revolution. That is, we don't know whether Mao's own rebellion against his presumably despotic father marks a break away from the tradi-tional Chinese submission to parental tyranny or rather a reproduction of this Oedipal tyranny under a new guise. More specifically, we don't know whether Mao's growth and progress paradigm connotes a Marxian dialectic kind of progress by which the traditional Chinese father is eliminated, whether the old dominating Chinese figure suppresses progress even in con-temporary Communist China, or whether progress and continuity are possi-ble in spite of and because of the dialogue between the traditional filicidal Chinese father and his communist patricidal son.

We should thus reread patricidal and filicidal myths in order to discover possible links between the kinds of *solutions* to intergenerational tension that they implicitly or explicitly offer and the kinds of cultural progress, regress, or stalemate with which they may be associated. It is by keeping this "solution" perspective in mind that the comparison between dialectic and dialogic components available in various versions of the classic Oedipal and Isaac myth might be highly revealing. Though it appears that most of the thematic elements comprising the Oedipal myth were quite popular in med-ieval tales and fables, let us begin by comparing the Christian version of the Judas Iscariot legend and its Jewish counterversion, found in the legend about the biblical Joshua, the son of Nun. I shall introduce first the legend of Judas Iscariot, which, according to Otto Rank's much neglected impor-tant work on the incest theme (1912), "was declared by most researchers as the Christian interpretation [formulation] of the Oedipus fable" (p. 143), and which appeared first in Jacobus de Voragine's (1941) thirteenth-century *Golden Legend*, one of the most famous books in the Middle Ages.[2]

> There was in Jerusalem a man called Ruben . . . who had as his wife a woman named Ciborea. One night, when they had lain down with each other, Ciborea fell asleep and had a dream, from which she awoke moaning and weeping with fright. And she said to her husband: "I dreamt that I was bearing a son so evil that he would be the downfall of our race." And Ruben answered: "Thou sayest a wicked thing, not worthy to be spoken or thought. The devil himself, no doubt, has set thee raving." But she replied: "If I conceive a son of our union this night, it will be proof that my dream was no devilish illusion but a revelation of the truth!" And when nine months from that night, she bore a son, both she and her husband were sore afraid,

and knew not what to do; for they were horrified at the thought of putting their own flesh and blood to death, and on the other hand could not bear to nurture the future destroyer of their people. They determined ultimately to place the infant in a little basket, and to leave him to the mercy of the waves of the seas. Thus he was borne to the shores of an island called Iscariot. . . . And the queen of the Island walking on the strand, discovered the basket. . . . Thus she had the babe cared for in secret, and pretended to be with child; and in time she presented the child as her son, and the whole kingdom hailed the event joyously. . . . At last, however, the truth came out, and it was known that Judas was not the true son of the king. Thereupon Judas, burning with shame and jealousy, secretly slew the king's true heir, his supposed brother. Then, fearing the penalty of his deed, he took flight with his cronies and went to Jerusalem, and there the prefect Pilate, recognizing in him a boon companion, conceived a warm affection for him. . . . And one day Pilate was looking out upon an apple orchard close by his palace, and began to long for a taste of the fruit. As it happened, the orchard belonged to Ruben, the father of Judas; but neither of them recognized the other. And Judas, aware of Pilate's desire, entered the orchard and started to pick apples. And when Ruben found him out, they began by vilifying each other and then came to blows: and Judas finally killed Ruben, striking him with a stone at the back of the head. Thereafter he brought the apples to Pilate, and told him all that had happened. And when Ruben's death became known, Pilate bestowed all the dead man's goods upon his favorite Judas, and gave him the widow in wedlock, she being none other than his own mother, Ciborea.

One evening Ciborea was sighing so mournfully, that Judas, her new spouse, asked her what had befallen her. She replied: "Alas, I am the most unhappy of women. I was forced to drown my only son, my husband was murdered, and now, to crown my misery, Pilate has compelled me to remarry maugre my grief!" Then she told him the whole story of the child, and Judas recounted his adventures to her. Thus they discovered that Judas had killed his father and married his mother. Then, at Ciborea's behest, the wretched man resolved to do penance, and sought out Our Lord Jesus Christ of Whom he implored pardon for his sins. . . . Our Lord made Judas His disciple, and chose him among his twelve apostles.

Let us now read the Jewish legend about Joshua, which, according to sources from the tenth century (see *Rav Pealim*, 1894),[3] was presumably rewritten in the eighteenth century.

The father of Joshua lived in Jerusalem and his wife was childless and this righteous man was praying in the presence of his wife and God listened to him. And it was so that while she was pregnant, this righteous man tormented himself and weeped day and night non stop; and this was bad in the eyes of his wife and she said to him: you should have been happy because God listened to your prayers. . . . and he told her . . . that he was told from Heaven that this son that will be born to him will decapitate him. . . . And it was so that when she gave birth and it was a son and his mother took for him a basket [ark] . . . and she put the child in it and she threw it into the river [Nile] and God arranged for a big fish [whale] to swallow the basket. . . . And it was the day when the king made a feast for his ministers and slaves and he caught this fish . . . and opened it and there was a boy crying. . . . and the boy grew up in the king's palace and he made him the hangman. . . . And after these things this righteous man [Joshua's father] sinned to the king of Egypt and the king ordered the hangman to decapitate him and take his wife, sons and property to himself as was customary those days. And as he approached his mother to copulate with her, then the whole bed filled up with milk from her breasts. And he became very alarmed and he took a spear to kill her because he thought that she was a witch and his mother remembered the words of his father the late righteous man and she answered him her saying: it is not witch-craft but the milk with which I nursed you because I am your mother and she told him the whole event and he immediately separated from her . . . as he did not know that it was his father and he repented. (P. 23)

Upon comparing these two "Oedipal" versions, which contain two entirely different role models, one is obviously struck by their almost total systematic resemblance, in spite of the fact that they were planted into two diametrically opposed cultures.

This resemblance should, however, not be too surprising, not only because legendary themes usually travel (though under various disguises) across cultures, but because, according to the usually ignored important work of Velikovsky (1960), for example, there is sufficient historical-archeological evidence to prove that "the legend of Oedipus grew from the real experiences of the Pharaoh Akhnaton" (p. 197), dating back to early times in ancient Egypt. If Velikovsky's assertion is indeed based on sufficient historical data, Oedipal-Pharaoh myths might naturally have spread in such Middle Eastern countries as ancient Israel, Greece, and Egypt (where the Akhnaton patricidal incident presumably occurred) because they were based on the belief that a pharaoh once really killed his father. The possibility that such a case of a pharaoh killing his father indeed occurred in a specific time and place in history might, however, challenge Freud's claim that the hidden urge to kill our fathers (because growth and progress are possible only after the killing of Father Laius) is a universal truism beyond time and space. In reality, it might be that in spite of the universal incestuous-murderous intergenerational tension, one culture might prescribe a dialectic patricidal father killing as a result of a belief in an Oedipal kind of metahermeneutic code that states that progress is possible only when the son rules *instead* of the old king; while other cultures might offer a dialogic rearranging of the intergenerational continuity that resulted in a son ruling *after* the old king, without having to destroy his cultural heritage, and in spite of the tension.

I should indicate here that in many medieval versions of the Oedipal myth, the father-killing theme is entirely lacking and the incestuous marrying of the mother ends in a dialogic rearranging continuity. An example is the famous Gregory legend in which the son, after discovering that he was married to his mother, not only repented but was allowed to become Pope (see *Gesta Romanorum*, 1891).[4] The fact that Freud, nonetheless, chose the patricidal Oedipal myth as a key narrative for the construction of his dialectic paradigm of growth and progress might be revealing. The careful selection of the Oedipal metacode paradigm demonstrates that it was not only the incest theme but its concomitant theme of patricide that Freud believed characterized human development.

Moreover, while in the famous medieval legend about Pope Gregory, an incestuous relationship between mother and son was actually enacted, in the Jewish version of this legend, which appeared under the title "Mamzer Talmid Chacham" (the Talmudic Scholar Bastard) in various anthologies, the actual sexual performance of incestuous relationships was prevented at the last moment, as happened in Joshua's fable. In one version for example,

> the husband sat and heard the whole story, and he was utterly startled: it became clearly known to him that this woman was his mother. . . . and [he] gave praise and gratitude to God, for bestowing upon him great charity, so that he did not falter in committing such a grave sin to depend sexually on his mother. (Ben Yechezkel, 1951:369)

It was thus not possible that Freud chose the patricidal story of Oedipus as his paradigmatic key narrative because he was unfamiliar with Judas's legend, since it was cited by his student Otto Rank, and as he was most probably acquainted with Pope Gregory's legend, about whom Thomas Mann wrote his famous novel, *The Holy Sinner*. Rather, these different solution patterns demonstrate once again the Jewish search for a *dialogical* solution of incestual tensions featuring intergenerational relationships—a solution that Freud eschewed.

Furthermore, in this context it is most important to point out that evidence showing how the dialogical norm of intergenerational continuity was fostered in Jewish tradition is available already in ancient Midrashim. By emphasizing how its antiincestuous nature differed from the dialectic gentile mode of progress, the ancient (first or second century) *Midrash Tanchuma* (*Vayshev*:a) stated:

> Why did the Scripture engage in writing their [the gentiles'] genealogy . . . but . . . to publicize that they are all the children of incest and so He says, "the sons of Elifas Teman and Omer, Zefo and Gaatam Kenaz and Timna and Amalek . . . (Chron. I 1:36) and [in the Torah it says] Timna was Elifas' mistress" (Genesis, 36:12). It teaches us that he [Elifas] married his daughter . . . and later He says, [about someone else's genealogy] Ana the son of

Zivon . . . it teaches that Zivon copulated with his mother and she gave birth to his Ana so that he was his brother and son. . . . But God brought Israel close to Him . . . as it is written "Yet I had planted thee a noble vine, wholly a right seed." (Jeremiah, 2:21)

We shall return to compare the two major key archetypal narratives of Oedipus and Isaac that obviously exerted the major phenomenological impacts on modern psychosocial thinking, the first due to Freud's influence and the second due to Jewish commentary, but it is the subtle yet symbolically significant differences in solution trends, which one might already recognize in the almost identical versions of the Judas and Joshua myth, that seem highly revealing in terms of their respective dialectic or dialogic implications for the possibility of progress.

While the oracle, basket, and patricide themes appear in both stories, in the Christian legend of Judas, the warning dream repeats twice that the birth of Judas symbolizes not only the killing of the biological father but also "the downfall of our race" and the idea that Ciborea and Ruben, the Jewish parents, "bear to nurture the future destroyer of their people." Whereas the Christian Judas story indeed ends by telling how this "wretched man" [Judas] . . . sought out Our Lord Jesus Christ [who] . . . made Judas His disciple and chose him among his twelve apostles," the Jewish myth of Joshua seeks another solution. Not only is there a last-minute rearranging of the intergenerational relationship between Joshua and his mother, whom he recognizes *before* committing incest with her (while according to one version Ciborea bore two children to Judas), but it is in fact this very dialogic encounter with the mother that brings him back to Judaism to become the heir of Moses, who, as is known, bestowed upon him the historical task of transmitting the Judaic culture to future generations.

It is thus this Hegelian dialectic notion of progress, embedded on the one hand in the conception of the organic impossibility of self-renewal (Ciborea bearing the seeds of national self-destruction) and grounded on the other hand in the theological idea that Christian progress is possible only after the Oedipal-Paulinian killing of the Laius-Moses religious kingdom, that is symbolically blatant in the myth of Judas. This dialectic paradigm of growth is nonetheless precisely the model Freud adopted in his Oedipalization of Moses when he said first (1967):

"The Mosaic religion has been the father religion; Christianity became a Son religion. . . . The Old God the Father took second place, Christ the son stood in his stead." . . . Paul, by developing the Jewish religion further, became its destroyer. . . . It could scarcely be chance that the violent death of another great man [Moses] should become the starting point of the creation of a new religion by Paul. (P. 111)

Then, to lead us back from his cultural analysis of social progress to the major theme he aimed to present, Freud (p. 175) offered us the following psychological generalization. "The way in which the new religion came to terms with the ancient ambivalency in the father-son relationship is noteworthy . . . the son, who had taken the guilt on his shoulders, [by] becoming God himself . . . [functions now] in place of the [old God] father."

It is consequently not Freud's generalization that the story of Oedipus "moves us all because . . . it is the fate of all of us . . . to direct . . . our first murderous wishes against our fathers" (ibid.) that should interest us, but it is the concluding solution that one could become the king of Thebes only after killing the father Laius or that social progress is possible only after the Paulinian killing of father Moses' religious legacy, that becomes now most revealing.

To accentuate the difference between Joshua's solution in which patricide was not used to *substitute* the father but to facilitate progress by reestablishing the dialogical continuity between them, let us look at another example of dialectic progress.

In demonstrating how the dialectic structure of intergenerational relations operates among the Pawnee Indian Shamans of the North American Plains, Levi-Strauss (1963) used the following Pawnee myth, which he termed the recurring theme of the "pregnant boy":

> An ignorant young boy becomes aware that he possesses magical powers that enable him to cure the sick. Jealous of the boy's increasing reputation, an old medicine man of established position visits him on several different occasions. . . . The medicine man offers the boy a pipe filled with magical herbs. Thus bewitched, the boy discovers that he is pregnant. Full of shame, he leaves his village and seeks death among wild animals. The animals teach him their magical powers, by means of which the boy, on returning to his home, kills the evil medicine man and becomes himself a famous and respected healer. (P. 234)

While in both the pregnant boy myth and in the Joshua legend, patricidal progress is triggered by filicidal pressure, only in the Joshua myth is there a last-minute avoidance of incest and repentance about the inadvertant patricide that rearranges intergenerational continuity between the "righteous" man and his repented son. On the other hand, the "pregnant boy's" growth into a "famous and respected healer" is possible only through an eliminating dialectic negation process by which the "evil medicine man" is advertantly killed and "substituted" as would be the "evil" capitalist by the Marxist working class.

With this attempted differentiation between dialectic and dialogic key narratives of progress, we should now reconsider the limitations of some filicidal propositions (especially those related to the archetypal Isaac story) that focus merely on intergenerational tension instead of on the implied solution.

THE ISAAC PARADOX: AS A DIALOGICAL
GROWTH MODEL

I have said earlier that although in medieval times dialectic and dialogic components permeated the many available versions of what may be generally termed the Oedipal myth, the more predominant phenomenological impact on concrete patterns of growth and socialization doctrines should be sought in the original Oedipal and Isaac stories simply because these were used more than any other myths to interpret behavior, at least in the Christian and Jewish cultures. To contradistinguish from the term *conflict*, which is usually used in relation to the Oedipal complex to connote the unbridgeable tension between father and son, I have chosen the term *paradox* to explain dialogic intergenerational tensions, because paradoxical relationships may, by definition, be interconnected and rearranged in spite of their initially "seeming" inner contradiction.

To revisit theoretical arguments using the "Isaac complex," let us first return to David Bakan (1972) who on the one hand traced contemporary child-abuse manifestations to ancient Isaac-type child sacrifice practices, but who on the other hand agrees with Wellisch (1954) that the last-minute prevention of actual filicide in Isaac's biblical case may have served as a counteracting theme to the ancient infanticidal impulse or to the Roman *Patria Potestas* (see Bakan, 1966) phenomenon that gave the father unlimited authority even to execute his children.[5]

While these two possibilities of father restrainment and his abuse of power against his child are certainly not mutually exclusive, it is in fact only from the "progress perspective" that one might determine the extent to which such European cannibalistic legends (which Bakan uses) as Jack and the Bean-stalk, or Hansel and Gretel are associated with universalistic or culturally idiosyncratic trends of child abuse and cultural regression or rather with authoritarian patricidal styles of dialectic progress. By contrast, in other cultures (e.g., Jewish) a key narrative theme such as the biblical Isaac story may precipitate a dialogical style of progress via continuity in spite of the intergenerational tension.

Similar to Bakan's undifferentiated documentation of the child-abuse hypothesis with European and biblical filicidal stories, Sheleff (1981) used the Persian tale of King Rustum, who unwittingly killed his son Soharb, to introduce his thesis about the *universal* pervasiveness of adult hostility to youth.

Again, since Sheleff focused only on universalistic trends of intergenerational *tension* and not on culturally differentiated modes of their *solution*, we do not know from the impressive evidence he adduced (a) how this Persian myth might be causally related, as Sheleff claimed, to adult hostility in the West, and (b) whether, when, and where such filicidal pressures caused cultural and social decadence, stalemate, or rather patricidal, reactions of dialectic or dialogic styles of progress that are triggered by these challenging filicidal hostilities.

Finally, lack of awareness about the plausible meaning of a myth in specific sociocultural contexts in terms of its impact on possible manifestations of dialogic versus dialectic modes of progress characterize Shoham's (1977) use of the Isaac complex.

To highlight the very dark spot of how societies' struggles for existence are accomplished by subduing, glorifying, and socializing their fittest heroic sons to sacrifice their lives for their countries and their ideologies, Shoham traced Isaac's "Akeda complex" to the ancient child-sacrifice practice by citing from those rare Jewish commentaries (Midrashim) that imply that Isaac actually died (according to Shoham, like Jesus on the cross) on the altar.

It is, however, precisely by reviewing the evolvement of diversive cultural possibilities of dialogic versus dialectic patterns of progress from the background of such ancient child-sacrifice practices that the one-sided consideration of filicide, without its counterreactive trend of parricide, becomes partially misleading.

A careful reading of the predominant Jewish Midrashim would thus reveal, for example, a systematic effort to establish the possibility of dialogic progress and intergenerational continuity in spite of the ancient actual, and the contemporary psychological, impulse toward infanticide.

While there is no denying of filicidal pressures and intergenerational tension, the Akeda is presented in most Jewish Midrashim somewhat as a Kierkegaardian (1954) test of faith in order to inculcate in the "Jewish Isaacs" the parricidal stubbornness of not discarding their faith in the biblical promised multiplying progress and dialogic continuity with Abraham "even when a sharp sword is laid upon their neck," as the famous Talmudic saying goes (*Berachot*, 10:a).

It is thus with this dialogic continuity dimension of progress in mind that we may now understand, contrary to Shoham's narrow interpretation of contemporary child sacrifice, why on the one hand even those rare Midrashim that "kill Isaac" bring him back to life (see Shpiegel, 1950) in order to facilitate the fulfillment of the promised dialogic continuity, while on the other hand massive child sacrifice modeled by the Akeda was relatively permissible only during the Middle Ages, when, for instance (ibid.), Jewish continuity was concretely threatened by the Crusaders' coercion of Jewish children to convert to Christianity.

Thus, what we possibly now have is two models of progress:

1. the dialectic paradigm in which the idealization of the actual filicidal killing-sacrificing of the son-Jesus may trigger progress via the actual Oedipal elimination of the father generation, so that the son rules *instead* of the father;

2. the dialogic paradigm that idealizes Isaac's "patricidal" faith in a last-minute avoidance of Abraham's "filicidal" pressure to facilitate continuity of the son ruling *after* the father.

From a semantic point of view, the following differentiation between dialectic and dialogic solutions seems now in order. Although tension between two opposing elements has been commonly referred to as *dialectic tension*, according to the foregoing "solution"-oriented analysis, we could suggest now that while tension must by definition be dialogic, it is only the synthetic solution (in which the "I" thesis and the "it" antithesis are swallowed into a new synthetic entity) that makes the synthetic kind of progress dialectic, but if growth of an "I" is accomplished while the "thou" remains a "thou" or even an "it" in spite of the tension between them, we have a dialogic solution of continuity and progress.

It is of interest to note here that while both of these models should make growth and progress possible, according to Ricoeur (1970), for example, in Freud's archeological or rather biological model, *identification* and especially *sublimation* do not present even distinct synthetic processes of desire-facilitating dialectic progressions in cultural and artistic creativity, but essentially, regressive desexualization processes of energy discharge and or responses to suppressions by the superego.[6] Thus while the psychoanalytical decomposing negation of the past (parents) should have facilitated, according to Ricoeur, synthetic (sublimating) outlets of creativity, Freud's archeology only uncovers, but does not clearly integrate, past guilt or desexualized energy with new creative potentialities.

In his analysis of a typical Freudian text on sublimation, Ricoeur (1970) concluded that

> artistic sublimation is mentioned but not developed, instead, a parallel example of reaction-formation is developed—scopophilia. Finally, nothing justifies our saying that the values, esthetic or otherwise, toward which the energy is channeled or displaced, would be created by this mechanism. (P. 487)

In reacting to Freud's paper "On Narcissism," Ricoeur (ibid.) reacted similarly: "The more Freud distinguishes sublimation from other mechanisms . . . the more its own mechanisms remain unexplained."

At any rate, from the present formulation of dialectic progress as a "substitution" of the old, we may recognize in Freud two sequential phases of synthetic dialecticism that do not represent a neutral archeology, but two opposing processes of conquest:

1. the first, dialectic filicidal phase of *identification* in which the negating sexual desires of father and son result in the father's synthetic swallowing of the son (who "becomes" the father) by "killing" his sexual ego.

2. the second parricidal dialectic phase of the son "killing" his father on the "psychoanalytic trial bench," as a result of which the Oedipal son may rule *instead* of his father-Laius.

Although this second individuation phase of "becoming conscious," which parallels Hegel's second "blossoming phase," already entails Hegel's deterministic third phase of self-destructiveness (decay), it may in fact generate growth of the son if the filicidal pressures during the first phase were sufficiently challenging to promote the teleological accumulative progress of the father's "spirit," which may not be "elevated" by the son who has to kill his father to allow for his own conscious growth.

In other words, if we reformulate Hegel's "genesis" stage (the first in Hegel's three-phased progress paradigm) as *identification* with father, the fathers challenging filicidal pressures (Oedipal "castration" threats) might indeed hasten the son's progressing process into Hegel's second phase of consciousness. It is, however, this very second phase of "becoming" or of acquiring consciousness, which, according to Hegel and Freud, contains the self-destructive seeds of personal decay precipitated (from our perspective) by the archeological uncovering of the patricidal original sin guilt, which encompasses and constitutes the third phase of decline. The third phase of self destruction must follow the second phase because self-annihilating guilt would logically follow the second-phased killing of parents on the "psychoanalytic trial bench" according to Freud's archeological model for uncovering repressed guilt, embodied in psychoanalysis.

The Oedipal killing of parents on the "psychoanalytical trial bench," to which I alluded earlier, refers to the therapeutic implication that only through individuation and separation from dependency on parents (to whom one is attached by Oedipal parricidal guilt) may one reach the Western norm of maturity and normalcy.

Indeed, Peter Berger (1963) observed, for example, that

> many Americans seemingly spend years of their life . . . retelling over and over again (to themselves *and* to others) the story of what they have been and what they have become . . . and in this process killing their parents in a sacrificial ritual of the mind. . . . It is no wonder, incidentally, that the Freudian mythology of parricide has found ready credence in American Society and especially in those recently middle-class segments of it to whom such rewriting of biographies is a social necessity of legitimizing one's hard won status. (P. 60)

Since, accordingly, the predestined original-sin-based parricidal wish (Freud, 1967) is an inevitable component of growth, most Freudian-influenced therapies train people not only to become conscious of their parricidal guilt, but also to cut off their umbilical cords and tie them around their parents necks in order to legitimize their "hard won status" and qualify as "independent Westerners."

As I introduce my metaphoric use of parental killing on the "psychoanalytic trial bench" as a central second-phase of consciousness in the Freudian-Hegelian growth paradigm, a typical therapeutic illustration is in order. Thus, the following excerpt from Fritz Perls' (1969) Gestaltist therapeutic dream analysis seems not an exception but the rule in most neo-Freudian therapies.

> F: (therapist) So find somebody else to kill . . . .
>
> J: (patient) My mother . . . how can I kill her? I want it to hurt. . . . Oh! I killed her. . . . Into the swimming pool, all filled with acid, and she dove in. There's nothing left. . . . You deserved it. I should have done it a long time ago. There aren't even any bones left. She just disappeared. . . . And then I sorta felt *good*. I should have done it a long time ago.
>
> F: Say this to the group.
>
> J: It felt good! I should have done it *a long* time ago (p. 221, 22).

It seems that one need not be a therapist in order to realize that the therapist's encouragement of this thirty-five-year-old patient to "say this to the group!" is geared to help her to kill her mother symbolically and publicly in order to become "healthy" by separating from her according to the prescribed Western-American social norm.

Nonetheless, it should be noted that like dialectical overoppressive filicidal pressures, which may result in obedient-submission to parents that would hamper progress (see Neumann, 1962), dialogic father-son relationships that entirely lack filicidal pressures—like those described by Malinowski (1927) among the Trobriand Islanders or like the Hasidic father who overcontracts himself to play with his child (see Rotenberg, 1983)—could result in stalemate or decadence rather than progress, as Buber (1946) indeed claimed occurred in the Hasidic movement.

In general one may expect, however, the dialogic mode of progress to surpass the dialectic growth pattern because in the latter, progress energy must first counteract the "negative energy" invested in "killing" and separating from the Oedipal parent by putting him on the psychoanalytic trial bench. However, since during this second analytical phase of becoming conscious, energy must be used also for the archaeological process of uncovering this unavoidable patricidal "original sin" guilt, one may wonder how much "positive energy" might be left for progress after so much "negative energy" is invested in the mutually conflicting processes of parricide and self-blame. True, the presentation of "orthodox" Freudian psychoanalysis as a dialectic parricidal "trial bench" for parents and as a subsequent self-destructive confession box for offspring may, ironically speaking, represent in itself an extremist "Oedipal thesis" aimed at "killing" Freud's theoretical (paternal) authority, which would paradoxically then serve as a testimonial case supporting his dialectic theory of growth. It can obviously be proved that some efforts were made by such neo-Freudian therapists as Heince Kohut and D. W. Winnicott to soften the parricidal element in their Oedipal versions in order to reestablish dialogically the possibility of intergenerational continuity. One is reminded, however, that the hypothesized association between the parental overrestricting superego and neurosis, which one may become conscious of but which one cannot erase but must learn to accept as a reality principle, may have contributed in recent decades more than we would like to believe to the perpetuation of many political parricidal movements. Thus, the emergence of the Marcusean (1962) anarchistic "pleasure principled" rebellion of youth against their parents' "reality principled" authority in the sixties and the "counter culture" parricidal encounter-therapy groups that accompanied them may be highly revealing cases in point. In this sense, it was Freud's own dialectic parricidal metacode of Oedipal progress that defeated his self-contradicting preaching to enforce society's reality principle. It is thus because of the observed differences between the American Western style of progress via parricidal burying alive of obsolete old parents in old age home asylums (see Goffman, 1956) and a Japanese Eastern style such as the "amae" system of progress that reestablishes intergenerational dependency (see Doi, 1973) that the introduction of the "Abraham-Isaac" dialogic model of progress becomes significant.

Thus, unlike Freud's Oedipal, castrating, sword-threatening continuity, which triggers patricide, Abraham's Akeda-sword must be understood as an urging-immunizing sword of Damocles assuring dialogic faith in the promised continuity that enhances investments in progress in spite of, and "even when a sharp sword is laid upon the neck." In other words, faith in progress and continuity must be assured not only when Rothchild Jr. inherits his father's wealth but even when Rothchild or Rockefeller goes bankrupt or threatens to disinherit his son.

To give the reader some concretizing illustrations of how the dialogical style of continuity may be empirically observed even in spheres where dialectic pressures were also immanent, in the next chapter the Talmudic system of discourse and the Jewish-Israeli kibbutz style of integrating immigrants will be presented as essentially dialogical processes.

NOTES

1. The only explanations for connecting the castration threat to the Oedipus complex can be found in such vague statements as the following, offered by Freud in his *Collected Papers* (1900b): "Analytic observations enable us to perceive or to infer the connection between the phallic organization, the Oedipus complex, the threat of castration. . . . They justify the statement that the Oedipus complex succumbs to the threat of castration" (p. 273). It should be of major interest to suggest here that Freud's evasive

reference to this arbitrary connection between the filicidal castration threat and the patricidal Oedipus complex, which may presumably be discovered in "analytical observations," might be related to the possibility that Freud derived the idea about the filicidal castration threat from anti-Semitic sources that he, as a Jew, had good reasons to hide. In a scholarly book about nightmares that gained little attention, Freud's biographer Ernest Jones (1931) demonstrated how the Christian idea of Satan and the devil was gradually associated with the father-son complex, in which the son dreads that the "bad father" (devil) will castrate him. Trachtenberg (1984) has shown then that the idea of a Jewish Antichrist—"bad fathers" or Satans castrating Christian children can be seen in plates available from medieval times. Trachtenberg (p. 243) indicated further that the anti-Semitic blood libel—castration charge was revived during the Third Reich when pictures of Rabbis sucking blood from an "Aryan" child were published in the official Nazi newspaper *Der Sturmer*. In the medieval plates provided by Trachtenberg, the "bad Jewish fathers" castrating the little Christian boy (Jesus?) are associated with the Jewish symbolic custom of circumcision (here symbolizing the attempt to prevent Christian continuity and propagation). Indeed, in his last book, *Moses and Monotheism* (1967) Freud stated that "among the customs through which the Jews marked off their aloof position, that of circumcision made a disagreeable, uncanny impression on others. The explanation probably is that it reminds them of the dreaded castration idea" (p. 116). To complete his outrageous effort to combine the filicidal and parricidal mythologies into one theory, Freud forged history twice. Thus, while he insisted against all historical evidence that the Jews killed Moses in the desert (the Oedipal element), he also attributed to Moses the introduction of circumcision (the castration element), although it is well-known that this custom has symbolized God's covenant with Israel since Abraham. "Moses 'sanctified' his people by introducing the custom of circumcision, we now understand the deep-lying meaning of this pretension. . . . Circumcision is the symbolic substitute of castration" (p. 156). One may wonder then not only why and how Freud, as a Jew, combined the anti-Semitic rooted idea of castration with the Greek Oedipal notion, but how he presented both as a universal phenomenon that is to characterize every father-son relationship although it becomes obvious on the basis of the above evidence that the "castration-libel-myth" could have been, at most, only an idiosyncratic invention.

2. De Voragine's *Golden Legend*, which is today in the public domain, was reprinted in 1973 by the AMS Press in New York. The reader is referred, however, to the 1941 edition because it so happened that while the index of the AMS book includes the item: "Judas Iscariot's birth and parentage," the legend cannot be found in its indicated page or elsewhere in the text itself. Nonetheless, if one considers the number of available translations, copies, and editions of the *Golden Legend*, such deletions may be well understood.

3. In regard to the assumption that this legend can be traced back to the tenth century, Professor Ginzberg (1968) offered the following comment:

> *Rab Pealim*, 12 a, giving as a source a Midrash quoted by the Kabbalist R. Nathan [i.e., R. Nathan Shapiro, author of *Megale Amukot*], but the published writings of this Kabbalist do not to my knowledge contain this form of the Oedipus legend, nor is it found in any other Jewish source. The reference to *Sefer Hamasiyot* of R. Nissim Gaon [tenth century] by the editor of *Rab Pealim* is a poor guess, as this narrative does not occur in that book. (VI:169)

I should like to add that after personally examining all available editions of *Megale Amukot* and *Sefer Hamasiyot*, even in the first Ferera edition of *Sefer Hamasiyot* to which Eisenstein (1969, L: 209) refers the reader, no trace of this legend can be found. It is possible, however, that it was appendixed to one edition and later lost or that Rabbi Nathan Neta, to whom *Rab Pealim* refers us, was not Rabbi Shapiro, as Ginzberg assumes (as there was no family name mentioned) but another rabbi, because there were several rabbis named Nathan Neta. The legend can be found, however, also in *Lev Avot Hashalem* (1970:32) which contains Midrashim (legends) on the book, *Ethics of the Fathers*.

4. A similar story in which incestual tension is overcome through a last-minute dialogic salvation of *tikun* that rearranged interpersonal relations can be found in the Talmud (*Gitin*, 58:a). The story tells of the son and daughter of Rabbi Yishmael who were taken as captives by two different masters who decided, upon meeting accidentally, to have these children married to each other. However, when they were put in a room together for the night, each one sat in a corner and wept, because, as offspring of a *Kohen* (priest), neither wanted to marry a servant, and, indeed, in the morning they recognized each other and thus prevented incest. Moreover, in the Jewish-Hasidic version of the Gregory fable, *The Talmudic Scholar Bastard* (see Soybelman (1913:21) also never copulated with his mother-spouse.

5. Here I would like again to remind the reader that according to Talmudic interpretations of the biblical law, a "stubborn and rebellious Son" (see Chapter 1) is to be put to death if the parents can prove to the court that their son's stealing, gluttony, drunkenness, and other symptoms of delinquency were not caused by the environment or by their own educational faults. Nevertheless, according to many sources and commentaries that I adduced with Bernard Diamond (see Rotenberg and Diamond, 1971), the many restrictions established by the Talmud, which make it almost impossible to execute such a "son," and especially the biblical stipulation that the father cannot execute him but has to bring him to court, were developed largely for the purpose of restraining the unlimited authority that the father had possessed in ancient times.

6. One should not overlook the potentially important distinction, on which I shall elaborate elsewhere, between the material "dialectic sex model" and the spiritual "dialogic flirt model," which follows from Freud's biological orientation. The metaphoric definition of spiritual "flirt" as dialogic refers to the infinite romantic energy that motivates interpersonal progress, while the material definition of sex in its strict physiological sense refers to the finite biological synthesis that characterizes the culmination of such a dialectic act. While Freud (1961) stated that "genital love leads to the formation of new families and aim inhibited love to friendship" (p. 50), his overemphasis on the biological-sensual origin of both kinds of love seems to miss the great potential for spiritual growth inherent in "romantic flirt," although his concepts of "displacement" and "sublimation" lead, as is implicit in the Jewish concept of "impulse" or (*yetzer*), to spiritual possibilities of progress in spite of his biologism.

6 The "Non-Melting Pot"

In the foregoing chapter I have shown how "dialectic" growth grounded in the conflict-based Oedipal myth is possible only via the killing and "replacing" of the old and no-more-fitting thesis, ruling class, or father, whereas according to paradox-based myths such as Isaac's Akeda, a dialogic "I and thou" coexistence and continuity between father Abraham and his son Isaac is possible in spite of intergenerational tension.

To illuminate the empirical differences between these two modes of progress, in this chapter the patterns of what can be termed Jewish *spiritual progress* (Talmudic learning style) and Jewish *material progress* (Zionistic actualization styles) will be analyzed.

Before we proceed with our discursive distinction between these two patterns of dialogic progress, let me concede that this differentiation is somewhat arbitrary because as a countervailing force to the Hegelian organic emphasis on dialectic progress, dialogicalism must primarily be a spiritual metaphor of growth.

Let me elucidate how such implicated differences might practically follow from the two opposing metaphors of progress.

In his vehement refutation of Arnold Toynbee's "fossilized" conceptualization of the Jewish entity, Maurice Samuel (1956) provided ample evidence demonstrating that while Toynbee praised Yochanan Ben Zakai's leading role in Jewish spiritual revival, he refused to recognize this recurrent trend in Judaism as a symptom of progress and self-renewal that would stand in diametric opposition to Toynbee's "fossilized" conception of Judaism.

Very briefly, it is well-known that Rabbi Yochanan's Academy at Yavneh, which was reestablished during the first century A.D. at the time of the Vespasian siege and the physical destruction of Jerusalem after Rabbi Yochanan

111

escaped from the city in a coffin, became the symbol of Jewish spiritual progress reflected in the Talmudic thought system that Rabbi Yochanan revived in Yavneh's Academy.

Nonetheless, Toynbee, whose fossilized conception of Judaism was rooted in Hegel's organic metaphor of progress, insisted that Yochanan Ben Zakai's "Yavneh" symbolized a Jewish conversion from (physical-organic?) violence to the way of gentleness, stating: "In act and word Jochanan ben Zakai was proclaiming his *conversion* from the way of violence to the way of Gentleness; and through his *conversion* he became the founder of the new Jewry which survived—albeit only as a fossil" (quoted by Samuel, 1956:86).

Thus, if in the dialectic mode of progress, organic-physical persistence outweighs spiritual renewal, in dialogic continuity it is essentially the spiritual growth system that primarily determines the possibility of such material progressions as Zionistic actualization.

Another illustration of how the overemphasis on organic-mechanistic development may hamper or ignore the potentiality of spiritual progress is Freud's dialectic theory of instincts.

In his book, *The Utopian Flight from Unhappiness* (1974), Kalin concluded the following in regard to what he termed Freud's inconsistent theory of instincts:

> Freud's final dualism pits life (Eros) against death (Thanatos) but his account of pleasure, . . . collapses the alleged distinction between the two primary instincts. In the mechanistic model pleasure consists in a diminution of tension. The ids' desire for absolute pleasure therefore coincides with its quest for Nirvana, the state of complete tensionless existence. Since life vacillates between the production and reduction of tension, however, only death brings real equilibrium: hence the pursuit of unconditional pleasure constitutes a drive toward death . . . basic drives have a regressive tendency. The Death instinct in particular inclines the self toward the past because it seeks to restore the tensionless or inorganic state that precedes life. (P. 172)

Thus, again, if pleasure or spiritual progress is formulated in organic-mechanistic terms of dialectic movements, it takes on a regressive direction. However, if emphasis is not on the biological-mechanistic aspect of Eros culminating in physical Nirvana ("death") that characterizes the synthetic state in the sexual act but on spiritual "flirt" featuring the dialogic phase of Eros, the dynamic tension of hypothesis between the "I" and the "thou" may facilitate constant spiritual growth because of its ability to remain unfulfilled.

This is not to say that Freud's dialectic growth model is void of spiritual growth potentialities in spite of his biologism. However, by keeping in mind that in dialogicalism, it is the spiritual that shapes the material, we may now proceed to discuss the dialogic possibilities of spiritual growth inherent in the Talmudic-style thought system and then discuss the dialogic possibilities of "material progress."

"PILPULISTIC CHUTZPAH" AS DIALOGIC PROGRESS

In his treatise about the biblical historiosophy of the Jewish neo-Kantian philosopher Herman Cohen (1842-1918), Eliezer Schweid (1983) demonstrated how Cohen (1971) perceived the Bible as an accumulative system that progresses systematically from the descriptive myth to the reflective epic so that a moral order is constructed from the epic without destroying its previous mythic form.

The mythic phase refers to a divine description concerning the happening of events and the creation of things in the infinite present. The epic phase refers to a reflective, contemplative story about the past and seeks to derive from it the moral conclusions necessary to proceed from the present to the future.

Thus, while biblical commentaries must correlate with the original text so that the lower layers may hold the upper layers added to the rising construction, later hermeneutic attempts to reharmonize and rearrange the present with the past do not contradict earlier exegesis, according to Cohen, because they do not erase but only develop the potential that earlier narratives contain. Hence, what evolves is an accumulative developmental continuum of thought.

To demonstrate how moral thought develops from the mythic to the epic in the Torah, Cohen showed how in the epic Book of Deuteronomy, which reflects on the mythic events described in the Book of Exodus, the (neo-Kantian) principle of moral autonomy is established, according to which: "It is not in heaven. . . . But the word is very nigh unto thee, in thy mouth, and in thy heart, that thou mayest do it" (Deut., 30:12–14).

Even more revealing in the apparent contradiction between the biblical "early" and the "later" that Cohen reconciles as progress in the moral system is the collective responsibility of "the fathers have eaten sour grapes, and the children's teeth are set on edge," declared by early prophets, which Ezekiel (18:2) challenges by setting forth the principle of individual responsibility of "the soul that sinneth, it shall die" (Ezek. 18:5)

Instead of erasing and replacing the old collective inherited punishment code by an individual mode of responsibility, Cohen indicated that the early[1] punitive system referred to collective injustice—such as cheating, depriving, and oppressing the weak and the poor—in which the individual member of the collective cannot be identified and blamed separately. This collective injustice, which characterized collective life in ancient Israel, is, however, never obsolete and so Ezekiel (who was the first prophet in exile) could introduce in his time the higher level principle of individual morality that demands that each person take full responsibility for his own sins and repentance (see Schweid, 1983) and that became more relevant during postexilic individualized life.

Thus, through a temporal dialogue between seemingly contradictory positions, spiritual-moral progress is accomplished, not by abolishing or synthesizing the old-past principle of collective responsibility to let the new higher moral-autonomy principle take its place, but by adding to it a new dimension through the hermeneutic paradox-based "rearranging" method of *tikun* (see Rotenberg, 1983), which establishes that under condition A (e.g., collective injustice) one should activate principle a, while under condition B (individual sin), principle b might be applicable.

The temporal dialogue is, accordingly, not a process by which the past is internalized and hence negated, as Sartre (1960) posited, but it is a standing vis-à-vis an "it" in an "I-thou" coexistent fashion of dialogue. While the pantheistic unification[2] or the swallowing-internalization of the past would convert it into a Sartreian unchangeable totality, the temporal dialogue with it allows its reintegrative change.

This dialogic system of progress in time, in which the "thou" (e..g., past, old principle or the other) is not internalized, eliminated, or synthesized by the new "I" (e.g., new principle) to allow the enhancement of "reciprocal-individualism" (see Rotenberg, 1978), might indeed be recognizable now in the Talmudic learning tradition.

From this spiritual progress perspective, we may consider once more the much quoted rabbinical statement asserting that "Any controversy that is for the sake of Heaven shall eventually be of lasting worth (endure) . . . which controversy was for heaven's sake? Such was the controversy of Hillel and Shammai" (*Fathers*, 5:17).

This citation, which concurs with other famous Talmudic declarations (about the possible coexistence of opposing opinions), such as the one stating that "these and those are God's living words" (*Gitin*, 6:2), raises the immediate question of how it could be possible that a legal controversy would not be settled one way or the other, that is, either according to Hillel or according to Shammai.

A careful examination of such proclamations would reveal, however, as indicated in Chapter 1, a strong dialogic element concerning time and space that is systematically implanted in these assertions. While it may accordingly be imperative at one point in time to settle a legal dispute according to the more lenient view of Hillel, Shammai's stricter position is not discarded but preserved for possible application at some future time when either circumstances will demand strictness or when people will reach the higher and more progressive level of moral development.

Indeed, one may notice that while Jewish legal development has been largely guided by the Newtonian idea that "dwarfs can see further because they stand on the shoulders of giants," the countertendency to settle controversies according to the biblical principle of "thou shalt come unto . . . the Judge that shall be in those days" (Deut., 17:9) has maintained equal popularity.

That is, on the one hand, one may recognize not only the tendency to preserve but to overdepend on the early Talmudic "giants" legalistic power, but on the other hand, one may identify an increasing trend to rely on those later "Judges that shall be in those days," namely in the present, so that legalistic progress shall not be obstructed. Thus, the power of the early "giant" Talmudists is not abolished but the fact that the later "dwarfs" can see "further" connotes the possibility of dialogic progress because it lends the latter increasing legalistic power (see Tashma, 1979), not by stamping on the giants' corpses but by standing on their shoulders. While legal matters must be settled, even temporarily, according to one view or the other, the dialogical pattern of what I termed "spiritual progress" might now be best recognized in the Talmudic learning method known as "*pilpul*," in which the mind may grow although nothing must be settled or abolished.

The term *pilpul*, which is derived from the Hebrew word *pilpel*, meaning literally "pepper and spice," refers to the predominant Talmudic method of learning, according to which two distinct complementary types of students were evident. The *palpelan* who was more known as *oker harim* (the uprooter of mountains) refers to the spicy-peppery sharp debator who has the ability to analyze and criticize biblical and Talmudic commentaries through hair-splitting arguments from which no necessary deductions for practical purposes must be drawn. His counterpartner the *Sadran* (arranger or systematizer) is usually known as *Sinai* because this type of scholar presumably knows the law as it was presented at Mount Sinai.

According to Dov Rappel (1979:1), the original epistemological meaning of the verb *pilpul* refers to turning a point from one side to the other side, and it may be identified by three traits:

a. against every argument "A" it is possible to introduce a counter argument "not A".

b. both arguments entail equal logical plausibility and

c. the argument in each case is purely formal. The practical consequences of accepting "A" or "not A" do not contribute to [legal] decision."

While this is not to say that pilpul as a thought and learning system, was viewed favorably by all Talmudists during all times, and while this does not mean also that the pilpul system was exclusively Jewish, one of the major differences between the Jewish pilpul and the Christian style of debate was, according to Rappel, rooted in the following:

> In the Jewish debate the question regarding the legitimation of any one of the opinions was never raised. By contrast in Christianity there was always the suspicion that one of the sides will defeat his fellow so that by proving that his opponent is wrong, the later's position will be declared as heretic. (P. 18)

Thus, these two types, *oker harim* and *Sinai*, which by definition must supplement each other (see Greenstone, 1914) through the ongoing dialogue that they are to maintain between their respective approaches, in fact also epitomize the possibility of "spiritual progress" through what may be termed "dialogic *Chutzpah.*"

It is by the "pilpulistic" method that the young "Mountain uprooters" ("Okrey Harim") are trained and urged to challenge with "chutzpa which is even towards Heaven effective" (Sanhedrin, 105:a) the seemingly established interpretations of their senior "Mountains" ("Sinais") who are "not in Heaven . . . but . . . in thy mouth and in thy heart that thou mayest do it" (Deut., 30:12).

Thus, "spiritual growth" through "dialogic chutzpah" may be viewed as the method of institutionalized socialization by which the young, because "the Torah has 70 faces," that is, infinite interpretation possibilities, learn to challenge the old without having to destroy them by declaring their opinions heretic or by "synthesizing" the Scripture dialectically.

As Greenstone (1914) noted in his account of "pilpul,"

> Every word, every letter has a particular significance, and it is left to us to discover the hidden meaning. Thus, a wide field was opened up for the keen intellect wherein to exercise its powers. Liberty of individual interpretation, permitted by R. Akiba and his school, might have led the study of tradition, in less skilled hands, to most absurd results. Fortunately, common sense and the conservatism prevalent in the academics helped to check the flight of the imagination and to regulate the method of study. (P. 155)

Indeed, according to the "pilpulistic" method, a *sevara* (a logical deductive assumption) must not be synthesized or eliminated if challenged by an *ipcha mistabra* (a counterassumption). This is so because according to the paradox-based rearranging method of *tikun* (see Rotenberg, 1983), there might be infinite ways of resettling and reharmonizing seeming contradictions so that the resultant coexistence of "those and these are God's living words" functions mostly as mind sharpeners. Thus, while *teyku* (*no legal settlement*) and the creative hypothetical *kushya* (question) and not the final totality of synthesis are the predominant and desirable states in life, "pilpul" must be viewed only as a methodological possibility and a means for "spiritual progress." Spiritual progress as an end would obviously depend on what Sartre (1960) termed the dynamic "totalizing" ability to ever extend and widen the pilpulistic dialogue so that the growing knowledge emerging from life will not turn into a synthetic dead "totalite" (practico-inerte) but be included in its ever-widening circle.

As alluded to above, because no side has the ultimate power to label its opponent heretic,[3] the circular "pilpulistic" method of dialogue might lead also to adversive polarizing debates that might weaken and tear apart the social system. Indeed, one might say that the popular saying that two Jews represent at least three political parties reflects a reality of bitter inner struggles that were characteristic of the history of Jewish communal life to the present day both in Israel and the Diaspora.

As we have discussed above at some length the dialogic nature inherent in Midrashic narrative thought system, it would seem unnecessary to dwell further on the pilpulistic method that is encompassed in what we term *Midrashic hermeneutics.* The major goal of our brief presentation of the pilpulistic dialogue was only to introduce it as a spiritual system of growth that might have exerted paradigmatic influences on possibilities of material-communal progress. In this sense, it is assumed that without the hermeneutics inherent in the *Babylonian Talmud,* the *Babylonian Tower* of Jewish materialism will always collapse.

By assuming that the spiritual system of dialogue might have exerted paradigmatic impacts on communal life, I am certainly not oblivious to competing influences that Jews (especially European) might have absorbed, especially from the dialectic thought system permeating Europe since the Enlightenment. Thus, to explicate the dialogic possibility of communal-material progress, a brief genealogical examination of the term *kibbutz* would seem useful now.

KIBBUTZ VERSUS "MIZUG" AND MATERIAL PROGRESS

The term *kibbutz* means literally "collecting" or "ingathering," and while in modern times it has been used in association with both *kibbutz Galuyot,* referring to the Zionistic process by which the scattered exiles return or immigrate to Israel and with the Zionist collective farm known as the *kibbutz,* in previous times it referred to a group of married *yeshiva* (Talmudical college) students who learned together without the help of the *yeshiva* principal (see Even-Shushan's Hebrew dictionary, 1975).

It is remarkable that while in the Bible and in the Talmud we find a clear use of the term *kibbutz* only in reference to the Zionist ingathering of exiles, as, for example, "I will even gather (*vekibatzti*) you from the people . . . and I will give you the Land of Israel" (Ezek., 11:17), in modern sociological literature, a gradual switchover to the more popular term *mizug galuyot* may be noticed.

The term *mizug* refers literally to a process by which several elements melt or dissolve in order to be reblended into an new synthesized, fused entity. While the term *kibbutz* bears strong dialogical connotations, since the process of ingathering refers merely to the coexistence of assembled individuals or collectivities and not to their necessary fusion, the concept of "mizug" is by definition dialectic, as it demands the synthetic reblending of the exiles.

It is beyond the scope of the present work to tackle problems concerning the study of integration and absorption of immigrants in Israel, but from our conceptual point of view, it would be important to suggest that the term *mizug galuyot* appears to be an apparent derivation of the American dialectic "melting pot" conception.

A concomitant of the dialectic process of Christian *missionarism* would seem to be for Protestant America to use the "melting pot" technique to *erase* the immigrant's *race* and negate and dissolve his ethnic-cultural *past* in the great "melting pot" fire so that he may be "born again" as a new synthesized American.

As Israel Zangwill (1909) described it poetically, "America is God's Crucible, the great melting pot. . . . The real American has not yet arrived. . . . I tell you—he will be the fusion of all the races, the coming superman" (p. 37).

To assess how the "American-dream" melting pot formula has succeeded, one has to read such studies as Glazer and Moynihan's (1970) *Beyond the Melting Pot* or to examine the massive failures of the desegregation projects that gained momentum in the sixties (see Cloward and Piven, 1974). True, in America the blacks were the first to raise the "anti-melting pot" flag, and by following the lead of Alex Haley's *Roots*, they were also the pioneers of the "roots" search for ethnic identity. However, other white minorities, and among them the Jews, were quick to follow, as Chaim Waxman (1983) indicated in his study of America's Jews: "Once blacks had publicly rejected the ideology of the melting pot and adopted the ideology of cultural pluralism, white ethnic groups were quick to follow suit" (pp. 132–33).

Thus, ethnic minorities finally realized that while the lower class *melts*, there is always a hidden upper-class missionary who *molds*.[4] Accordingly, *missionarism* may be defined from the present perspective as a process by which an antithetic B's identity is dissolved and recreated by and according to a synthesizer A's identity. Having been indoctrinated by the same Hegelian dialecticism that came out of the European Enlightenment, the early Zionist conceptions of resettling Palestine were similarly based on the ideological notion that progress is possible only by negating and erasing the Diaspora and the past. One has only to skim through Yechezkel Koyfman's (1952:159) critical review of such Zionistic writers as Y. C. Brenner,[5] who in stating that: "we the free Jews have nothing to do with Judaism," represented in Koyfman's view, the famous Zionist idea of progress through *shlilat hagalut* (the negation of the Diaspora).

The natural translation of the original dialogic "kibbutz galuyot" concept into the dialectic notion of "mizug galuyot" imported by the European Enlightened and American-influenced early settlers who comprised the absorbing establishment in the early fifties may now be well understood, especially if one considers how they negated their own past "fiddling on alien roofs" to recreate the earthly farmer type at "home."

While the book that published the lectures given at the sociological conference that assessed, in the late sixties, the integration of immigrants was entitled *Mizug Galuyot*, one may best grasp the extent of disappointment in the application of the dialectic "mizug" conception to the integration of immigrants in S. N. Eisenstadt's (1969) introductory lecture to this conference.

Eisenstadt, who as a leading Israeli sociological authority not only provided the major studies about "the Israeli ways" of absorbing immigrants but who probably also influenced its policy and operation, differentiates, in retrospect, between three absorption phases. The underlying assumption of the first "absorption phase" was, according to Eisenstadt, that in Israel "there is in existence a social centre, perhaps quantitatively small but qualitatively crystalized who is called upon to absorb those incoming immigrants into its midst and imprint upon them its established image" (p. 6). In this "absorption phase," the new immigrants were expected to "melt" their "imported" ethnic identity in order to be "remolded" by the local crystalized and homogeneous establishment. However, this exact duplication of the American dialectic "melting pot" notion, failed to integrate the new immigrants, according to Eisenstadt, because they simply *refused* to be *fused* by relinquishing their old identity.[6]

According to Eisenstadt, it was only as a result of the failure of what we would term the *dialectic-missionary* (absorption) phase that the absorbing establishment moved to the second phase of "mizug galuyot," which was based on the assumption that the new immigrant groups comprise several complete autonomous cultures that negate and clash with the predominant culture in Israel.

While during this dialectic "mizug" phase, there was a growing recognition of the cultural conflict between these opposing ethno-cultural groups, the assumption was still that in the dialectic "melting-molding" sequence, more awareness about differential cultural origins should be sufficient to enhance the integration process by which the immigrants, not the "old timers," would be reshaped. The error in assuming that various immigrant groups constituted complete separate cultures made it, however, useless, contended Eisenstadt, to change the absorption ideology toward a more pluralistic separation between them, because even during the second "mizug" phase, the natural tendency to change by being reblended into the old existing "Israeli" image did not increase. By contrast, maintains Eisenstadt, the "differential treatment" of various ethnic groups seemed to increase tension, which sharpened, polarized, and widened the socioeconomic gaps between the European establishment and the mid-Eastern immigrants. Eisenstadt thus called for a third phase, which could be unequivocally called the "dialogic phase of progress," that should be accomplished through the egalitarian readiness of both the old and the new to change simultaneously and to grow together.[7] Accordingly, it would not be the established "old who mold" so that the new would do what they were *told*, but it would be a progressive transformation of all groups. During this phase of "dialogic progress" via simultaneous ethno-cultural re-creation, polarization would be minimized and, as Eisenstadt says,

> There exists a chance for organic growth . . . in which there is certainly room for pluralistic patterns . . . but which does not reach polarization and which does not cause social and cultural stagnation. This chance will materialize only to the extent that out of the two preceding phases, the absorption and the "mizug" phases, the Israeli society will reach the level of building together of integrating various immigrant groups, new and old timers, and together they will know how to construct new differentiated patterns in the realm of labor, culture and society. (P. 13)

While the foregoing analysis focused more on the dialectic elements that permeated the "mizug" conception of growth, rather than on the dialogic components that are to feature the "kibbutz" notion of progress, I think that the possibility of "material progress" available in Eisenstadt's category of "organic growth" through the common re-creative change of all social units may indeed be identified in the ideology of the organic kibbutz system.

I shall thus conclude our illustrative discussion of what should be carefully phrased as only the *possibility* of "dialogical-material progress" by demonstrating briefly how, in spite of dialectical pressures, the kibbutz idea, essentially maintained a dialogical conception of growth mainly in its *communal* (material) structure.

I say the kibbutz "idea" because as a dialogic·idea it includes, as we shall see later, also the semicollective rural settlement termed *moshav*, where, in my opinion, the dialogic possibility of "reciprocal-individualism" (see Rotenberg, 1978) is epitomized in time and space because their members retain their individual and collective property and identity simultaneously.[8]

In his now classical anthropological study of the kibbutz, Spiro (1971) argued that the collective structure featuring the communal life-style in the kibbutz, (which we use now as a general case for the dialogic possibility of material progress), can be traced to the Jewish East European small town known as the *shtetl*.

> The following description of the *shtetl* applies, without qualification, to Kiryat Yedidim [the fictitious name of the kibbutz he studied]. . . . Locked doors, isolation, avoidance of community control, arouse suspicion. . . . "Home people," *Heymisheh mentschen*, . . . are free to come in whenever they like at any time of the day. . . . Withdrawal is felt as attack, whether physical or psychological, and isolation is intolerable. "Life is with people." . . . Everywhere people cluster to talk, at home, in the market place, on the street. Everyone wants to pick up the latest news, the newest gossip. . . . The freedom to observe and to pass judgement on one's fellows, the need to communicate and share events and emotions is inseparable from a strong feeling that individuals are responsible to and for each other. (P. 32)

Thus, the Jewish shtetl, which according to a well-known sociologist can be viewed as the cradle of the "Israeli Statel" mainly on the basis of its reciprocal "alter-centered" (other centered) welfare organization (see Rotenberg, 1983), could constitute, according to Spiro's comparative description, a dialogical archetype of the kibbutz that demonstrates the possibility of material progress because it exemplifies how the communal kibbutz system evolved from the shtetl not by negating it but rather by developing its collective orientation.

If in the shtetl a social mechanism organizing and activating mutual-aid institutions must operate constantly so that the Jewish egalitarian mutual-responsibility norm of *tzedaka* (see Zborowski and Herzog, 1952) will function smoothly to maintain the total community, in the collectivized kibbutz, egalitarian provision for each individual's needs is structurally built into its very system.

Nonetheless, here we must introduce counteropinions that describe the kibbutz as a dialectic reaction *against* the shtetl. Diamond (1957), in his study of the kibbutz founding fathers' perception of their past, presented, for example, the kibbutz system as a "dialectic negation" and reaction against the shtetl culture in which these early kibbutz settlers were reared.

Thus, if, according to Diamond, the shtetl-ghetto as a prototype for Jewish communal behavior was conceived as a pyramid of castes locked within the larger, encircling, Gentile class-structured society, major institutional patterns characterizing the communal life-style in the kibbutz are explained as revolutionary reactions against the pyramidic shtetl.

Thus, while *chalutziut* (pioneering spirit), *shivayon* (egalitarianism), asceticism, and self-employment in manual labor were in part functional mechanisms for efficient, economic, and speedy colonization of Palestine, they nonetheless constituted, according to Diamond, reactions against the hierarchical structure of the shtetl, in which the Talmudic scholars and the rich merchants were ranked highest while the poor and ignorant manual workers were ranked lowest. But here we must insist that, according to our perspective, it is in fact Diamond's very description that leads to an opposite conclusion.

Although Diamond is essentially correct in portraying the kibbutz ideology as a dialectic negation of the humiliating, nonproductive or even parasitic Diaspora life (*shlilat hagalut*), his repeated emphasis of the overreactive ambivalent nature of the early kibbutz settlers reaction to the shtetl converts, in fact, at least the *communal* (material) aspects of the kibbutz system into a perfect case study of dialogical progress and continuity.

That is so not only because this ambivalence reflects typical intergenerational "Akeda" tensions between past and present that are necessary for dialogic progress, but because the shtetl culture was in fact predicated on the *same* communal ideology of Jewish alter-centered egalitarian mutual aid and mutual responsibility that the shtetl endeavored to nurture and that the kibbutz succeeded in developing and implementing.

After all, it was this egalitarian ideology of granting multiple and equally prestigious actualization outlets so that the Hasidic ecstatic prayer, and the poor Talmudic scholar would be on the same salvation level as the rich merchant who is to support them (see Rotenberg's "Issachar and Zebulun" model, 1983) that was said to have maintained and explained the survival-equilibrium of the Jewish community. If the shtetl failed to live up to this egalitarian communal ideology due to persecutions, prohibitions to work in various professions, or other reasons, or if it survived as long as it did *because* of its communal ideology and in spite of the above obstructions, it is still a fact that the kibbutz communal structure perfected, rather than destroyed, this very same ideology with an opposing individualistic antithetic doctrine of egoistic salvation.

Now, since *all* people who joined the early kibbutz communal experiment had to change and grow together, due to the simple fact that none of them had lived in such a setting before, the kibbutz, or rather the *moshav*, conforms in essence to Eisenstadt's "organic growth" model of integration (especially if newcomers and old-timers found together a new *moshav* or kibbutz) that did not require an obliteration of the past but rather a common progressive transformation through an ongoing dialogue with it. I added the semicollective category *moshav* (alluded to earlier), which is akin to the Jewish shtetl, because it was probably the *moshav* in which the dialogic "kibbutz" idea culminated and that became the main vehicle through which new immigrants were absorbed and that greatly facilitated the organic growth and the transformation of the whole format of the Israeli society.

In Eisenstadt's recent book (1985), which analyzes the transformation of the Israeli society and reevaluates the absorption process of immigrants into Israel, the relative failure of the dialectic model of progress with its indoctrinated rebellion against the past and its gradual substitution with what we term the *dialogic* mode of progress, is clearly evident.

Eisenstadt thus showed how growth in Israel, which may only be understood in terms of the total transformation that the Israeli society experienced, is largely characterized by a shift toward a more positive coexistence with the past. Accordingly, Eisenstadt argued that it was not only Westerners renewed dialogue with their past, via the "root searching" revival of the Holocaust experience,[9] that legitimized the concomitant past-anchored ethnic identity formation among "Oriental" Jews, but that, in fact, today the new political power distribution in Israel draws heavily on the dialogic coexistence of various *edot* (ethnic groups) that derive their strength in the *Moshavim* and in the small towns, largely by reviving their past traditions and heritage.

This self-renewing dialogue with the past may be illuminated by such evidence as was provided in Diamond's (1957) citations from the kibbutz communal diary of the early 1920s: *Sefer Hachayim* (the Book of Life): "We must remember what bound us in the Diaspora, common values. . . . We have to build a new society, this will bind us together once again" (p. 95).

While this is not to suggest that the contemporary kibbutz or *moshav* conforms to the dialogic pattern of progress outlined above, the foregoing discourse does intend to stress that the kibbutz ideology seems to encompass sufficient strength to periodically overcome dialectic-parricidal pressures, so that the dialogue with the past may persist in spite of the "sharp Oedipal sword hanging or pressing upon its neck."

The empirical elucidation of progress possibilities through dialogic coexistence on the spiritual (the Talmudic learning style) and material (the kibbutz or *moshav* style) level raises the question of the very possibility and significance of socialization for an internal dialogue on another level. That is to say, an examination of the meaning of an educational system for an internal coexistence between rational and mystic approaches to life seems to be in order. Thus, after reviewing the psychophysiological literature of interhemispheric brain functions and its implications for cult socialization, the next chapter will introduce Jewish hermeneutics as a balancing socializing system between emotional-mystical and rational-Talmudic types for interpreting life and changing behavior.

NOTES

1. While it may be understood that in his interpretation of the bible as a dialogic system of progress, Cohen's mythic phase is ranked lower than the epic state into which it develops, it essentially represents a qualitatively different phase from Buber's (1965:15) poetic *saga* stage, which is the archetypical experience "preserving the memory of what happens," and in this sense it is an earlier not a lower phase. Such dialogic preservations of the (past) mythical modes of thinking, which were described by Levi-Strauss (1966) and used by such Jewish thinkers as Cohen, Buber, Rosenzweig, and Fackenheim to stress that since such revelation experiences as Sinai persist phenomenologically into the "here and now" present, they also testify to their actual occurrence in the past, are rejected, however, by such Christian thinkers as Bultman for whom progress means the dialectic demythologizing abolishment of the past.

2. According to Horowitz (1977) it was only under the decisive influence of Franz Rosenzweig that Buber changed his early Eastern-influenced pantheistic concept of unification into a dialogue terminology in which the "I" stands vis-à-vis a "thou" but in which neither disintegrates into the other.

3. In a paper delivered at a conference on science, religion and the possibilities of world peace, I mentioned (see Rotenberg, 1986) that in contrast to fundamentalistic-

missionary styles of imperialistic impositions of world views, Judaism maintained a spiritual dialogue with "gentile" philosophies. Thus, the first-century philosopher Philo did not shun Hellenic culture, and medieval philosophers such as Maimonides did not hesitate to incorporate into their thinking Aristotelian ideas and Arabian philosophy with which they were able to maintain ongoing dialogues without feeling the need to either "proselytize" non-Jews or abandon their Jewishness. Indeed, the popular slogan "I love Socrates, I love Plato, but more than anything else I love the truth" (see Sever, 1961) was very popular among these Talmudic scholars. Nevertheless, it was the Greek Hellenists, the Crusades, and the Muslims who declared war against the Jewish "refuseniks" who would not convert and accept the predominant religion.

4. It is noteworthy that in the "polytheistic" East, which is marked by an interfaith coexistence and by a pluralistic religious tolerance, the founder of the Christian sect Makuya attacks Western "missionary imperialism" as follows:

> This nature of "religious imperialism," as it were, can be found without exception in Catholicism, Anglican and other Protestant sects. As a result, some American Christians, for example, are busy sending missionaries to Jews and pursuing their impossible efforts to make Christians out of Jews. . . . I never dream of assimilating the already established Judaism into Christianity. (See Teshima, 1981:44,49)

5. It should be stressed that this dialectic negation of the Diaspora was not shared by all "Enlightened" scholars. Achad Ha'am (1946) for one, launched, in my opinion, vehement attacks against Hegelian dialecticism, especially in such articles as "Past and Future." Moreover, in practice, the communal aspect of the kibbutz carried strong dialogic features (as will be argued below) in spite of the dialectic ideology that was imported into it by its early settlers.

6. A novel describing how European kibbutz people failed to impose their dialectic-imperialistic "mizug" conception of absorption on young Eastern new immigrants, is Eli Amir's *Tarnegol Kaparot* (1984).

7. The seemingly self-contradictory conclusions of Smooha (1975) and Peres (1978) who on the one hand argue that Israelis express an increasing desire for complete ethnic integration (mizug) but on the other hand point out the discontent and ethnic consciousness resulting from the growing socioeconomic gap between various groups, may be reconciled only by suggesting that the expressed desire for integration was again misconstrued by Smooha and Peres as a one-sided Westernization process and not as a simultaneous change of all ethnic groups.

8. It is probably this reciprocal-individualistic element that explains why the dialogic continuity between East European Hasidic egalitarianism with its multiple actualization ideal (the "uplifting of sparks") and the collective settlements in Israel can be identified in the religious *Moshavim* and not so much in the kibbutzim (see Fishman, 1972).

9. While for Emil Fackenheim (1978) the very fact that a return to Jerusalem was possible after Auschwitz serves as a living testimony to the Jewish futurist self-renewal power, it is highly questionable whether the popular Holocaust-influenced "root searching" and the lack of a futurist vision that characterizes contemporary Israeli literature reflects a renewal of the past or rather a spiritual-ideological decadence of the present generation, which is preoccupied with material living conditions.

7 The Hermeneutic Dialogue and Interhemispheric Balance

The tremendous vogue of reformulating psychotherapy and psychological observations of people's lives in narrative or hermeneutic terms raises the immediate question of how many degrees of freedom one may use in choosing one or several alternative reinterpretations of one's own or someone else's life story.

In Chapter 2 I demonstrated how Freudian hermeneutics operates as a "missionary" method, which because of its dogmaticism I termed also the *Karaite* system of fundamentalism, that constitutes a therapy by which one missionarizing-analyst imposes the "replacement" of an "irrational" subconsciousness and/or dream language with one fundamentalistic ("sex-aggression") interpretation that then establishes a rational-causal connection between past Oedipal guilt and present neurosis. In the foregoing chapters, I maintained that as a dialectic therapy grounded in a historicist conception of developmental necessity, its missionarizing class of analysts must, as in the Marxian system, replace the old, nonfitting interpretation of reality with a new, fitting one.

I have argued further that Freudian therapy, as a rational deterministic system, may permit only one fundamentalistic cause-and-effect interpretation, because allowing the analysand to choose freely any interpretation of his life story would be not only causally irrational but would also undermine the analyst's interpretive authority.

This chapter will focus on demonstrating how the dialogic element in Midrashic hermeneutics, which allows the coexistence of various interpretations, is not synonymous with complete freedom of interpretation but contains the components and mechanism necessary to balance matter and spirit or the mystic and the rational approaches to life within a given general, temporal, and spacial structure such as the Jewish culture.

125

Before introducing those elements of the Midrashic framework in which this approach to the hermeneutic balance may be found, it might be justified to ask why and in what way is the balancing of matter and spirit, or rather of rational and mystical interpretations of reality, expected to be advantageous in the first place? I propose here that in order to understand the need for a rational-mystical "hermeneutic balance" one should digress briefly to focus on the pertinent knowledge coming out of research on interhemispheric brain activity. I shall thus quickly discuss the possibility of a hermeneutic dialogue via interhemispheric balancing and then return to show how the Midrashic system offers a narrative or hermeneutic model that allows people to choose between Cabalic-mystic and rational philosophic interpretations of text and reality.

THE PROBLEM OF INTERHEMISPHERIC BALANCING

The literature summarizing neuro-clinical observations of brain functioning has repeatedly claimed that the parietal lobe on the right side of the brain is intimately associated with the perception of *spatial* relations that are wholistic gestaltist in nature. By contrast, evidence indicates that the left hemisphere (especially the angular gyrus), which in the West is presumably the more dominant side of the brain, is strongly related to such activities as mathematical operations requiring logical analysis or sequential ordering in *time*. The most important conclusions relating to the lateralization of the cerebral hemispheres seem however to be those deduced on the basis of recent experiments with animals and humans who had had their corpus callosum and anterior commissure sectioned to prevent the interhemispheric spread of epilepsy. While the left cerebral hemisphere was indeed found to produce speech and rational and analytic thought that processes *temporal* units and controls the ability to set opposites one against the other, the wholistic right hemisphere, it was claimed, organized the *spatial*, tonal, and other sensual and affective percepts, including those that constitute the *emotions*.

According to Gardner (1975), for example, for a number of years (during childhood) learning of diverse sorts may occur in both hemispheres, but after adolescence, each hemisphere becomes incapable of executing the activities of the other side, either because it no longer has access to its early learning or, more importantly, because early traces have begun to atrophy through *disuse*. Before going any further, it would seem important then, according to these findings, to eschew the identification of the left hemisphere as the dominant side as a Western bias, because it may be that while in the West high emphasis is put on rational analytic training, among artists and in non-Western cultures the right hemisphere may be more dominant as a result of increased affective and wholistic orientations. Here one should also ask how and why do various cultures maintain hemispheric balanced or imbalanced socialization systems; and, further, how and whether one can reactivate hemispheric functions after extended disuse?

Luria (1966) has shown, for example, that lesions or destruction of brain parts in the area that Geshwind (1965) termed the *inferior parietal lobule* inhibit the ability to compare diadic opposites and to generate antonyms, and d'Anquili (1983) has suggested, on the basis of the above-mentioned evidence, that the inferior parietal lobule on the left side "may not only underlie conceptualization but may be responsible for human proclivity for abstract antonymous or binary thinking which underlies the basic structure of myth" (p. 250). The human need to construct and reconstruct myths, maintain anthropologists, is a response to what Max Weber called the "imperfect world" or the "capricious universe" in which we reside and in which the antonymies or polar opposites with their coding systems determining what is good and what is evil constantly change. It is thus the process of myth making that serves as a hermeneutic instrument to bridge cognitively incoherent and causally unexplainable sequences in everyday reality.

It has been suggested further, although with no clear implicatory evidence, that the dual hemispheric brain functioning may be linked with Hess's model of the *ergotropic* and the *trophotropic* systems. Very briefly, the function of the ergotropic (derived from *ergon*, work) system is said to be related to *energy-expending* mechanisms, so that it encompasses not only the sympathetic nervous system that controls states of physical and emotional arousal, increased activity, and what is commonly called "getting high," but also such processes as increased heart rate, blood pressure, and other stimuli. The trophotropic system (meaning nourishment) is generally said to be associated with the *energy-conservation* mechanism of an organism, including the parasympathetic nervous system that regulates the basic vegetative and homeostatic functions. Accordingly, the trophotropic system maintains the baseline stability of an organism by reducing, for instance, heart rate and blood pressure, which is then manifested by general inactivity and drowsiness that results in a state described as "cooling off" by those who claim to have experienced "trance states." Elaborating on Hess's model, d'Aquili and Laughlin (1979), for example, ventured to link the trophotropic energy-maintaining system with the right hemisphere and the ergotropic energy-exerting mechanism with the left hemisphere, which, as we said, produces analytical, rational thinking. Although d'Aquili and Laughlin posit that a "spillover" reciprocity exchange system between the right and left hemisphere operates when either one of the hemispheres is overstimulated, they believe that "meditation" is initially and essentially a right-side trophotropic technique because it involves thought and desire reduction, as in ego-emptying Zen practice, while ritual ("the dance"), which usually requires repetitive rhythmic motor activity such as visual and auditory driving stimuli, is initially activated by ergotropic excitations.

To what extent are these propositions relating the ergotropic-ritual operations to the left hemisphere and the trophotropic-meditation practices with the right hemisphere empirically substantiated is a question with which one should deal separately, but the point that should interest us here is that the claimed "spillover" reciprocity exchange system might entail the components for dealing with polar opposites and for balancing cognitive-affective perspectives.

The criteria for setting and resettling polar and opposite dyads according to changing norms and circumstances derive from various cultural hermeneutic coding systems. It is, after all, the cultural *Zeitgeist* that legitimizes or disqualifies, for instance, in a rational Waspy country such as the United States, the reinterpretations of stressful contradictions in life at one time on the basis of Eastern affective-mystic codes (as manifested mainly during the 1960s) by the "psychedelic counter culture" and at other times permits reconciliation of irresolveable contradictions only via the use of such rational hermeneutics as psychoanalytical methods. In spelling out the cognitive and neurobiological transformation modes that man uses periodically to readapt himself to his ever changing environment, d'Aquili (1983) rejected what we would term the dialectic definition of transformation, such as the psychoanalytic method that calls for a *replacement* of cognitive and affective elements with a totally different set of elements. d'Aquili thus prefers what we would term a dialogical formulation of transformation that is similar to a Levi-Straussian structuralist transformation by which elements are not substituted but reorganized or *rearranged*.

The "spillover" model of d'Aquili and Laughlin would thus essentially mean that unexplainable dyads would not be resolved by drastically *shifting* from the rational left hemisphere, which is unable to provide answers to irreconcilable transcendental questions of life and death, to the *affective* emotional and timeless right hemispheric operation. Rather, it would basically call for a simultaneous stimulation and activation of both hemispheres to maintain the necessary homeostatic equilibrium.

In the present brain-balancing terms, this dialogic approach would basically call for a simultaneous stimulation and activation of both hemispheres to maintain the necessary homeostatic equilibrium, which could always be rearranged or reorganized.

But here again, the practical question remains: whether it is indeed the hermeneutic balancing system that bridges the unexplainable polar opposites such as good and bad through the simultaneous rational-left and emotional-right hemispheric activation alluded to above?

DRASTIC INTERHEMISPHERIC SHIFTING AND DEVIANCE

One can best understand the functionality or dysfunctionality of rational-emotional hermeneutic balancing by studying the possibilities for understanding and altering deviant conduct. More specifically, the problem may be illuminated by observing drastic switching from a rational reading code of reality to a mystic code, for example, from the analytic-rational left hemisphere to the emotional-gestaltist right side, as it is often manifested in conversion processes mainly among cult recruitees.

True, very little is known about how various hermeneutic systems providing reading codes for interpreting reality affect or reflect hemispheric brain functioning. However, if the findings mentioned earlier about functional divisions between left and right hemispheres are generally correct, one has reason to speculate that if in one culture the hermeneutic code used for training people to interpret their reality is based on *faith* in irrational magic or transcendental explanations of cosmic activities, then the process of comprehending reality must operate mainly through the right hemisphere, since *faith* is not an analytical but a wholistic emotional activity. On the other hand, if only a rational-analytic hermeneutic code is used to read and interpret reality, then this cognitive understanding of the universe should be processed primarily through the left hemisphere. Now, research on psychopathology has repeatedly demonstrated that schizophrenic thinking in the West in fact constitutes and provides a mystic hermeneutic code for reconciling those unexplainable polar opposites that the Protestant rational West usually leaves unanswered (see Sarbin, 1969). Moreover, Flor-Henry (1974) has found, for example, that the left-hemisphere dysfunctions were observed among those labeled "schizophrenic." Thus, while one may conceive the emergence of the "psychedelic" counterculture in the United States and Europe during the 1960s as a *shift* or escape from the overactivation of the rational competitive left hemisphere to the meditative blissful homeostatic and gestaltic hippie culture in which right-hemisphere brain activity predominated, one should also expect to find "psychotic" breakdowns resulting from a too drastic interhemispheric switchover in brain activity among those who experienced such sweeping shifts. Parenthetically, it might be said here that revolutionary and oppressed minority movements usually lean toward the "left" because without "rights" they feel "left out."

Although not reported by professional social scientists, citations of one or two cases used by Conway and Siegelman (1978) to document the phenomenon they termed "snapping" will elucidate the dangers inherent in instant switching in brain functioning. In one case describing the conversion of an American by an Eastern swami, the guilt and fear of disorientation resulting from a drastic switching to a sensual-pleasure-based operation of the brain (probably because it is a taboo zone in the West) is explicitly stated:

> I felt as if a huge pool had opened in my heart—full of soft air, and I was floating on it. It was the most intensely sensual feeling I had ever had. . . . My first reaction was a sharp pang of guilt, a feeling that I had stumbled into some forbidden region . . . in my brain, which would keep me hooked

on bodyless sensuality . . . until I turned into a vegetable. . . . Then I
forgot about thinking and just let myself drift. (P. 61)

The drastic shift from what would seem a left-side kind of rational thinking to a sensual, emotional-based right-side operation may be even more
clearly evident in the following account of a "deprogrammed" ex-Hare
Krishna convert:

The vegetables are amazing. . . . The guy who brought me into the cult was
a college graduate in philosophy, and he used to teach classes every day. He
went nuts, started saying weird things and began screaming at women all
the time. . . .
   There are people cracking all the time. . . . Some people would have attacks and become very violent. . . . After a while you just accept it. You accept insanity as a matter of course. (Pp. 181, 182)

It is not necessarily that the drastic sweeping changes converts experience
in contemporary religious cults or in communist reform or brainwashing
systems operate, as Conway and Siegelman (1978) indicate, "like an electric
shock, [because] the information an individual receives from some massive
physical, emotional and intellectual experience may be powerful enough to
destroy¹ deep and long-standing information processing pathways in the
brain" (p. 132).

It is also not crucial to verify from our perspective whether these drastic
changes are indeed reflected in left-right hemispheric brain activities.

Rather, it seems that the instantaneous switching from either the rational
or the emotional hermeneutic code to the exclusive use of the other code
would comprise the underlying cause for converts' mental breakdown
because it is possible that a drastic change in one's accustomed orientation
to life may be confusing.

Here it might be suggested that in the Christian West, which is permeated
by the notion of the unshakable "original sin" guilt, the only possible salvation from the rationally unexplainable "capricious universe" is through the
drastic *death-rebirth* "or born again" process that might, in fact, require
practically the instant change (see James, 1971) from a disappointing rational
(left-hemispheric?) predominance to the redeeming mystic (right-hemispheric?)
activation.

Indeed, our observations among the recently popular repenters (*baaley
teshuva*) movements in Israel strongly suggest that only among those (mainly Western-American) who switched drastically from one hermeneutic code
to another, may cases of emotional breakdown be noticed, while those who
chose the *teshuvah* style (rational or emotional) that fitted their natural inclination and who used both codes seem to manifest remarkable stability.

It has, in fact, been further observed that in special week-long seminars
geared to familiarize potential repenters with the Jewish religious way of life

and in these special Talmudical colleges (*yeshivot*) for repenters, clear trends of choosing either the rational or the mystic hermeneutic approach may be noticed. Very generally, it appeared that *baaley teshuva* with an Eastern (*Sephardic*) background seem to prefer the mystic interpretation of reality, whereas Westerners tend usually to seek the rational approach to religion.

Options for choosing one of these orientations by joining a Hasidic yeshiva with its predominantly mystic code or a "Lithuanian" yeshiva in which the rational code predominates seem, however, not to follow the Eastern-Western division.

Thus, in a study differentiating between "emotional" and "rational" styles of *teshuvah* (repentance) among women, Michal Fachler (1986) observed that by and large, the built-in hermeneutic choice option available in Judaism enabled these women to follow their natural inclination and select either a mystic-emotional or a Talmudic-rational-style program that seemed to coincide with their predispositions and past preferences in the secular world.

In this study, Fachler conducted depth interviews with fifteen women who joined a Hasidic program of *teshuvah* in which emphasis is more on the emotional-mystic and experiential approach to Judaism and fifteen women who joined a program in which emphasis is more on understanding Judaism through the Lithuanian, rational, Talmudic style of learning. While settings differed in orientation, interview schedules that were geared to elicit the phenomenological subjective meaning of the teshuvah process were identical for both groups. Below are excerpts from a typical interview with a woman who may be termed the "emotional type" and who joined a *teshuvah* program with a mystic-Hasidic orientation and one from a typical interview with a woman who may be referred to as a "rational type" and who selected a program with a scholastic orientation.

The "Rational" Repenting Woman

The subject stated that as a secular girl, she was always an inquisitive, argumentative type who had possessed natural intellectual curiosity and adequate general knowledge. As a high school graduate, she was contemplating studying nuclear physics or biology, in which she majored in high school. She was even interested in astronomy and archeology but less in the humanities. Her interest and approach to *teshuvah* began through listening to lectures on Jewish philosophy at the age of seventeen. According to her own assertion, it was precisely because she hated prejudices that she wanted to "see for herself" whether those religious teachers (who were condemned in her circle as biased missionaries) could provide logical proofs concerning the existence of God, and so on.

You can tell if a person is capable of proving a point. Some teachers were more dramatic, they don't convince me. One teacher was very scholastic and rational. He had great influence on me. He spoke about science, evolution and the philosophy underlying science. After I finished serving in the army, I went to this seminar. In this "seminar" I felt the intellectual breakthrough. For example, if according to the moral [Kantian?] imperative, a person always behaves as he feels, there is no absolute truth why not to steal or murder. There must be an absolute truth! Instinctual behavior doesn't necessarily produce the correct result. You have to understand the Torah through your mind. If Moses, (i.e., a human being and not God himself) had indeed "pulled an act" at Mount Sinai, and "mesmerized" the Israelites, with artificial audio visual devices, then some unavoidable mistake must have been discovered in the course of the years. For instance, in regard to biological stipulations concerning "kosher" and non "kosher" animals . . . I joined this program and became a *baalat teshuvah* only through intellectual persuasion. I couldn't have done it in any other way. There are "floating" ["freaked out"] *baaley teshuvah* [repenters]. This is not my style. I loved the secular life and the process of returning was very gradual; first internal and only then I gradually committed myself to observe the commandments. A sudden change is very dangerous. If a boy, God forbid, ceased all of a sudden to look at girls, this would be very dangerous for him. The program here is a very balanced program. Here one needs capabilities for learning. The Rabbi wants high school graduates, girls that are capable of studying at a university level. There was a girl who was incapable of studying and the Rabbi asked her to leave, but not without arranging for her a more suitable program.

The "Emotional" Repenting Woman

In Fachler's (1986) study, the subject left school at the age of fourteen, worked in a bank, then in boutique stores that she liked more. She always liked music, arts and crafts, and beautiful clothing. At the age of seventeen she left home to look for experiences, joy trips, and so on. She lived in India in various temples for six months, but it was emotionally exhausting.

I was not prepared for life in India. I first thought it is like Europe. Once friends made a birthday party for me in a very fancy hotel and outside the hotel people washed their laundry in the sewer. I cried terribly. There I became self-conscious. I was a very popular girl in the secular world, but I felt bored and empty. I did not absorb and did not radiate. Once I went to see a Guru and upon hearing that I am a Jewess from Israel, he asked me why I am coming to him for a mantra, if we have the "Shema Israel"? He shocked me because I came all the way to have mystical experiences and to become happier, but I wasn't. So at once I felt a craving longingness for Jerusalem although I never lived in Jerusalem and within a week I was in Jerusalem. I first stayed with a family to experience Shabbat. This filled my soul. Before that I never felt fulfilled. I first joined another *teshuva* program and loved the learning but they did not know how to apply what they study for every day life. When I joined this program [the Hasidic] I learned how to apply what I learn. Here emphasis is on praying, on ecstasy. When I am low, I can scream to God, and I know that he is with me. It has been now 10 years since I returned. My husband [who is also a *baal teshuvah*] was also in many *yeshivot*, but he did not find joy and happiness until he came here. If he felt emotional stress while being in other programs, they would tell him to *study*; here they tell him to *pray*. Here they teach you how to get up to sing and dance or meditate in the mountains in the middle of the night when you are low, and you know that you'll get high again. My girls learn music and I teach them how to dance and sing and love each other. In my home, I was trained to look at people's bad traits, here I learn to seek the positive in people. I never needed a rational persuasion to become a *baalat Teshuva*. I am very spontaneous. I sometimes act up and dance alone, my return was instantaneous and straight from the heart. I attend classes with the Rabbi's wife, it fills me with energy. It fills me with joy. What is important in observing the commandments, is *faith* alone without any sophisticated philosophizing. Simplicity, lots of joy and comrade love that's the secret of life.

While these cases might not be representative, they demonstrate, nonetheless, the basic difference between the typical *Karaite* (fundamentalistic) style of interpreting reality that characterizes most cultish resocialization programs and the institutionalized multiple choice system of interpreting life available in the Jewish Midrashic hermeneutics.

Accordingly, it is not so much the suddenness or the preference for one style for changing behavior that might prevent mental disorientation, but the compatibility between personal inclinations and the changing pace. Thus, antibiotics, football, and salami might be good things for people, but not for every person at all times and in the same quantities. Since both women described briefly above seem to be emotionally stable, married, and content for many years (five to ten), although they differed in style and pace of change, there is reason to believe that it is the Midrashic hermeneutic choice element that may safeguard possibilities for switching life-styles because it has been observed time and again that drastic interorientational switching in the "missionarizing-Karaite" cult system results more frequently in mental breakdown.

While propositions concerning the effectiveness of who chooses which hermeneutic code under what conditions require more systematic research, especially for those interested in correlating such choices with brain function, at this point one generalization seems plausible: Since drastic switching from one orientation to the other appears to be largely harmful, an interhemispheric or an interorientational mechanism for hermeneutic balancing should be very useful.

The Midrashic model for hermeneutic balancing that I am about to discuss may be better understood after a short introduction of the Hasidic-Cabalic contraction theory that I have developed in my book *Dialogue with Deviance* (1983). In introducing a synopsis of the contraction paradigm, I hope to show not only how this theory may be instrumental in understanding interorientation or interhemispheric balance but that it was, in fact, the mystic-Hasidic and not so much the philosophic-rational tradition in Judaism that encompassed the a priori mechanism for balancing material and spiritual interpretations of reality.

HASIDIC-CABBALIC CONTRACTION AND INTERHEMISPHERIC DIALOGUE

In his eloquent review of the literature exploring the functional interdependence between body, brain, and culture, Professor Victor Turner (1983) expressed the challenging quest for new descriptive work that will throw light on the question explaining, how the the current picture "of brain functioning and of the central nervous system accord with distinctive features of the varied religious systems that have *survived* to this point in time and exerted paradigmatic influence on major societies and cultures" (p. 237).

Thus, the presentation of the psychophysiological implications (pertaining to the claimed hemispheric origin of the mystical rational orientations) emanating from the Judeo-Hasidic contraction model would constitute more than just an intellectual exercise because it draws on the belief that Judaism represents a major case study of a religion that not only has "survived" but that has possibly also exerted some paradigmatic, that is, phenomenological, influence on other (mainly Western) societies.

We have said that survival via constant readaptation to the ever-changing environment requires not a dialectic hermeneutic system that *replaces* one fundamentalistic reading code with another but a dialogic system facilitating a choice between multiple interpretations of reality. The physiologist Davidson (1976) suggested, for instance, that "whether a right-hemisphere dominated experience would be classified as hallucinatory, psychotic or mystical" depends primarily on "beliefs and attitudes resulting from experience and training" (p. 372). One might assume, accordingly, that while drastic switches from ergotropic (energy expending) ecstatic rituals to trophotropic (energy conserving) meditation often resulted in healing psychosomatic or mental disorders (see ibid.), in most cases, such instant interhemispheric changes will cause, as alluded to, "psychotic" collapse or disorientation, because changing beliefs requires prolonged hermeneutic training in reading one's reality in one way or the other.

If we rephrase this proposition in our current brain-functioning terms, this would essentially mean that *survival* may largely depend on a double hermeneutic code that allows for a balanced simultaneous reading of reality through analytic-rational-left-hemisphere spectacles and through affective-mystic-right-hemisphere lenses. In Chapter 1, I argued that Midrashic socialization exposes and trains people for a "double bind" understanding of reality in mystical and rational terms so that the hermeneutic choice of selecting one's suitable interpretation is left open.

More poignantly, it seems, however, that it is the Hasidic-Cabalic myth of contraction that provides precisely those a priori double reading glasses that facilitate and require a simultaneous mystic and rational interpretation of reality that permits individuals to constantly readapt and replace themselves in space and time.

The Cabalic myth of divine contraction comprises a theodicy and an *imitatio Dei* model by which such polar opposites as good and evil may constantly be reconciled by maintaining both a rational scholastic system and mystic ecstatic procedures through which one may neutralize apparent evils and actualize goodness.

Unlike the Gnostic-dualistic unbridgeable dichotomy between the Kingdoms of Good and Evil, which originated in Persian Zoroastria and unlike the passive Neoplatonic conception of evil as the absence of Godness, the Cabalic theodicy of divine contraction (*tsimtsum*) explains the possibility of "seeming" evil and man's free will to overcome it, as resulting from God's voluntary active contraction. Accordingly, it is God's volitionary dimming of His own brightness that made the creation of the world and its apparent evils possible. Thus, according to the Jewish mystical Cabalistic doctrine of *tsimtsum* (contraction), God's self-shrinkage, condensation, or withdrawal into Himself to evacuate primordial space for the human world is a dynamic ebb-and-flow process of regression and egression, of *tsimtsum* and *hitpashtut* (embracing or expansion), of dimming His own light but staying in the background to bestow light whenever necessary.

Moreover, the process of contraction made it possible for the element of divine sternness (*midat hadin*) to emerge in the world, as Y. Luria is cited as saying, "in the power of sternness that was exposed there with the contraction" (see Tishby, 1975:24). But at the same time, unity and harmony are possible only through the coexistence of contrasts and the interaction between this element of sternness (*midat hadin*) and the element of divine compassion (*midat haracamim*), or between the material-rational and the mystic-irrational, because the world can exist only through the continuous dynamic interaction between matter and spirit, between good and evil, between the "I" and the "thou."

As a matter of interest, according to the Cabalic world of the ten *sefirot*, which, portrayed as a tree of a human body essentially represents the ten basic divine elements through which God manifests Himself in the world and facilitates its operation, left- and right-side elements correspond generally to empirical findings about hemispheric brain functioning.

Thus, *Chochma* (widsom), in the sense of God's meditation of Himself, is pictured on the right side, while *Binah*, referring generally to intelligence, is pictured on the left side. But more clearly compatible with accepted hemispheric division of brain activities is the fact that *Chessed*, referring to love and God's compassion, are conceived as on God's right-hand side while *Din* (severity) or rigorous judgement, that is, analytic rationalism in our terms, is perceived as a divine left-side component (see Scholem, 1974).

In order to understand how these twofold, mystic-ritualistic (which would hypothetically correspond to right and left hemispheric activities) and the rational scholastic interhemispheric implications follow from the notion of contraction, it is useful to notice how the metaphor of light is employed in training people to read reality.

Thus, according to Cabalism, especially later Cabalism, divine contraction is explained as a functional cathartic cosmic process known as "the shattering" ("breaking of the vessels"), which refers to a kind of divine breaking for the sake of differentiation and correction, as Y. Luria stated (see Vital, 1882, Shaar A.A. 1): "and here this contraction . . . is called breaking for the sake of correction." This functional cathartic "breaking of the vessels" (*shevirat hakelim*), which followed the process of contraction and which has many explanations in the literature of mysticism, presumably caused a diffusion or shattering explosion of the divine light, and the sparks of that light flew either back into its divine source or downward into the abyss and depths of the earth. In this way, it is said, the good elements, (i.e., the divine sparks) came to be mixed with the so-called vicious elements i.e., the shells (*kelipot*) (see Scholem, 1941). So man's salvation (*tikun*) requires a constant effort to restore the divine order by raising or uplifting to its divine source the holy sparks that are scattered in the world. According to the major Cabalistic document, the Zohar (which originated, according to the religious tradition, during the pre-Talmudic era and according to the scientists, during the late thirteenth century), man's corrective actions in this world actually lend strength to divine activities: "In the earthly activity the upward activity is awoken, if a man performs properly down [on earth] so strength is awoken properly upwards" (cited in Tishby, 1975: Vol. 2, 434). Moreover, according to Hasidism, which brought Heaven down to earth by reinterpreting Lurian Cabalism in an optimistic operational salvation language accessible to the masses, there is now actually no evil in the world. What appears to be evil is only disguised by "shells." Hence in every earthly matter (*gashmiyut*), such as eating, rejoicing, copulation, and even sinning, there are holy sparks that may or must be redeemed by peeling off the "evil" shells, so to speak, and raising them back to their divine source, and "correcting" part of the primordial breaking. Salvation means now that man must learn to interpret or "reframe" everyday reality so that he will be able to see the good element inherent in every possible event and experience. Moreover, salvation in terms of motivation means not only that man has the free will to choose between commission and omission of the evils of this world but also that he has the obligation and power to "correct" Heaven, which, through the divine process of self-contraction, lends itself to be influenced by man's spark-lifting endeavors inherent in the concept of *tikun* (correction). Here it should be stressed that the Talmudic term *Chutzpah* refers originally to man's dialogical corrective obligation and optimistic ability to argue with and influence Heaven's decrees.

HERMENEUTIC PLURALISM AND
INTERHEMISPHERIC BALANCE

While the theodicy-myth of divine space-evacuating contraction is intricate, what should interest us here is that the idea of God contracting Himself to allow for a bilateral intercorrective dialogue between man's materiality and God's spirituality becomes a multiple actualization model that man is urged to emulate. Thus, mystic "spark-lifting" rituals are not to replace the Talmudic rationalism but are to be employed simultaneously as hermeneutic codes for understanding and experiencing reality.

Indeed, from early childhood, the Jew is trained to repeat three times a day the biblical verse of "*Shema Israel*": "And thou shalt love the Lord thy God with all thy heart and with all thy soul and with all thy might . . . and thou shalt teach them diligently onto thy children and shalt talk of them when you sittest in thine house and when thou walkest by the way" (Deut., 6:5,6).

Thus, the ordinary Jew is exposed since childhood at least to two linguistic structures of "loving with the heart" and of "teaching" through the brain.

The point to be explained is, however, that while according to Jewish hermeneutic pluralism one could and should actualize Judaism through ritual praying of the heart and by teaching scholastic Talmudism, the functionality of this balancing system can be best understood by examining its application within a specific sociohistorical context. Although the Torah as a guide for reading life entails multiple interpretive possibilities, this balancing hermeneutic system has not always heeded. Thus, one should notice that according to Scholem (1941), by and large from the tenth to the fifteenth century, Maimonides's style of rational-philosophical Talmudism predominated Jewish praxis and thinking, although Cabalic mysticism was not unknown. And it was only the famous expulsion of Jews from Spain, which marked the crisis and breakdown of the "philosophical era" at the end of the fifteenth century, that might explain the explosive rise of Cabalic mysticism in sixteenth-century Zafat. But it is also only the seventeenth century Shabbateist false-messianic crisis, during which ritual mysticism predominated, that might explain the eventual lasting success of eighteenth-century Hasidism, which did not replace the Talmudic rationalist but struggled to guarantee a coexisting equal status for the ecstatic-prayer.

Thus, states Rabbi Yaacov Yoseph Hakohen (1963) of Polony the Beshts' (the *Baal Shem Tov*, who was the founder of the eighteenth-century Hasidic movement) contemporary, disciple, and exponent:

> Since similar to the individuality within one person the soul and form is not to feel superior over the body and say that it is a soul . . . and even more so the body is not to be arrogant over the soul as it holds the soul . . . as they need each other like a man and a woman, each being half a body, so it is in the collective, the Talmudic scholars and righteous are not to say that there is no need in the masses . . . and even more so the masses are not to say that there is no need for Talmudic scholars . . . since their livelihood is due to them. . . . And so each one is half and with both together matter and form whether in the collective or within the individual it becomes one full person. (P. 243)

Hasidic usage of Matter and Form, which to a great extent rebalanced Jewish original hermeneutic pluralism, could now be interpreted through the process of contraction as dialogical coexistence between the rational-analytic element of sternness (*midat hadin*) and the intuitive-emotional element of compassion (*midat harachamim)*.

Here the dialogic principle of a tikun-style reorganizing coexistence between the intuitive and the rational hermeneutics of life receives its concrete operational meaning.

To designate the interrelationship between the rational and the irrational, the recently popular Rabbi Nachman of Bratzlav, the Beshts' great-grandson, used, for example, the two concepts "inner mind" and "engulfing" or "encircling mind" (see Weiss, 1974:116). The rational mind refers to the inner mind (which, indeed, due to its rational basis, penetrated one's mind) and the encircling mind refers to the intuitive irrational (which, indeed, one cannot conceive and interpret logically in one's inner mind but is nonetheless there). The difference between the two intertwined forms of thinking is that the rational inner one refers to the "mind which one acquires through many introductions" and the intuitive one refers to the spontaneous mind, the "mind which comes to a person without any introduction."

The relationship between the "inner mind," which resembles the Bergsonian rational matter, and the encircling mind, paralleling Bergson's spiritual intuition, is not in that the intuitive is a nebulous preconscious knowledge but rather a clear creative spontaneous flash of the mind that has not yet been processed and substantiated by the inner rational mind. Here the popular expression of "open-mindedness" colors the vital relationship between the "inner rational mind" and the external "intuitive encircling mind." Thus, the "inner rational mind" is not closed or locked up but remains open and is constantly nourished by one's intuitive, creative "encircling" mind. Hence it is man's active hoping and waiting for the Messiah with creative "wondering" (see Heschel, 1966) but with nonetheless unceasing faith, and it is man's creative swimming in the ocean of intuitive hypothetical questions, not his landing on the safe shore of rational synthesis (see Weiss, 1974:120), that breathes life into the continuous dialogue between constrasting elements that are paradoxically and functionally interrelated. Moreover, according to Rabbi Nachman, rational final answers eliminate the creative free will: "The essence of work and free choice is that one remains in constant doubt" (see Weiss, 1974:146). Thus, in the rational synthetic "redeemed world" of the millenarian Messiah who has already come, there is no choice, because restorative past-oriented salvation refers to the rational known, while in the utopian future-oriented hypothetic world of *Kushya* (question) that has not yet been redeemed, free will is constructed on the paradoxical relationship between the mystic unknown world of the future and the rational known world of the past, which complement each other.

The idea of socializing people with more than one linguistic structure in order to live in a "double bound" world of contrasts that does require a functional "schizophrenic" dichotomy between secular-rational activities and intuitive mystic orientations, but in which hypothesis and not synthesis ascertains their dialogic coexistence, was possible only through contraction, as Weiss (1974) stated:

> The first momentum movement of creation was also the hour of appearance of the question and its beginning predominance in every reality, the vacuum that was created due to the act of contraction whereby the Godly contracted itself to provide space for the creation of the world . . . is the very essence of the . . . contradictory dialectics. (P. 120)

Thus, Jewish, and particularly Hasidic, ideology would train people to perceive the world through Maimonides's rational spectacles and through Nachmanides's Cabalic mysticism because life perceived as a creative hypothesis requires a priori constant dialogical interaction between irrational intuition and rational-empiricism. But how is this balancing system derived from the Midrash as a general hermeneutic guide offering individual choice for differential interpretation of reality? As indicated in the introductory chapter, it is well-known that the dozens of biblical commentary books that Jews have used for ages to concretize and contemporize the weekly portion of the Torah usually offer a choice between various mystic-Cabalic and Talmudic-rational interpretation of Scripture.

In addition, it has been pointed out that this hermeneutic choice, which enables people to adopt individually suitable interpretations of reality, is not synonymous with an existential freedom to attribute "any" meaning to reality. Presumably, however, it is constructed on the popular notion of reading the Torah through its "seventy faces." Thus, we must now examine the operational meaning of the "seventy faces" model for a hermeneutic multiple choice in the interhemispheric balancing terms with which we are concerned here. More specifically, the general model of Midrashic pluralism presented in the introductory chapter may now receive its concrete therapeutic meaning by considering how Hasidic mysticism was balanced with Talmudic-rationalism in theory and practice.

DIALOGIC NARRATIVISM OF "SEVENTY FACES"

While hermeneutics according to its Christian tradition, originally concentrated, as stressed in Chapter 2, on selecting and establishing from a multiplicity of sloppy and contradictory texts, *one* authentic (fundamentalistic?) true interpretation of the Holy Scripture (see Bauman, 1978), Jewish hermeneutics is said to be guided by the multiple interpretation principle predicated on the Midrashic notion that the "Torah has seventy faces" (*Midrash Rabba*, Numbers 13:16).

Thus, in regard to the biblical passage "The words of the wise are as goads, and as nails well planted are the words of masters of Assemblies, which are given from one Shepherd" (Ecc., XII:II), the Talmud (*Hagiga*, 3:a–b) offers for example, the following interpretation: "But [should you think] that just as the nail diminishes and does not increase, so too the words of the Torah diminish and do not increase; therefore the text says 'well planted,' just as a plant grows and increases, so the words of the Torah increase."

Accordingly, it seems that following such beliefs as "the words of the Torah increase and grow like a plant," the "seventy faces" notion of finding infinite ways for interpreting the Holy Scripture according to changing needs appears prima facie to be the norm regulating Jewish mundane life.

Indeed, the example of the seventeenth-century rabbi Natan Neta Shapira's (see Margalioth, 1977, 4) book *Megale Amukot*, which is comprised of 252 interpretations of only one single word in the Torah, would epitomize such infinite interpretation trends. Would this suggest then that the Jewish Midrashic hermeneutic system stands for complete freedom of individual interpretation?

The answer to such an implication is not a simple matter.

In *The Art of Biblical Narrative* (1981), Robert Alter stated that

> an essential aim of the . . . ancient Hebrew writers was to produce a certain indeterminacy of meaning, especially in regard to motive, moral character and psychology. . . . Meaning, perhaps for the first time in narrative literature, was conceived as a *process*, requiring continual revision—both in the ordinary sense and in the etymological sense of seeing again—continual suspension of judgement, weighing of multiple possibilities. (P. 12)

Suzan Handelman (1982), who cites Alter, asserted similarly that the term

> process . . . can aptly be applied to Rabbinic thought. As creation is considered to be a continuous and unified process, so is the Torah and so is its

interpretation. . . . Torah and every verse, letter and so on contains, therefore a plurality of meanings and references, applicable not only to Biblical time and place, but to all time and place. Through proper interpretation . . . the application and meaning appropriate for any contingency is revealed. Thus interpretation is not essentially separate from the text itself . . . but rather the extension of the text. . . . Hence one of the fundamental doctrines of Rabbinic Judaism is that the written Torah is accomplished by an oral Torah without which the written is incomplete and incomprehensible. . . . Since the Oral Torah is the revelation of the deeper aspects of the written, it also has divine status. (P. 39)

At first sight it would appear then, that as a process, Jewish hermeneutics constitutes, due to its "oral" nature, a system allowing for infinite free interpretations beyond place and time.

Indeed, the Talmud (ibid.) anticipates this pitfall when in regard to the second part of the biblical verse it adds the following discourse:

The masters of assemblies these are the disciplines of the wise who sit in manifold assemblies and occupy themselves with Torah, some pronouncing unclean and others pronouncing clean, some prohibiting and others permitting, some disqualifying and others declaring fit. Should a man say: How in these circumstances shall I learn Torah? Therefore the text says: All of them are given from one Shepherd. One God gave them; one leader uttered them from the mouth of the Lord of all creation blessed be He. . . . also do thou make thine ear like the hopper and get thee a perceptive heart to understand the words of those . . . who prohibit and the words of those who permit, the words of those who disqualify and the words of those who declare fit.

Thus, except for establishing the principle of plurality within unity (All . . . given from one Shepherd), we have here again a prima facie support for complete hermeneutic freedom, even in regard to legal matters (understand the words of those who prohibit and . . . of those who permit).

True, here we may find the epitomizing essence of the Talmudic guiding principle for dialogic interpretation in the sense of "these and those are God's living words' (*Eruvin*, 13:b). Here we might come to conclude also that the notion of "the Torah having seventy faces" culminates in an existential hermeneutic system according to which people are free to attribute infinite meanings to text or to personal experiences. To avoid such a misleading interpretation of the "hermeneutic dialogue" into anarchic terms of a hedonistic "here and now" existentialism, let us see how the dialogic principle of interpretation as a system may be understood from a psychological perspective, only in terms of how it balances matter and spirit or the legal-rational with the mystic irrational.

THE DIALOGIC EQUILIBRIUM BETWEEN MATTER
AND SPIRIT

Suzan Handelman (1982) is probably right[2] in asserting that by and large the

> validity of the "oral law" is at the heart of the conflict between Judaism
> and Christianity, [because] Christianity rejected the oral law entirely, ad-
> hering to the written text alone [p. 32]. . . . while for Judaism, a text is, as
> Rawidowicz claimed not a finished independent, self-sufficient text but one
> which is open and has to remain open to *interpretatio*. (P. 42)

Nevertheless, what Handelman, like many other critics, seems to overlook or fails to emphasize are the different levels of "hermeneutic
freedom" that evolved in the mystic and rational schools in Judaism and
the interrelationship between them.

True, a fundamentalistic adhering to the written word was considered, as
alluded to earlier, almost blasphemous in Judaism, but this did not rule out
logical or straightforward legal interpretations.

The tenth-century rabbi Sa'adia Ga'on (1970:219), who was known as the
most authoritative opponent of the Karaite sect, which rejected the oral law
and hence adhered only to a fundamentalistic strict interpretation of the
written Torah, established that

> everything in the Bible is straight forward (*Kipshuto*) except for what can-
> not be interpreted straight forwardly for one of four reasons: either be-
> cause the sense rejects it . . . or when the mind rejects it . . . or when there
> is another verse contradicting it . . . as well as whenever we have a stipula-
> tion in our tradition we shall interpret it according to the narrative concur-
> ring with the tradition.

For the present, it is of less relevance to discuss here the four specified circumstances that would require the use of divergent narrative rules. However, what follows clearly from Rabbi Sh'adia's (known as the "Rasag")
authoritative stipulation is an imperative rule legitimizing and in fact requiring a coexisting dialogue between various kinds of interpretations, that
are not only to be used differentially but sometimes also simultaneously.

Hence, while the Talmudic dictum of "these and those are God's living
words" must end with the legally binding statement "but the law is according to Beit Hillel" (Eruvin, 13:b)—this does not mean that within the law
one is not urged to find diversified mystic-symbolic meanings to the same
law. Here it might be said that the Talmudic paradox "He is been coerced
until he says I want" (*Yevamot*, 106:a) may come to mean that only within
a generally coercive legal system does the Midrashic free will to interpret acquire its legitimization for existentially actualizing attributions of meaning.
It is thus the dialogic coexistence between the *finite* material reality or
logical-legal "he is been coerced" interpretation (because the law must be

enforced) and the mystic-Cabalic *infinite* free willing "I want" inherent in Midrashic narrativism that constitutes the basis for a balanced therapeutic system. Put differently, it is only the spiritual interpretation available in the "Babylonian Talmud" that might restore communicative order to the chaos that the collapsing of the material "Babylonian Tower" caused.

Thus, while the conception of "seventy faces" might still be seen as a finite idea paralleling the notion of the seventy languages into which the Bible was translated, in the Cabalic-mystic sense expressed by a sixteenth-century Cabalist like Yoseph Elashkar (quoted by Idel, 1985), "seventy faces" connotes infinite interpretation possibilities. "And how good and pleasant is their saying also that the Torah has seventy faces and they did not say seventy interpretations, because . . . each face has seventy faces and from now on there is no end to it." (P. iv)

Indeed, the coexisting dialogue between the mystic and the rational interpretation of the Torah is vividly elucidated in the fact that the Jew could usually relate simultaneously to philosophical rational interpretations of Scripture offered by such scholars as the twelfth-century Maimonides and to thirteenth-century mystical narrations of Nachmanides. Nachmanides, as is well-known from the introduction to his classic commentary on the Torah, stated, for example, that all secrets of creation were revealed to Moses either explicitly or implicitly in the letters of the Torah and thus that even the numerical value of the letters (*Gematria*) or the semiotic form of the letter entails the secrets of creation and the world.

Thus, the structural principle of attributing meaning by rearranging letters into new words—so that seemingly opposing elements might be logically and structurally related—marks the infinite hermeneutic system of mystic Cabalism, as summarized by Idel (1983):

> The Torah has as many Kabbalistic meanings as the Kabbalist is able to find in it. Zoharic Kabbalah introduced the large-scale use of symbolistic interpretation. . . . Abraham Abulafia, using the techniques of gematria and letter combinations explains a single verse in various directions. . . . Whoever knew the techniques of interpretation could take part in disclosing the infinite, mystical dimension of the Torah. (P. 71)

This dialogic coexistence of the finite logical and the infinite mystical dimensions of interpretation, which, I hope to show, contains the necessary components for a balancing therapy in space and time, might be understood also in terms of the difference between metaphoric and metonymic modes of interpretation.

Handelman (1982) indicated that while in the metaphoric mode of interpretation the analogy resembles the property that I seek to explain and thus may be used as a substitutive term for the said property, the metonymy requires that a property may be qualified by two independent categories that do not cancel each other.

Thus, the metaphoric mode of interpretation would constitute from the present perspective, a dialectic system that due to its substitutive nature would characterize Christian hermeneutics, while metonymic narration, in which two predicates may coexist simultaneously, could be viewed as an interpretative dialogic method featuring Judaism.

Indeed, Handelman stated:

> that Christian thought is predominantly logical and metaphorical, whereas the Rabbinic mode may be characterized as metonymical and propositional. . . . The coexistence of different interpretations and the proliferation of meanings can be seen as an extension of the propositional. . . . In Greco-Christian thought, metaphor . . . is a transfer of one word or name or idea for another. Resemblance here passes over into substitution, identification, cancellation and the differences . . . are effaced. . . . The cancellation of the literal meaning of the "Old Testament" was in fact, one of the major points of dispute between Jews and Christians in the interpretation of Scripture. (P. 55)

If we are to return now, after our somewhat lengthy roaming detour in the fields of biblical hermeneutics, to the psychological arena, we may say that the metonymical dialogue of coexistence betweeen the mystic and the rational predicates seems to entail the secrets of a dynamic balancing way of life in space and time.

Such a therapeutic balancing perspective may be best understood through a structural interpretation of the Hasidic-Cabalic notion of the rearranging *tikun* (correction) concept, which I shall discuss very briefly below.

REARRANGING "TIKUN" AND THE PARADOX

A famous Hasidic story tells of a simple farmer who came into the synagogue in the midst of the High Holiday prayers and sat down to chant the alphabet, which was all he was able to read in Hebrew. When asked by the respectable, frowning members of the community exactly what he was trying to do besides cause a turmoil, he is said to have answered, "Unfortunately, I only know how to read the alphabet. I trust that God, who knows what I want to say, will rearrange the letters into proper words." As mentioned earlier, the mystic-oriented hermeneutic method of the Cabala allowed infinite interpretation of Torah that may be derived through such techniques as "letter combinations."

Indeed, the Cabala attributes great significance to the symbolic meaning of reconstructing words by rearranging their letters so that they take on a new, usually contrasting meaning. Thus, by rearranging the word *ani* (I or me) into *ain* (nothingness), the imperative verb of *iyun* (self-designification) is derived. Rearranging seemingly contrasting elements thus constitutes the paradoxical essence of the monistic notion of *tikun*. In the monistic world, all elements may in principle be functionally interrelated. Their seeming dysfunctional, contrasting, and often clashing appearance results mainly from the improper connection between them. Thus, *tikun* (correction), in the monistic (wholistic) world of paradoxes, is actually a matter of rearranging seemingly contrasting elements. The Hebrew word *nituk* (separation) becomes *tikun* by rearranging its letters. God's holy sparks, which fell down into the depth of the earthly abyss, are merely misplaced, hence the creative "spark-lifting," correcting (*tikun*) process is a matter of restoring order and reintegrating the original monistic whole by replacing and rearranging the divine sparks where they belong, up in Heaven. Indeed, the symbol of fertility and creation upon which the perpetuation of life and existence depends is explained in the Cabala (see Tishby, 1975) as a process emanating from a proper arrangement between the two contrasting symbolic creatures, male and female. Life, creation, and continuity are possible only when male and female are arranged together in certain physical positions. Thus paradoxical *tikun*, which would facilitate creative continuous relationship between seemingly polar contrasting elements, requires the prevention of *perud* or *nituk* (separation or disconnection) and the creative connecting rearrangement of male and female or any other paradoxical, contrasting elements, In this way, *tikun*, be it sociohistoric, therapeutic, or political, can make evil the throne of goodness in a Beshtian sense by using the rearranging "spark-lifting" transformation process of attributing new existential meaning to previously distressing phenomena or by creating new gestalts out of old dysfunctional structures that were perceived as unchangeable givens. Thus, creativity means indeed nothing else but the creation of new compositions out of old elements.

I have discussed at some length the Hasidic twofold affective-cognitive or rational-intuitive model for rearranging the ever-changing paradoxical, that is, seemingly opposing elements in life, because I believe that it was the Hasidic interpretation of Cabalism that has contributed more than anything else to what we would term here the reinstitutionalization of Jewish interhemispheric balance.

It is thus not only that the intuitive irrational creative questioning is relegitimized via the original Jewish notion of hermeneutic pluralism, but it is the mystical rituals of ecstatic praying that now receive its structural reorganizing meaning of *nituk* (separation) which becomes once again *tikun* (correction). Thus, everything that appears as "evil" or unexplainable is reconverted and given new meaning through reoperationalizing the contraction myth in "spark-lifting" terms of *tikun* (correction).

The hypothesized interhemispheric balancing dialogue, according to which the presumed right-side emotional activation is utilized to reenergize or refacilitate the analytical left-side Torah teaching, may be illuminated in a typical citation from Rabbi Nachman's biography (see *Chaye Moharan,* 1952) describing how he would emerge from the state of melancholy "smallness" (*katnut*) to the state of enlightenment "greatness" (*gadlut*). According to his biographer, once Rabbi Nachman began

> to teach Torah from the situation of simpleness [depressive "smallness"] . . . he revived himself during this state . . . by reliving [the experience] of his trip to the Land of Israel . . . and he explained that now he knows nothing . . . and then he said that he is happy that he has had the privilege of being in the Land of Israel. . . . And then he was in great joy and reprimanded Rabbi Naftali for being a bit ashamed to play music . . . and then he was very happy. (P. 85)

From the state of depression, Rabbi Nachman ascended first by reliving affectively a past joyful experience (his trip); then he began to revive others by urging Rabbi Naftali to play music (activating the presumed right hemisphere) so that finally he could return to the rational business of teaching the Torah (alleged left-hemisphere activity) in a state of "greatness." Thus, right-hemispheric "energizing" becomes instrumental for left-hemispheric rationalism.

Space and time do not allow us here to describe in full some of the doctrinal techniques (*hanhagot*) permeating the Hasidic literature that instruct man how to utilize ergotropic (in Hasidic terms "ascent") and/or trophotropic (in Hasidic terms "descent") methods of meditative ritual practices, including dancing, chanting, and even joking and drinking, as well as intuitive mystic methods for interpreting reality through the act of telling symbolic legends and parables to be found in or patterned according to the Jewish Midrashic tradition in which Hasidism is rooted. The point is, however, that these mystic practices, which according to brain researchers are right-hemispheric techniques are not conceived as dialectical substitutions for the presumed left-hemispheric rational-analytic Talmudism, but only as complementing expressions to be used dialogically with it, so that the resulting dual hermeneutic model could then be used to train people a priori to interpret and experience life through both hemispheres.

It should thus be stressed that while during its early phases, right-hemispheric actualization may be said to have predominated Hasidic praxis, one may say that this was so only due to its bitter struggle for recognition and legitimation by the Lithuanian Talmudists, the *Mitnagdim* (opponents).

Gradually, however, one may notice how a balancing process of what may be termed the Hasidization of the Lithuanian *yeshivot* (Talmudic colleges) and the "Talmudization" of the Hasidic *yeshivot* takes place. Thus, if my late father, who was a descendent of a famous Hasidic dynasty, had to "rebel" by attending a Lithuanian yeshiva in the course of becoming ordained as a rabbi because "in the Hasidic yeshivot they practiced the rituals all right, but they did not study seriously," as he would say, today, especially due to the influence of people like Rabbi Shlomo Carlebach, Hasidic singing and dancing is characteristic of most Lithuanian yeshivot, and rational Talmudism is part and parcel of Hasidic yeshivot.

It is thus only the *predominant* emphasis on the mystic orientation prevalent in Hasidic yeshivot in contrast to the relative stress on Talmudic rationalism characteristic of other yeshivot that helped the *baaley teshuva* to choose according to their natural inclination. In essence, however, a balancing dialogic coexistence of the mystic and the rational characterizes both institutions.

In summary, our dialogic model of interhemispheric balancing hypothesized that

1. drastic interhemispheric switching from rational to mystic or from a mystic to a rational reading of reality may result in mental breakdown or a cognitive disorientation, as could happen among Western recruits to mystic cults or, conversely, if a primitive tribe member were transplanted all of a sudden to a rational Western country;

2. the a priori inculcation of a balanced left-right hemispheric activation may be functional for living in a "schizophrenic" world of contrasts providing that the cultural hermeneutic for reading life is sufficiently flexible and pluralistic to allow for constant readaptive concretizing and rearranging for new interpretations of reality;

3. the above presented paradigm for "interhemispheric balancing" is obviously at this stage highly speculative and in need of repeated and diversified empirical validation;

4. the dialogical components of the model, which is by no means exclusively Jewish, may nonetheless be identified in the Jewish Midrashic tradition offering a multiplicity of hermeneutics for reading reality.

The proposed interhemispheric or simply interorientational balancing model may not only explain Jewish survival in space but also in time. The task of developing such a temporal balancing model is, however, beyond the scope of this presentation. In closing this chapter, one final thought: I have introduced a very, very hypothetical, and probably "idealistic," model for interhemispheric balancing. Perhaps it is not accidental that we speak yearningly about the possibility of a better balancing dialogue between the Eastern and the Western hemispheres in our troubled world. As this chapter was devoted to this much-needed bridging point between body and mind, between Descartes' rational *cogito* and Heidegger's intuitive *Dassein*, maybe it would be better to advance coexistence in the world by enhancing left-right hemispheric *harmony* instead of perpetuating East-West interhemispheric *antagony*.

The foregoing discourse about possibilities of "interhemispheric" balancing of the rational-mystical perspectives on the intrapersonal space level, which was illuminated by some empirical case studies, may lead us now into a discussion about the differences between "converting" and "returning."

Thus, the next chapter will focus on demonstrating how "dialectic conversion" (from one religion to another), which characterizes most cult systems differs radically from a "dialogic returning" to one's roots. The conceptual differentiation between those processes, which operate mainly on the intrapersonal time sphere, will be elucidated again by a presentation of selected case studies taken from clinical contexts and from our research on rehabilitation systems for ex-convicts.

NOTES

1. According to Conway and Siegelman, the dialectic assumption that under certain conditions, new information may destroy and *replace* old information, is traceable to W. Ross Ashby's Law of Experience. Ashby's cybernetic model seems to concur with or draw on Karl Pribram's holographic model that constitutes an optic-photographic paradigm for explaining how various intersecting patterns of information flow are processed and stored in the brain.

2. While Handelman's summarizing presentation of Midrashic hermeneutics seems correct, her discussion of Harold Bloom or Freud's rabbinic style of interpretation is self-contradictory because these essentially constitute dialectic replacement systems and not, as she claims, a multiple choice hermeneutics that maintains an ongoing dialogue with the "text."

8 Linear Conversion versus Cyclistic Teshuvah: An Empirical Differentiation

In this chapter, clinical and empirical implications emanating from the distinction between the dialectic process of conversion and the dialogic process of returning will be explored. Our discourse will thus be accompanied by illustrative clinical case material and empirical findings from our own studies of rehabilitation programs for ex-convicts. I begin by observing that following the recent influx of cult-based salvation-therapy movements, most recent social studies of religious conversion seem to have concentrated on providing causal models of this phenomenon.

It appears, however, that social/psychological-oriented studies of conversion focusing on relativistic-situational factors such as social influence add very little to what we already know from research on the impact of primary group pressure on behavior change.[1] Likewise, psychologically anchored studies attempting to detect antecedent conditions leading to conversion, such as personal stress and socialization patterns, encounter difficulties in demonstrating how such predispositions experienced by preconverts differ qualitatively from those characteristic of the lives of other Westerners.

The difficulty in explicating religious conversion experiences in secular social scientific terms comes through clearly if one examines how endeavors to present alternative positivistic-sequential accounts of conversion processes criticize each other.

Thus, while the sociological cause-and-effect approach to conversion studies has been used throughout most of the 1960s and the 1970s by models offered by Lofland and Stark (1965) and Lofland (1966), Heirich (1977) has shown, for example, how control and noncontrol samples do not differ significantly when control groups are compared on most of the classical predispositions (mentioned by Lofland and Stark or by others), such as the experiencing of personal stress or the facing of a critical turning point or in mode of upbringing.

Moreover, and more importantly, Snow and Phillips (1980) have demonstrated, for example, that since most conversion studies are usually dependent on ex post facto research methods, even when preconversion tension is recalled by converts, the reported stress appears to be a retroactive reinterpretation of their biography caused by the conversion experience rather than leading to it. As a matter of fact, while Lofland and associates do not admit explicitly that their causal conversion model failed to yield substantiating replicable studies, Lofland's own "conversion" from a positivistic linear orientation to a phenomenological retroactive account model for studying conversion seems complete. Indeed, in their 1981 study of "conversion motifs," Lofland and Skonovd (1981) stated that since "conversion experiences which investigators are reporting . . . are not simply a matter of the 'theoretical goggles' worn by the researcher . . . we explore the . . . 'conversion careers' . . . or 'motif' experiences . . . which describe the subjective perceptions of the convert. What converts stress in their accounts" (p. 374).

In other words, while Lofland and Skonovd's declaration that "we explore the 'conversions careers' . . . which describe the subjective perceptions of the convert. What converts stress in their accounts" marks a radical switch from the early causal model to a retroactive account model. By presenting the "conversion motifs" perspective, Lofland and his alternating associates cleverly succeeded in maintaining their "modeling" leadership role in conversion studies, although Lofland never fully admitted or "accounted" for the failure of his previous causal model.

The failure of the traditional causal-linear paradigm guiding social influence or stress and socialization studies to yield sound empirical expositions regarding the "when" and "what" causes "whom" to convert led Heirich (1977) to propose a new, more "comprehensive" causal paradigm of conversion. He suggested (p. 674) investigation of (a) conditions that "destroy" one's fundamental understanding of one's "root reality" (meaning of existence) and (b) the circumstances under which one will internalize a new-alternative sense of "root reality." Comparing Heirich's proposition to Snow and Phillips' criticism, one may notice that both offer to conceive of conversion as a problem of interpretation or narration of biographies.

The difference between their approaches is only that Heirich conceives of conversion as a process in which the inability to reinterpret one's "destroyed" interpretation of one's past reality will lead one to seek a new interpretation for life, while Snow and Phillips assume that the very conversion experience triggers-causes a reinterpretation of one's past that, in fact, reverses the sequence of cause and effect.

In other words, the observation that conversion may require the "destruction" of one's previously interpreted "root reality" or that it may involve a retrospective dissonance reducing reinterpretation of one's past places the causal approach to conversion in the midst of the controversy confronting narrative psychology.

It thus raises two (intertwined) cardinal questions:

1. To what extent is conversion or personal growth and change a linear or a cyclistic cause-and-effect process of interpretation? and

2. To what extent may differential perceptions of a "convert's" past as a cause or as an effect be influenced by the very religious belief system in which he or she was bred or that he or she adopts?

The first, more general question challenges the applicability of the physical linear (sequential) cause-and-effect paradigm to the cognitive-emotive process of personal progress. It doubts whether a cognitive experience such as stress operates in a physical-mechanistic fashion that must thus be the causal a priori "A" that precedes the resulting progressive or "converted" behavior "B," and proposes instead that on a cognitive level, the causal process is reversed so that it is the a posteriori reinterpretation in a present A that by causing a change in perception of a past experience B may proceed or progress to any future C.

The second question, which follows from the first, simply implies that conversion as a cognitive interpretation process may be differentially understood according to the way respective religions guide their converts' reorganization of self in time and space. Put differently, the second question's implicit assumption is that in order to understand whether in a religious change process, present interpretation of reality *may* be used to cause a perceptual change of one's past or whether the past *must* be perceived as the cause of one's present, one ought to examine how interpretation of a novice's past is conceived in various religions.

For example, while Buddhism differs from Christianity in its belief in the transmigration of souls and in its seemingly cyclistic conception of Karma, these two religious systems conceive suffering in cause-and-effect terms. Indeed, Mircea Eliade (1974:98–99) observed, for example, that the Indian conception of suffering appears to be only an extension of the Christian "this world" "original sin" causal orientation to a Karmatic "other worlds" causality paradigm, so that qualitatively these two religious views do not differ. "The Indians quite early elaborated a conception of universal causality, the Karma concept, which acocunts for the actual events and sufferings of the individual's life and at the same time explains the necessity for transmigrations. . . . The sufferings of one's present life . . . are in fact the fatal effect of crimes and faults committed in previous lives."

Thus, the search for variables that are to expound the nature of religious change, as for example the possibility of determining whether the process leading to a new religious state is cognitively an a priori or an a posteriori causality sequence, must begin by operationalizing the dynamics of religious, and not secular, experiences.

In the light of the foregoing perspective, it would appear now that it was their own secular causal models of conversion that led such veteran researchers as Lofland (e.g., Lofland and Skonovd, 1981) to shift from studying objective antecedent conditions leading to conversion to assessing the subjective and hence differential motifs or styles of the very conversion experiences that include the religious root meaning of these intellectual or emotional motif experiences.

Such religious root meanings of conversion, that is, specific religious change dicta, which were either internalized during socialization in one's mother religion or inculcated by the new absorbing religion, may thus be understood as what I termed metacodes or Platonic ideas that differentially affect the very experience of conversion.

More specifically, if we agree, for example, on the almost obvious, that the desire for religious change involves some measure of discontent with one's past, due to failure, stress, sinning, and so on (since otherwise, why should one seek the particular change), there is still a difference between the acquired or "inherited" metabelief that one can "repent" and "return" to one's original religion by correcting this negative past and the belief that a derogatory past is essentially an integral part of man's unchangeable "original sin"-based suffering in the world, so that in order to change, one has to "convert" to another religion. On the empirical level, these differences may then be recognized through the "vocabulary of motives" (see Mills, 1974) that subjects use to describe their religious change experience.

Thus, while a "convert" might say, "my past is dead" or "I was born again," the "returnee" might say, "I now understand the meaning of my past, " "I have returned to my roots," "I came home." Accordingly, conversion may be understood as a dialectic process of linear progression, since the negation of one's past causes its replacement by a new religion, while "returning" may be understood in cyclistic terms in which one returns to one's past via the dialogic process of reinterpreting it. In fact, linguistic differences between cyclistic and linear cultures are not reflected only in the "vocabulary of motives" used to explain or reinterpret one's own behavior, but often comprise the very structure of social relationships. Levi-Strauss (1963) demonstrated, for example, how in the Zuni kinship system, the use of the same term for grandmother and granddaughter, "who occupy symmetrical positions in relation to a third individual" (the mother or father) reflects a "cyclical historical structure" in which "each period repeats . . . the preceding period" (p. 75). Thus using the word *grandson* may mean a cyclistic "homecoming return."

The analysis and study to be presented below addresses itself to the very needed yet much neglected distinction between the dialectic case of converting-progressing in a linear fashion from one (past) religion to a new (present) religion and the dialogic-cyclistic case of returning (*teshuvah*) to one's presumed original religion or past.

LINEAR CONCEPTIONS OF CONVERSION AND PROGRESS

While William James's (1971) account of the Christian intrapsychic process of inner psychological conversion and growth is not directly relevant to our discussion of the sociological proliferation of cultish movements, his conceptualization of conversion in the "born again" terms of a "death-rebirth" process entails important implications for our distinction between linear conversion and cyclistic returning. James's assertion that in "Buddhism and Christianity . . . man must die to an unreal life before he can be born into the real life" (p. 171) would establish that conversion-progress is possible only through a complete obliteration of one's past. Indeed, the term *conversion* would concur then with the Hegelian notion of progress via negation and dialectic substitution, according to which "conversion" has nothing to do with a repenting return to one's parent religion but is a process in which one discards or transforms the old obsolete entity (self or religion) for or into a new form. In other words, in this case the past leads-causes the present in a deterministic-teleological process of historical necessity, and thus this past "root reality" must be substituted (converted) by a new present, but it may not be reinterpreted.

A compelling example of how the Christian and the Buddhist styles of conversion converge in their common dialectic-linear kind of negating of one's past would be the increasing popularity of Zen Buddhist cults among the American hip counterculture movement since the 1960s. Indeed, in his studies of thought reform processes, Robert Jay Lifton (1967) observed in the early 1960s that "the Zen Buddhist plunge of the American beatnik has in it some of the same elements of total rejection of one's past, in exchange for another's past" (p. 534).

In his study of conversion to the Black Muslim religion cited by Sarbin and Adler (1970-1971), Eric Lincoln observed that "the true believer who becomes a Muslim casts off . . . his old self and takes on a new identity. He changes his name, his religion, his homeland, his 'natural' language, his moral and natural values, his very purpose of living" (p. 607).

Now, since the impossibility of "returning" by reinterpreting one's past, which usually precipitates a substituting-conversion to another group, cult, or religion, is also generally implicated in the unchangeable Christian "original sin" kind of attitude to the past, it is rather surprising that even those comparative conversion studies that include the *teshuvah* phenomenon (e.g., Ullman, 1982) have hitherto ignored the possible fundamental difference between Western linear conversion and Jewish cyclistic returning.

To be sure, by my metaphoric use of the "original sin" kind of attitude toward the past I am referring again to the phenomenological impact exerted by such notions as the Christian belief that the original sin is an unshakeable hereditary vice. Such "interpretations of original sin as an original guilt of little children in the wombs of their mothers" often become, however, as Ricoeur (1981:269) asserted, "true symbols" that are transmitted from one generation to the other. Accordingly, the significance of such symbols in the present context lies in the following assumption. If such symbolic reductionism of religious metabeliefs is plausible, then people who absorbed such symbols as the "original sin" one might be unable to believe in human alterability and in the possibility of correcting one's past. Consequently, they might be driven to desert or obliterate their failing past by converting to another religion.

Thus, let us turn now to contrast the linear conversion style of personal change with the cyclistic return (*teshuvah*) process.

TESHUVAH AND THE ROOTS OF CYCLISTIC ACCOUNTING

Janet Aviad (1983:93) was generally right in indicating in her pioneering study of the Jewish *teshuvah* movement, that "this sense of 'returning to the fold' may well be the most distinctively Jewish component of the teshuvah process, setting it off from other 'conversion' phenomena."

While Aviad has not differentiated analytically between the underlying causality paradigms that make returning or converting possible, her distinction between the "seeking" and the "homecoming" (returning) styles of *teshuvah* fits generally our differentiation between the linear (dialectic) and the cyclistic (dialogic) processes of "becoming" religious.

The possibility of maintaining a reinterpretive "homecoming" dialogue with the secular (sinful) past is described by one of the returnees cited by Aviad.

> Part of my being is the experience I had in the secular world. To deny that would be to deny part of me, which, whether it was legitimate or not, that was who I was, I never saw the process of teshuvah as destroying my being but as redirecting it. . . . My personal history was the bridge. It was not necessary to cut, but rather, to maintain connections without destroying either side or negating my personal being. . . . The change is rational and step by step. It can be without a trauma. (P. 109)

While we may then distinguish various patterns of change within the *teshuvah* movement, its essence is a "returning" to one's collective past through a reinterpretative dialogue with the personal past to which one returns.[2]

Most significant in the process of "homecoming" to one's religious collective identity, which by definition requires that one's autobiographic reinterpretation will be accepted by the collectivity to which one returns, is the destigmatizing element inherent in the reranking of deviations and sins.

This is to say that the more a "homecoming" return to a religious identity permits one to rank certain violations of religious norms (which are not being stigmatized by the secular society) as constituting more severe crimes in comparison to stealing, for example, the more chances there are that the cognitive consonance between one's present and one's past positive self-identity (resulting from this re-biographing process), will be more genuine, effective, and consequently, lasting.

Indeed, in one of our studies of ex-criminal *baaley teshuva*, comparative contraction and minimization of past criminality seemed to epitomize the possibility for a destigmatizing rehabilitation of returnee's biography. In this study, which was undertaken in conjunction with the preparation for this book, one ex-convict stated, for example, that

> the laws of the State of Israel exist 37 years. The laws of the Torah exist for thousands of years. The secular person, who does not observe the laws of the Torah is a bigger criminal than the one who sits in prison. The delinquent had troubles [in his past] therefore he turned out like that. The secularist did not experience troubles.

Comparative contracting minimization in re-biographing was even more paramount in the following citation taken from the study mentioned above:

> Our secular society is distorted due to vested interests. What is the difference between a surgeon who performs abortions, who is simply a murderer of babies, and a thief as I was? . . . The thief is perhaps less of a sinner but in this society the physician will be bestowed with honor and be recognized as a respected person while the thief will be degraded and thrown into prison.

Here again, it is not only that one's dream about becoming an "Indian chief" is meaningless unless other tribe members had the same dream, but for comparative destigmatizing purposes, tribe members must also dream that the "surgeon-abortionist" is a blasphemic false witch doctor.

To be sure, cyclistic returning is not characteristic only of the Jewish *teshuvah* process. Harrison (1974) has identified, for example, such a cyclistic renewal of the past in his study of recruits to Catholic Pentecostalism who "returned" to the faith of their youth, from which they had fallen away.

Moreover, in their study of Jewish *baaley teshuvah* (returnees), Glanz and Harrison (1978) noticed that through a process that in the present terms would constitute a biographic rehabilitation of the past, "*baale teshuvah* see their transformation as a reaffirmation and realization of their true iden-

tities . . . [because] the full break with the past so characteristic of true conversion occurs rarely among *baaley teshuvah*" (p. 137).

Thus, the difference between "returnees" who search for *alterations* in
their identities and converts who choose an *alternative* identity is a very
crucial one.

RETURNING AS A REVERSED CAUSALITY PARADIGM

According to the cyclistic *teshuvah* process, therapeutic progress is possible
through a cognitively reversed causality paradigm in which the movement
from the behavior change (repentance) in a certain present legitimizes the
remolding interpretation of the past from which one moves on in a Hasidic
"ascent through descent" (see Rotenberg, 1983) spiral fashion to the
future.

Indeed, typical "ascent through descent" kinds of autore-biographic reinterpretations of the past that were recorded in our studies of ex-criminals included such accounts by "returnees" as the following:

> My dark past, is a social matter I always thought that I will stop [criminali-
> ty]. . . . It is possible that it is from Heaven . . . that I was redirected by
> Heaven to circle around so much in crime. . . . Today, if I would go to
> prison, I shall say it is for the good, that God wants me to sit there and
> study [Torah] there . . . I cannot be born again but I can forget things.

The combination of reinterpreting the criminal past (being redirected by
Heaven to circle around in crime so that if one is sent to prison one will see
good in it) with the activation of a selective memory (I can forget things),
which concurs with Nietzsche's (1980) critical and pragmatic use of history,
comprises in essence the cognitively reversed causality system of retrospective accounting that underlies the teshuvah process. Thus, a recurring theme
in our interviews that characterized re-biographing was the identification
with the collective "ascent through descent" theme inherent in the biblical
story of Exodus. Accordingly, an ex-convict returnee's response to the
question—How do you feel about your criminal past?—would run
somewhat as follows:

If the Jews had to "descend" to Egypt, where, according to the Midrash
(Commentary), they indulged in all possible forms (forty-nine "gates") of
profane behavior, in order to "ascend" to Israel and become a nation, so
the *baal teshuvah's* (returnee's) criminal or sinful past may be reinterpreted
as a necessary "descent" for the sake of "ascent."

Thus, re-biographic accounting of the past begins with the "repented"
behavioral change in the present, which then legitimizes a reinterpretation
of one's past. Put differently, the repentance experience in the present
becomes by definition the causal vehicle by which the past (the effect) is actually changed and redefined.

Soloveitchick (1983), a contemporary leading authority in Jewish philosophy and *Halacha* (Jewish law), states unequivocally:

The law of causality, from this perspective, also assumes a new form. We do not have here the determinate order of a scientific, causal process, nor does the relationship of active cause and pre-determined passive effect prevail in such circumstances. . . . The future imprints its stamp on the past and determines its image. . . . The cause is interpreted by the affect, moment *a* by moment *b*. The past itself is indeterminate. . . . It is only the present and the future that can pry it open and read its meaning. . . . The main principal of repentance is that the future dominates the past and then reigns over it in unbounded fashion. (Pp. 114-15)

George Herbert Mead (1959) seems even more radical in his cognitive reversed causality paradigm in which the "emergent event" in the present may not be determined by the past but, in fact, shape it.

A present then, as contrasted with the abstraction of mere passage is not a piece cut out anywhere from the temporal . . . uniformly passive reality. Its chief reference is to the emergent event, that is, to the occurrence of something which is more than the processes that have led up to it. . . . It marks out and in a sense selects what has made its peculiarity possible. It creates with its uniqueness a past and a future. As soon as we view it, it becomes a history and a prophecy. (P. 23)

Concomitant with Nietzsche's selective memory approach to the past, Mead concludes decisively that

It is of course evident that the materials out of which that past is contructed lie in the present. I refer to the memory images and the evidences by which we build up the past, and to the fact that any reinterpretation of the future we form of the past will be found in the present. (P. 29)

By demonstrating how Soloveitchick's[3] and Mead's perspectives on the cognitively reversed causality process converge, I intend to argue that the "teshuvah-return" model contains paradigmatic implications for personal change and for the correction of one's past failure that reach beyond the religious context that may have bred various therapeutic models.

More specifically, I contend that in order to assess the logical truism inherent in the proposition that on a cognitive level the present determines the past or vice versa, one has to examine, as I suggested earlier, the underlying religious metacode that biases the secular norm of accepting one causal paradigm or the other.

Nevertheless, from a phenomenological-existential point of view one might be misled into arguing here that conversion is neither a linear nor a reversed causal process because it is the here-and-now "affective bond" acceptance offered in cults (including *teshuvah* cults) that contributes more than anything else to one's switching religions.

Indeed, the "affective bond" motif, which was the only residual variable from Lofland and Starks (1965:379) early linear causality model because it "was widely adopted and rapidly documented," appeared, misleadingly, to be a good predictor also for Lofland's and Skonovd's (1981) later phenomenological conversion model. Here one must point out, however, that Lofland and other students of conversion usually selected transient and esoteric cults, making it difficult to assess the durability of the mesmerizing-brainwashing and mystic-experiential effects that often attract, only temporarily, adventure-seeking youth.

Although it is difficult to determine a priori which change is transient and which is lasting, our studies, which focused on two collective-oriented settings that Jewish youth have been joining for many years, show that it is ultimately only the religious belief or its secularized ideological metacode that determines whether "affective bonds" may or may not undo the causal "original sin" kind of "once a thief always a thief" social blaming. To provide the reader with some illustrative examples of how the dialectic metacode of criminal causality outweighs secular social psychological predictors of conversion such as the "affective bonds" variable, selected results from our study about ex-convicts participating in two collective rehabilitation programs will be presented below.

EX-CONVICTS IN THE YESHIVAH AND IN THE KIBBUTZ

To facilitate a phenomenological evaluation of how one's subjective feelings in regard to the perception of one's present, past, and future affect one's identity, two totalistic settings, the *kibbutz* and the *yeshivah* rehabilitation programs for ex-convicts, were selected. By totalistic settings, emphasis is not only on the narrow Goffmanian valuefree sociogeographic "live-in" dimension described in his "total institution," but also on the Sutherlandian dimension of "differential association" according to which prosocial change depends on the predominating positive value system of the affective group to exclude any possible negative influences infiltrating from the outside. Since both the kibbutz and the yeshivah (the Talmudical college) comprise totalistic "differential association" settings in which the predominating value system is prosocial in the broadest secular-socialistic sense (the kibbutz) or in its collective-religious sense (the yeshiva), in theory, it could be only dialectic versus dialogic meta belief codes that would make personal and social re-biographing possible or impossible. In other words, since in these settings the egalitarian "affective bonds" value prevails, one's stigmatic past should not discriminate between the groups unless one is guided by an underlying metabelief about re-biographing.

In Chapter 6 I discussed the controversy over the question of whether dialectic ideas imported by secular European Marxists and/or American Hegelians have exerted decisive influences on the kibbutz notion (in terms of collective living and absorption of newcomers) that possibly outweighed its originally Jewish dialogic foundations. Put differently, I have essentially implied that while the kibbutz ideology is embedded in Jewish ideological roots, it remains an empirical question as to whether dialogicalism or dialecticism predominates its everyday life.

Since the nature of a social system may be best assessed by studying its attitudes toward and its methods for producing or reducing deviance, a comparative examination of the kibbutz and yeshiva absorption programs for ex-convicts seemed most promising, especially since both systems comprise totalistic settings that are presumably grounded in the same egalitarian dialogicalism.

While not all the details of this research are of interest in the present context, some results and demonstrative case material appear highly significant and relevant here. Very briefly, in this pilot study, fifteen male ex-convicts who found their way into a yeshivah for *baaley teshuvah* (repenters) and thirteen male ex-convicts who were accepted in a kibbutz were selected at random for semistructured (open-ended) depth interviews. As alluded to earlier, interviewees were asked to describe their subjective experiential feelings about how they conceive today their failing past, present changes in life-style, and future hopes and aspirations.

Possibilities for internal dialectic versus dialogic time perception were sketched schematically and categorized as outlined in Table 2.

It appears that only by comparing such collectivities as the yeshivah and the kibbutz can one hold constant and control the possible impact of "affective bonds" in order to determine whether in spite of the proclaimed egalitarian acceptance based on the "here-and-now" behavior change, ex-convicts perceive their failing past dialectically or dialogically.

Table 2
Dialectic and Dialogic Time Perceptions

Model	Dialectic-Linear "Conversion"		Dialogic-Cyclistic "Returning"	
Category	Death-rebirth	New leaf	Re-biographing	Existentialism
Time				
Past	Obliteration	"Original sin" guilt	Reinterpretation	Discounting
Present	Born Again	Dissonanced Behavior	Consonanced Behavior	"Here and now" Actualization
Future	Dictated grace	Teleological reading	"Messianic" writing	Discounting

Since the reader may be generally familiar with the models and categories schematized in Table 2, it would seem sufficient to stress only that, theoretically, linear conversion should concur with the "death-rebirth" model in which one negates one's past identity to accept a new identity dictated by divine grace or by the new cult that one joined. Realistically, it is possible, however, that on a secular social-psychological level, past failures are carried like an "original sin" guilt cross, so that the "new leaf" rehabilitation formula creates a dissonance between one's past failure and one's present changed behavior. Thus, in this category, bridging between one's past and future would be possible only through a teleological reading of this future that was already predetermined in the past. By contrast, cyclistic returning would theoretically follow the re-biographic pattern, in which case the descending into and the reinterpretation of the past reestablishes (in theory) identity consonance, which allows one to ascend and write the script of one's "messianic" (redeemed) future. It includes, however, also the existential mode, because this category contains the archaic "eternal returning" cycle described by Eliade in which hedonistic yet creative living in the present is possible by annulling the past and the future.

Now, although various intercategorical combinations are naturally possible, it would seem unduly burdening to discuss them here. The most relevant findings available from our study were, however, the following. While the ex-convicts absorbed in the kibbutz setting have by and large exhibited an existentialistic "here and now" orientation, this dialogic trend was colored by scattered configurations of dialectic "new leaf" and death-rebirth attitudes toward their past and future. On the other hand, the *baaley teshuvah* in the yeshivah setting demonstrated an overwhelming and consistent trend concurring with the "re-biographic" perception of their past, present, and future.

Thus, a typical ex-convict in the kibbutz would not obliterate the past but try to discount it by emphasizing the present. More specifically, our findings indicated time and again that while in the kibbutz, egalitarian acceptance was essentially based on one's "here and now" efforts to work and conform, over these "affective bond" feelings, the "once a thief always a thief" sword of threatening suspicion was constantly swaying. Said one ex-convict, "I was born to crime, I don't know whether I can get out of it. . . . I love life in the kibbutz but I am constantly afraid that I shall be blamed for something I did in the past which will destroy my present."

More specifically, while the dialogic existential "here and now" focus would be reflected in such a declaration as "what is important is to get ready to work and now that the present is important, [as in my case] a person has the ability to change; I have control; I decided." Nonetheless, the same subject also stated "Delinquency is a stigma and nothing will help. It will always remain." Thus, ex-convicts in the kibbutz expressed a "here and now" change that was in sharp dissonance with their past identity. Indeed, ex-convicts in the kibbutz would often express either a dialectic desire to erase the past: "The past is, from my point of view obliterated. . . . For rehabilitation, it is best to forget, to disconnect one self from the past," or a dialectic "death-rebirth" assertion: "My childhood was sad, I wish I could relive it in a different manner, in a good loving family."

It should be stressed that since single "outsiders" joining the kibbutz are usually "adopted" by a foster family, this "affective bond" should, and sometimes does, contribute to one's eventual full acceptance as a member of the kibbutz. It appeared, however, that due to the probational aura that was imbuing and underlying this "egalitarian" acceptance, ex-convicts in the kibbutz were unable to express hopes and plan their future, because, apparently, the degree of anxiety about maintaining such "affective bonds" (e.g., with the foster family) in the present increased with the degree of perceived attractiveness of such family bonds. Thus, an ex-convict stated:

> Today my relationship with the foster family is very important. . . . This relationship infuses me with strength to carry on. . . . I don't think about the future, the future is too far away, emphasis is on what happens today, to do what is expected of me, I don't know what's going to happen, I don't know what's going to happen in 10 years time, it's too frightening, I don't know what to expect from the future, many things that are not under my control may happen. For example, the police may press charges against me concerning a crime I committed in the past, but was never caught. . . .

And similarly, while one would express the typical gravitation toward the present-oriented actualization by saying "What's most important is the here and now, I have a home," yet another would express concern about the future by saying, "I am afraid to think about the kibbutz. I am afraid of disappointment, this is not yet my home, and I am not the one to determine whether it will be or not."

In contrast to the ex-convicts' existentially mixed time perception pattern exhibited in the kibbutz setting, apparent association between normative reinterpretation of past failures and egalitarian "affective bonds" was consistently expressed by those subjects in our study who joined the repenters yeshiva program.

A most revealing observation would thus be that in some of the yeshivot, the rabbis could not remember precisely who was an ex-convict and who was not. Thus, a typical ex-convict who would never hide his criminal and prison background from other yeshivah students (mostly repenters), would offer an "ascent through descent" reinterpretation of his failing past that not only placed him on an equal level with his comrades but that enabled him to reconnect this past with his future aspirations. Here are some typical examples.

> I want to remember this [criminal] period in my life so that I shall be reminded from where I came and to where I was able to go, from a low pit to a high roof [position].

> I don't want to erase my past, the past helps me today to know what life is all
> about, nobody can sell me out! It helps me to scrutinize matters correctly, so
> judge when things are serious and when they are not. I am not a new person,
> life fills me with joy. . . . I am happy that today I know why I live. I was sub-
> human and therefore I don't look down at no one because I was on these low
> levels myself. This is my greatest joy. The future depends on me. . . . I have
> only to do my best.

And another ex-convict in the study stated similarly:

> I don't have to forget my past. . . . Out of bitterness came forth sweetness. . . .
> I shall determine my own future, the future is not predetermined. . . . I was in
> a state of descent for the sake of ascent; if I would not have spent time in
> prison, I would not have been able to understand truth.

While the citations of the baaley teshuvah are somewhat redundant because I
have used similar statements in different contexts previously, the reader is
alerted to the observation that most of these ex-convict baaley teshuvah were
able to use Midrashic paraphrases for their re-biographic reorganizing of
personal time.

Accordingly, if in the first citation, the famous Talmudic slogan "from a
high roof [position] to a low pit" (*Chagiga*, 5:b), which refers to one's disgrace-
ful fall from a high respectable position, was reversed and rephrased in "ascent through descent" terms, in the last citation, the biblical (Judg., 14:14)
verse "from the strong came forth sweetness" was paraphrased by inserting
the word *bitterness* in place of the word *strong*.

In conclusion, the findings that were selected from our pilot study for presentation here must obviously be taken with reservations because insufficient
time has elapsed to permit generalization about the lasting effectiveness of the
yeshivah as a rehabilitation model for ex-convicts.

If, however, the acquisition of a new linguistic structure may indeed reflect a
deeper socialization process, we may have plausible evidence to believe that it
was the Midrashic metacode of re-biographing that, in the yeshivah case, affected the collective norm of egalitarian acceptance and not vice versa. Since
both the yeshiva and the kibbutz are prosocial totalistic settings that are essentially grounded in similar dialogic egalitarian values, it would appear that it is
under the influence of dialectic metacodes of causal linear progress that hidden
dualistic class systems and the disbelief in the possibility of re-biographing
might continue to flourish in the kibbutz.

After indulging in the specificity of case material, let us return now to the
generality by examining how criminological theories deal with the problem of
linear (dialectic) versus cyclistic (dialogic) causality on a cognitive level.

THE "NEUTRALIZATION" OF, VERSUS THE "ACCOUNTING" FOR, A DEVIANT PAST

While thus far we have a strong case for supporting the a posteriori model of
cognitive causality that concurs with, Mill's, Mead's and Soloveitchick's posi-

tions, one of the more crucial and concrete problems engendered by the reversed causality paradigm pertains to the criminological questions of how people "whitewash" their asocial behavior and whether its concomitant model of re-biographing in fact legitimizes such "whitewashing." While such expositions as Scott and Lyman's (1968) analysis of how criminals "account" retroactively for their asocial behavior by using "excuses" or "justifications" follows Wright Mills' a posteriori[4] perspective, Sykes and Matza (1957) present an a priori linear model of criminal causality according to which people choose beforehand their alibi-oriented techniques in order to neutralize their subsequent criminal conduct.

By using an acceptable vocabulary of motives, Sykes and Matza thus contend that criminals might subsequently use such techniques as denying the injury, denying the victim, or denying their responsibility in order to neutralize a specific deviant act. Nonetheless, the difficulty of accepting this a prioristic alibi model remains in that one can never prepare all of one's neutralizing techniques because the present contains unexpected "emergent events," as suggested by Mead.

Moreover, according to Mills (1974), people's tendency to account for and attribute motives to their past conduct must operate a posteriori as a constantly changing process of retrospective reinterpretation because: "a man may begin to act for one motive; in the course of his act he may adopt an auxiliary motive which he will use to explain his act" (p. 116).

Thus, while Sykes and Matza's a priori neutralization may be discounted by Mead's and Mills's more compelling a posteriori accounting models, the possibility that people might prospectively or retrospectively "psychopathically whitewash" their deviant past poses a serious question concerning the genuine corrective possibility inherent in re-biographic teshuvah.

Mead's (p. 29) insistence on the dynamic nature characteristic of the reversed causality model seems, however, to defend indirectly the therapeutic-corrective possibility available in re-biographing. True, the present molds the past, but since the present is constantly changing, it cannot introduce a fixed explanation of the past that could then legitimize any "psychopathic" neutralization or accounting for past evil, because this past has to be constantly confirmed or validated by, and correlated with, present evidential behavior so that past and present may be conceived in consistent terms.

> We are not contemplating an ultimate unchangeable past that may be spread behind us in its entirety subject to no further change. Our reconstructions of the past . . . never contemplates the finality of their findings, they are always subject to conceivable reformulations, on the discovery of alter evidence.

Indeed, the constant dependence of biographic rehabilitation on one's past or present behavior is expressed symbolically in the motto underlying the teshuvah process, which stipulates that

> Any one who confesses in matters [of past crimes] without deciding in his heart to discard [them] resembles a person that purifies [immerses in a ritual

bath] while holding in his hand a rodent, since purifying can not be effective for him until he throws away the rodent. (Maimonides, *Teshuva*, 2:3)

The point is that clinging to a rodent, which in Judaism symbolizes pro-
fanity and a criminal past (*kupat sheratzim*), and which requires purification if one touches it, becomes a symbol for the meaning of re-biographic
repentance in the sense that one has to prove constantly by his ceaseless
"purifying" (immersing-repenting) behavior that he is no longer clinging to
impurity (holding on to the profane rodent).

It thus appears that Soloveitchick, Mead, and Mills are in agreement that
causality must be understood on a cognitive level as a dynamic dialogic process in which the constantly changing presents are shaping the pasts.

To be sure, in discussing the applicability of cognitive attribution theory
to psychotherapy, Garfield and Bergin (1978) suggest, for example, that
"changing the causes attributed to problems brought to therapy is a key
task in equipping clients to control important events in their lives" (p. 117).
Thus, contend Garfield and Bergin, "Psychotherapy as an attempt to change
causal perceptions assumes that causal attributions are unstable and are al-
terable with new information" (p. 118). Following the above "flexible" linear causal attribution techniques of therapy, it is possible then that it is the
legitimization of the deterministic attribution of linear causality that invites
the psychopathic "whitewashing" and shaking off one's responsibility and
not the cyclistic reversed causality that demands constant "immersing" to
"purify" the past "rodent." Why then do criminologists such as Sykes and
Matza or sociopsychological-oriented psychotherapists such as Garfield and
Bergin cling to the linear model? For an answer we must uncover the causal
ideologies underlying clinical psychology at large.

LINEAR AND CYCLISTIC APPROACHES TO PSYCHOTHERAPY

Before we begin to contrast the differential implications for psychotherapy
inherent in the linear and cyclistic causality perspectives, one major observation seems in order. While in psychotherapy, according to both linear-
conversion and cyclistic-returning, re-biographing may occur, only the latter permits a favorable reinterpretation of the past, while the former insists
that it must always be a negative-sinful past that caused present neurosis.[5]

Since the Western historicistic linear conception of progress as well as the
Calvinistic Protestant-based work ethos[6] allow in principle a favorable interpretation of the past, it is only by demonstrating how the physical-mechanistic model of traumatic causality was reified by applying it to the cognitive
sphere that one may understand why in psychodynamic therapy, linearity

must always be based on a correlation between a negative cause and its subsequent effect.

I agree with Stanley Leavy (1980) that

> where Freud took the giant step was not to abandon the doctrine of causality, but to extend it to a new reach: the symptom did not need a physical process to explain it, like tumor or inflammation. The cause might be an event. "Trauma," originally purely physical, meaning a wound, might now designate a causal event, but as an event it is a historical explanation: the patient is ill because something happened in the past, and what happened had a mental significance from the beginning. (Pp. 5-6)

Thus, while Freud's extension of the linear model of causality from the mechanistic-physical traumata realm to the mental-cognitive trauma spheres represents a par excellence reification of the term *trauma* (referring originally only to a physical wound) we still do not understand why psychoanalytic therapy relies primarily on "excavating" the presumed causal impact of only detri-"mental" memories on present neurosis. That is, if the bulk of subconscious or preconscious mental experiences from early childhood are now assumed to comprise causes of adult life, the analyst could, in fact, reconstruct selectively only pleasant memories (in the same way that he reconstructs selectively guilty Oedipal "memories") that might assist the patient in overcoming present difficulties. True, mechanistic-linear causality is very convincing*; if I see a car speeding toward me, I would rush to clear the way because if the car would hit me, that is, wound me, this wound could subsequently cause my death. Must we consequently accept also that if the car did not hit me, the sheer fear of being hit must cause subsequent problems?

Some clinical cases might illuminate the difference between mechanistic and cognitive causality. A caseworker told me that once she treated a thirty-five-year-old woman who was the mother of five children, all fathered by different men, whom she did not even remember. The relationship between this woman and her parents, who were originally slaves who had come from the South, was described by her in such absolutely negative terms that it was a "mission impossible" to dig out even one tiny good memory from that childhood experience. Being unable to alleviate the woman's poor financial situation or reach out to her in any other way, the caseworker felt quite helpless and frustrated until one day the woman walked into her office with a bag of potatoes that happened to be very cheap that day. In an attempt to communicate on any level, the caseworker launched into a discussion with

---

*Here it should be mentioned in passing that according to recent retro-causality theories, the laws in the physical sciences must not conform to linear causality.

the woman about the various dishes, including fried, boiled, or mashed potatoes, that could be prepared. As they talked, the woman remarked spontaneously every once in a while something to the effect, "I remember how my mother used to fry [boil, etc.] potatoes like this [or that]." The caseworker was then able to call the woman's attention to the fact that she was smiling pleasantly while she recalled these memories of her mother's cooking. Once the woman became aware of *some* pleasant memories, treatment took a new direction, in which pleasant memories from the past became the motivating energizing impetus for overcoming difficulties in the present.

When asked, upon termination of treatment, to articulate and summarize what she got out of treatment, the patient said to the caseworker: "You gave me new sweet memories of my past. Whenever I feel depressed and desperate during night or day, I think about you and the good memories from my home imbue my mind and these thoughts infuse me with strength to go on."

With a psychoanalytic orientation, it would have been probably imperative to concentrate on this woman's hostile feelings toward her parents until she had accepted a reinterpretation of her biography in which her Oedipal relationship with her parents became the "traumatic" cause of her inability to relate to men, her present predicament, and so on.

Additional examples of positive re-biographing in therapy might be drawn from such "uncommon therapists" as Milton Erickson. Jay Haley (1973:180) cited a case of a woman who came to Erickson and expressed fears of having children because she felt that she herself had had such a miserable childhood that she did not "know anything good about childhood" that she could pass on to her prospective children.

Through a series of hypnotic therapy sessions that lasted several months, Erickson introduced an "invented pleasant person" called the "February man," whom he then "planted" into this woman's childhood memories by using an age-regressing hypnotic psychodrama method. During each therapy session, Erickson would thus perform an age-regression hypnotic induction and then, by playing the role of the pleasant "February man," Erickson would conduct with this woman (who always enacted a different age in her childhood) pleasant conversations. Erickson made sure to coordinate the appearances of the pleasant "February man" with important dates in this woman's life, such as birthdays and holidays, so that as she progressed in age it became convincing to talk in a "natural" way about childhood and teenage interests, and this, in turn, reinforced her self-confidence.

It is difficult to establish the extent to which the selective retrospective "planting" into this woman's "memories of the past the feelings of an emotionally satisfying childhood" (p. 182) was the direct cause of subsequent consequences. It is also difficult to assess how advisable it is to "invent" a new past instead of selecting good memories. One may, however, plausibly assume that the fact that eventually this woman enjoyed the growth and development of three healthy children that she had borne testifies to the fact that in order to turn her into a happy mother, it was unnecessary to "excavate selectively" from her past any negative Oedipal memories of her high-society mother, who was always away from home, or of her over-compensating rich father.

To be sure, then, it is not just that pleasant memories are tabooed in all psychodynamic therapies, but that the predominant orthodox or classical psychoanalytic method of biographic reinterpretation is constructed on the negative-unpleasant causal role of psychosexual guilt and hatred memories in childhood.

To give the reader an illustrative clinical example in which the admitted predominance of the psychoanalytic orientation was used to reverse the self-chosen autobiography of a returnee (*baal teshuva*), let us consider also the following case study.

In his treatment report, Moshe Halevi Spero (1982) described a case of a returnee (*baal teshuva*) who was referred to him due to "personal conflicts" between his new religious beliefs and his periodic feelings of depression and loneliness, presumably resulting from lack of direction. This twenty-two-year-old man, who allegedly came from a home in which both parents were unstable alcoholics, insisted, according to Spero, on reinterpreting the process of his becoming a baal teshuva by comparing himself to the two major Talmudic role models, Rabbi Akiva and Reish Lakish.

This constructive self-chosen "ascent through descent" re-biographing, which was admittedly used for "reducing the cognitive dissonance which usually arises in the wake of contrast between former and current ideals, values, identifications, affiliations and self images" (p. 156), appeared quite reasonable since Rabbi Akiva, who became one of the sharpest Talmudists, began his religious studies and practices at the age of forty and Reish Lakish became a Talmudic sage after being a highway bandit. However, Spero preferred to reverse the re-biographic process by "excavating" "over the course of several months," this man's negative Oedipal "deeply suppressed hate for his parents" (p. 152). Since we are not told whether this negative "re-biographing" was more effective in resolving this man's "personal conflicts" (most probably because psychoanalysis is not a cure but a process of becoming conscious of the cause) compared to the relative adaptation of a person coming from an alcoholic unstable home, as he did, might have achieved through the self-chosen process of positive re-biographing, the question is not which of the two re-biographed versions contains the "narrative-historical truth." Rather the case demonstrates once more how a self-chosen cyclistic dissonance-reducing version of re-biography is rejected in favor of the predominant Oedipal linear-causal model, which is then a prioristically superimposed in reconstructing the biography.

168 / Rewriting the Self

While both those who use the Greek Oedipus and the Hebrew Talmudists, employ legendary heroes in an exaggerated fashion to foster re-biographing, in the first case, the manipulative ("missionary") therapeutic process reifies (obscures) the legendary basis for reinterpretation that deepens the rupture between past and present, while in the second case, the folkloristic self-chosen heroes (who were real historical figures) are not obliterated but used in a way that could reestablish cognitive consistency between past and present.

Thus, on a cognitive level, cyclistic reversed causality could work in the service of psychotherapy. Psychoanalytic linearity appears, however, to control not only the living people who seek therapy but also deceased personalities undergoing the postmortem process of psychobiography.

THE LINEAR BIAS IN PSYCHOBIOGRAPHY

To learn how the predominance of the psychoanalytic linear orientation to the past is prominent not only in the therapeutic profession, one need only skim through William Runyan's (1984) excellent analysis and review of the psychobiographic method. Runyan demonstrates how most psychobiographies of creative celebrities, such as Woodrow Wilson, Emily Dickinson, Wilhelm Reich, and others focused primarily not on how possible positive experiences may explain the subsequent contributions of these celebrities but how their negative childhood experiences provide causal explanations for their eccentric personality features.

Accordingly, it is very difficult to understand why Emily Dickinson's general seclusiveness and tendency to avoid people must have resulted from the "cruel rejection by her mother," although "there exists no record of any concrete instance in which Mrs. Dickinson took such an attitude toward her daughter" (p. 198). That is to say, that without the a prioristic acceptance of the psychoanalytic physical "traumata" dogma, one would attribute Dickinson's seclusiveness to her desire to concentrate on creative writing, especially if there was no historical evidence to refute this hypothesis.

In the same vein, it is even more difficult to connect Wilhelm Reich's impressive lifelong creativity to his traumatic experience of his mother's suicide, which he presumably caused inadvertently. But here again, although it is possible that suffering may generate creativity, no equal status is given to an alternative hypothesis, because Runyan's own psychodynamic bias comes through loud and clear when he admits, "my reading of the psychobiographic literature suggests that, in spite of errors sometimes arising from doctrinaire application of psychoanalytic theory . . . it has a role of fundamental importance in psychobiography" (p. 221).

A most absurd case of a psychoanalytic linearization of biographic reconstruction is Avner Falk's (1985) recent attempt to reinterpret the heroic Israeli leader General Moshe Dayan's courageous behavior as an underlying death wish caused by the Oedipal symbiotic relationship he had with his mother during early childhood. While it is obviously possible that the tremendous social reinforcement of Dayan's first "courageous" act, during which he lost his eye (even if it was accidental), became the cause of subsequent courageous behavior, Falk's selective linear biographic reinterpretation adheres to the popular psychoanalytic theory that even the road to a heroic paradise is in fact a hell paved with bad childhood experiences.

In summary, by returning to our proposed differentiation between linear conversion and cyclistic teshuvah, it would seem plausible now to posit that it is not merely the extension of the reified medical-physical *traumatic* model of linear causation to the mental sphere of *trauma* that makes positive rebiographing impossible (or at least difficult).

In other words, it is not the inability to exorcise Freud's ghost but it is rather vice versa, that the religious paradigm of conversion has at least partially affected the linear orientation of psychobiography and psychoanalysis.

The religious linear conversion perspective that I have in mind is the final "doomsday" or "judgment day" conception of time inherent in "original sin" based religions characterisic by and large of even recent Protestant thought (scc Dillenberger and Welch, 1954) that conceives of man's life as a declining "fall." In such cults or religions adhering generally to an "original sin" conception of life, society's or man's basic sin and guilt are seen as the cause of his subsequent irreversible and unshakeable suffering and falling-decline.

Since in such religions, future-hope refers to a timc beyond "the end of the present age," which cannot "be established by any human effort" (p. 282), it is only by a "born again" death-rebirth conversion to another cult or religion that the unchangeable sinful-guiltful past is eradicated and therapeutic-salvation made possible. By contrast, positive reinterpretation of the past is possible in the returning-teshuvah style of becoming religious.

We may conclude then that the two major ideal types, linear conversion and cyclistic returning, may be identified in processes of therapy, secular actualization, and becoming religious.

The association of these types with other cultural and behavior correlates and their possible subdivision into various subtypes remains, however, a task for future research. However, to complete our cyclical excursion into people's time-oriented possibilities for hermeneutic psychotherapy, I shall venture to tackle now the final and most difficult task of this book by exploring Midrashic narrativism of the future.

NOTES

1. It is of great interest to note here that Edwin Sutherland's old theory of "differential association" has accounted in its simplistic elegant formulation for the two

most crucial variables that seem to outlive most modern theories purporting to explain how one learns criminal and anticriminal behavior. These two intertwined variables, primary group pressure (or reinforcement) and the group's predominant value system, differ from what I termed *metacode* only in that I assume the latter (which originates in religion) to exert influence preceding and succeeding the impacts of concrete groups.

2. While the process of "converting" from the gentile world to Judaism is essentially dialectic, there are Talmudic opinions that retroactively include the *ger* (convert to Judaism) among those that were purified during the revelation at Mt. Sinai. Thus, in discussing the nature of idolators, the Talmud poses the rhetoric question:

> Why are idolators lustful: Because they did not stand at Mt. Sinai; for when the serpent came upon Eve he injected a lust into her, the Israelites who stood at Mt. Sinai, their lustfulness departed; the idolators; who did not stand at Mt. Sinai; their lustfulness did not depart. R. Aba son of Raba asked R. Ashi: What about proselytes? Though they were not present, their guiding stars were present. (*Shabbat*, 146:a)

Accordingly, since Jewish ahistoric conception of the revelation experience at Sinai demands that every Jew should consider himself as if he was present at Mt. Sinai, retroactively the re-biographic purification included the proselytes whose fate or star was already present at this experience. In another Talmudic passage, we find a more straightforward statement implying that proselytes were actually present at Mt. Sinai, where they accepted the commandments. In discussing how Moses adjured Israel to observe the Torah, the Talmud states

> We find in the case of Moses our teacher, when he adjured Israel [to keep commandments] he said to them: know that not according to your mind do I adjure you, but according to the mind of the Omnipresent . . . as it is said "neither with you only do I make this covenant and this oath but with him that standeth here with us this day before the Lord our God, and also with him that is not here with us this day" (Deut., 29:14). Hence we know only those who were standing by Mt. Sinai were adjured; the coming generations and the proselytes who were later to be proselytized, how do we know that they were adjured then? Because it is said "and also with him that is not here with us this day." And from this we know only that they were adjured for the commandments which they received at Mt. Sinai; how do we know that they were adjured for the commandments which were to be promulgated later, such as reading the Megilah? [the story about Mordechai and Haman on the Purim festival] Because it is said "they confirmed and accepted" (*Megilat Esther*, 9) they confirmed what they long ago accepted. (*Shavuot*, 39:a)

This last Talmudic statement then retroactively counts the proselytes among those who accepted "long ago" even those commandments that will be added in the future.

3. Rabbi J. B. Soloveitchick (see Peli, 1980) who, as indicated, differentiated between "blotting out the evil past" and transforming or "rectifying it," has in one place conceded that a person "who repents, erases with one blow, his whole past may become estranged as if he belongs to another eon, a different world" (p. 272).

Surprisingly, however, elsewhere Soloveitchick interpreted Maimonides' (*Tashuvah*, 2:4) famous stipulation that the *baal teshuvah* "changes his name to say I am someone else and I am not the person who committed these things" as follows: "What is considered in the words of Maimonides, 'another person' . . . is as though he has undergone a complete transformation. . . . Through repentance . . . man is reborn and he gains a new heart, a renewed spirit. . . . One man enters the bath of ritual immersion and another emerges from the water'' (p. 67).

While the above interpretation of Maimonides' ''name changing'' formula, seems indeed to contradict Soloveitchick's observation concerning the impossibility of erasing one's past, I think one should understand Maimonides' name changing notion not in ''death-rebirth'' terms but as a problem of social destigmatization.

The idea of name changing may be understood as a social identity problem if one reads on in Maimonides' teshuvah regulations: ''One day a person may be despised by the Lord, abhored and loathed and cast far away and the next he is loved and desired and close at hand, a friend.'' If emphasis is on being ''loved . . . desired . . . close . . . [and] a friend'' it is certainly not in one's own eyes but in the eyes of others, who are also not permitted to remind the repenter of his past (*Teshuvah*, 7:8). Here might be the proper place to add that Soloveitchick's reversed-causality model has been recently criticized by Norman Lamm (1986). Lamm's distinction between cyclistic contemplation of *teshuvah* and the linear process of actual sinning concurs with my distinction between cognitive and physical causality (i.e., trauma and traumata).

4. It is surprising, however, that Mills, who became inadvertently the father of criminological theories by explaining how people a posteriori account for their deviant conduct, attempted to present a linear theory according to which motives (in spite of their retroactive changing nature) cause subsequent actions. Indeed, Gordon Marshall (1981:24) challenged Mills precisely on this linear causality perspective: ''Mill's presentation . . . asserts that motives are 'causes' by dint of their being antecedent to the actor committing the act . . . but Mills fails to consider possible alternative functions of motivational rhetoric after the fact.'' Marshall (p. 26) hence contends that in spite of his ''attack on the varieties of psychological determinism . . . Mills cannot quite exorcise the ghost of Freud.''

5. Here I should again acknowledge Otto Rank's (1978) pioneering contribution because Rank was probably the first of Freud's students who ''dared'' to criticize Freud's therapeutic model, which, according to Rank, was based on two fallacious assumptions. The first was that present neurosis must be explained in historic-causal terms in which the infantile Oedipus complex must be evaluated in pathological terms, and the second was that in his desire to introduce psychology as part of the natural sciences, Freud mixed biological linear causality with psychological cyclic causality in which one constantly alters the past in the light of the present.

6. While it might appear now that re-biographing is possible according to both the Jewish-Midrashic ethic and the Calvinist-Protestant ethic, it is important to stress that Midrashic interpretation of one's failing past is based on spiritual corrections of one's behavior, unlike the Protestant ethic, in which re-biographing is based solely on material achievements.

9 The Midrashic Dialogue between Past and Future

While the anticipation, prediction, and projection of the future has been variously treated within such very different domains as theosophy and social planning, therapeutically oriented psychologists have tended to avoid tackling the "not yet here and not yet now." Thus, except for reinforcing and enhancing people's ability to plan their future realistically, "living in the future" or the possibility of having faith in a specific future is usually dismissed by psychologists as nonrational or even dangerous speculation associated with such nonverifiable notions as apocalypse, eschatology, teleology, utopia, messianic hope, or prophecy. It is ironic, however, that, in fact, "rational" scientists appear to have greater faith in the mysterious future than so-called irrational mystics because it is the former who believe in causality and deterministic prediction while the latter may have greater trust in multiple alternative outcomes occurring by chance. Indeed, George Henrik von Wright (1974) has shown, for example, that the assertion "it will rain tomorrow!" is causally deterministic only in the *ontic* sense that clings to the scientific laws of linear succession that presumably operate in nature. Accordingly, von Wright claims that an "open future" is possible only in an epistemic sense in which the "logic of tomorrow" consists of "perhaps" free will and on alternative probable outcomes.

While the "scientific" treatment of the future may thus contain a "double bind" message, Western eschewal of a psychological confrontation with the future is not due to its nontangible mysterious nature, but may possibly stem from its organic conception of human life and its consequent fear of the decaying process characteristic of oldness. Raised with a Hegelian-Freudian biological conception of man's linear development through the three phases of genesis, blossoming, and decay, Western man is taught to believe that after reaching his blossoming stage of consciousness and organic

172

fitness, he is doomed (programmed) to physical decline, while his spiritual fruits will leave him to join the accumulative progression of the World Spirit.

Indeed, consider how aging Western people are not only constantly busy trying to fake organic fitness in order to avoid being fired or retired but also are being excommunicated from most institutions "selling" spiritual growth. At an academic conference I once met a Western woman in her sixties who seemed unaware of how she kept telling me secretly and apologetically that she was studying for her Ph.D., and only after discussing seriously her uneasiness in the student role did we both recognize how the Western social norm urging *only* the young to acquire career degrees affected her.

It is not only that there is a need to invest in the young because their "future, which is their society's hope" is still ahead of them; rather, it is a matter of simple observation that while in Indian, Arabic, Chinese, or Jewish mystic and spiritual societies, the old usually play (in certain domains) *the* main leading roles, in Western hippie communes or spiritual growth centers, elderly people can usually not be found at all.

It must then be the cultural attitude toward, or rather the interpretation of organic fitness and spiritual achievements, that determines the relationship between youth and age; between past and future.

Put differently, it is the balanced meaning attributed to matter and spirit in space that entails also the possibility of a therapeutic dialogue between my past material-rational "I" and my own mysterious and hence irrational spiritual "it" or "thou" that lies ahead of me in my future.

To be sure, since Freudian therapy is grounded, as shown earlier, in an organic-biological conception of man, it must by definition dismiss the future as "an illusion" because the future constitutes a declining process of *exit* during which the old father's spirit is elevated (synthesized) by the Oedipal son while the father's organic decay spins him out of the spiral "future game."

There is a story about two Jews who, instead of going to the synagogue on the first evening of Rosh Hashanah (the Jewish New Year's Eve), would march to the cemetery one after the other. For many years this practice continued without either one exchanging a word but one day these two met and the follower asked the leader why he was going to the cemetery when everybody else was in the synagogue. The man's answer was that while everybody was busy welcoming the New Year, he felt a need to set a tombstone in the cemetery on which he inscribed one sentence: "Here is buried the past year!" He then asked the follower, "And why are you following me every year instead of going to the synagogue?" "After you leave the cemetery," answered the follower, "I turn over the stone you erect and inscribe on it 'Here was born the new year!'" Thus, the same tombstone commemorating the past might be turned into a cornerstone for building the future.

In this chapter it will be shown not only how Midrashic hermeneutics may be used as a mechanism for balancing matters and spirit in space but also how a dialogue between one's finite past and infinite future is possible in time. It will thus be demonstrated how it is only through the hermeneutic dialogue with the future that oldness can be kept from marking an exit from the rational and organic fitness phase of the finite past and present and turned into an *entering* stage into the mystical-spiritual phase of the infinite future.

Although the association between modernization and the relative decrease in the status of the aged is well-known from comparative anthropological studies of gerontology (see Cowgil, 1972), and while, likewise, one does not have to travel back in time to ancient Greece to note the differences between Spartan appreciation of physical fitness and Athenian reverence for spiritual achievements, the discourse to be presented below will attempt to interpret the interrelationship between spiritual and physical fitness into a psychological perspective on the possibilities of dialogue in time. Our first task must thus be to explore the Midrashic possibility of maintaining a therapeutic dialogue with the past.

CONTRACTING PAST FAILURES THROUGH HUMOROUS REREADING

In his introduction to Zunz's (1974) classical work on the Jewish Midrashic system, Chanoch Albeck stated that the study of the *Haggadah* "was divided into *peshat* (rational explanation), *derush* (concretizing interpretation) and *sod* (symbolic mystification). The *peshat* investigates the past, the *derush* introjects the present into the transmitted word and the *sod* investigates the eternal and the future" (p. 25).

This classification of the Midrashic system of narration obviously contains a time orientation. But what is the normative relationship between these hermeneutic categories, especially from the psychological perspective in which we are interested here?

In essence, the stipulation demanding a rational *peshat* attitude only toward the "no more here and now" factual and finite past, which allows a mystification of the "not yet here and now" infinite future, appears to be prima facie quite balanced and reasonable, although one might say that "you have to be *realistic* (i.e., rational) also about your future expectations."

Thus, the rational approach to the past may mean that one must *read* one's past and not *write* it, because the act of reading refers to a given text while the act of writing creates the text. While this is not the place to take up the dispute with the apocalyptic teleologists who would insist that even the future may only be "read" and not written because it is predetermined, here it is imperative to demonstrate how the rational reading of one's past as a factual *peshat* does not contradict the principle of contracting past failures by reinterpreting them. And, more important, it would be crucial to show here how the posited dialogue between the rational reading of my past failing

"I" and the writing of my future "thou" is possible. I would propose here that the difference between a *hermetic* strict reading and an open *hermeneutic* reading of one's factual past lies in the humorous transformative reading tradition of "tragic" events that evolved in Judaism from Midrashic narrativism.

In humorous reading of past failures, one does not change the facts according to an irrational mystic code, but transforms their meaning by contracting the negative elements ad absurdum so that failure may turn into an "ascent through descent" asset. With the strength inherent in one's ability to be strong enough to accept one's weaknesses, one may enter then into a dialogue with one' future.

But how is the therapeutic-mitigating through humorous rereading of past failure possible without changing facts or events? In other words, how does the *hermeneutic* approach to the past differ from the *hermetic* method without "reading into" this past or rather writing into it new facts? Let us consider the following hermeneutic exercise dealing with the general possibility of rehabilitative repentance as an illuminative contraction principle underlying the therapeutic narrativism available in the Midrash. The much-cited Talmudic (*Berachot*, 10:a) statement "Yitamu Chataim min Ha'aretz" (and sinners will cease to exist on earth) is popularly reread so that the word *Chataim* (originally referring to sinners) is reread to refer to *sins* only. This hermeneutic rereading technique, which now entails a nondeterministic and an optimistic overtone, is repeatedly used by Jewish moralists to emphasize that Judaism believes in the repentability of man, because the "ceasing" refers now to the sins and not to the sinner. This rereading, which is used very frequently as a rehabilitative slogan, contains nonetheless a logical drawback that could suggest that if there are no sins on earth, there obviously could not be any sinners. To reconcile this apparent logical inconsistency, one may suggest, for example, that the rereading of this Talmudic statement should focus not on the word *Chataim* (sins) but on the word *Yitamu* (will cease), which in Hebrew may mean also: "will become innocent" (*tamim*). Thus, past events that were perceived as failure do not have to be eliminated or erased but "contracted," that is, put in perspective, so that they may be seen as "innocent" childish episodes that one ridicules retrospectively in the light of present corrective aspirations concerning the future. Here the Cabalic notion of space-evacuating contraction (see Rotenberg, 1983) receives its temporal applicable meaning, which might have far-reaching effects for rehabilitation perspectives. An innovative rereading that concurs with Midrashic hermeneutic norms may, in principle, turn a Talmudic statement into a socialization dictum.

The *Yitamu* contraction of past failure (seen now as ridiculous innocent minor events) may evacuate and expand the now available and accessible space for future aspirations, anticipations, and success. This illustrative hermeneutic exercise is then the essence of Midrashic narrativism; every word can be read and reread in seventy ways so that the above Midrashic derivation may turn into guiding slogans for the humorizing contraction of past failure.

Indeed, this "rational rereading" technique, which should be distinguished from the Cabalic mystic methods of infinite secretive combinations and permutations of the Torah's letters (see Idel, 1985), constituted the bedrock for Jewish contraction of past failure, which we have discussed in different contexts in this book. But how could Midrashic contraction affect the psychology of everyday life? How could this idiosyncratic method of rereading be translated into a dialogue between past and future accessible to the common man? A careful examination would reveal that a variety of dramatizing and humorizing techniques evolved from the Midrash. Citing the Jewish sages, Heiniman (1982:9) stressed that in order to compete with the Roman-Hellenistic theaters and circuses, "the *derashot* [sermons] came not merely to provide teaching and guidance but also for entertainment and aesthetic enjoyment. And, indeed, in the course of hundreds of years, the *darshanim* [Midrashic experts] succeeded in attracting and fascinating their audience."

Heiniman (ibid.) emphasized further that the "uniqueness in the opening [of the *derasha*] was not only in form but also in the *darshan's* talent to rhyme from one issue to the other until he reaches the desired subject by using play of words, taking advantage of resembling tones and word or idea associations, etc" (p. 13).

It follows, then, that in a cultural tradition kept for hundreds of years, in which the Hebrew word *higuy* (pronunciation) is derived from the same root as the word *higayon* (logic), it should not be too surprising to find that every Jew turns into a linguist who plays on words, puns, and even tones that might transform, reverse, mitigate, and sweeten the meaning of the seemingly dictated bitter reality.

In *The Death of Tragedy*, George Steiner (1961) wrote that "tragedy is irreparable. It cannot lead to just and material compensation for past suffering. Job gets back double the number of she-asses; so he should for God has enacted upon him a parable of justice. Oedipus does not get his eyes or his sceptre over Thebes" (p. 8).

Thus, contrary to the way Christians such as Carl Jung read Job, the Jew who rejects the notion of the "original sin," who lives in an "a-tragic world" as Baruch Kurtzweill (1969:38) phrased it, reads Job as an optimistic parable that demonstrates how the suffering man may use "*Chutzpa* towards Heaven" and enter into dialogue with God, who eventually accepts his justified complaints and compensates him.

Survival, in terms of the possibility of expanding future aspirations, would thus depend on one's ability to contract and transform past failure to such dimensions that by rereading it, its bitter sting would be neutralized or midgetized. The road from the Midrashic narrative or "narrowing" approach to past failure, which contracts King David's adulterous sin (as I have shown earlier), to the Hasidic and folkloristic humorous story, is thus naturally paved. While there might be many rereading methods of contracting past failure, the case of humorizing past failures should be of special interest from the present therapeutic point of view.

A good example of how intergenerational continuity is rearranged by using a humorous tonal "c'est le ton qui fait la musique" rereading technique, nique, is the following popular Jewish joke:

> A son of a poor Jew residing in a poor small town (*shtetl*) in Russia, who went to study in the big city, sends his father a cable saying: "Father, send trousers." Since the local butcher could read Russian, the parents asked him to read the cable, which indeed he did like a butcher, and it sounded as if the son demands-commands his father to send him the trousers. The father, appalled, disappointed, and startled by his son's disrespect, refuses to send the requested pair of pants. The boy's Jewish mother's instinct told her, however, that apparently her son is suffering from the winter's cold, so she convinced her husband to try the local pharmacist who could also read Russian, because "possibly the butcher misread the cable." Indeed, after the pharmacist read the same words with a pleading respectful voice, the father said: "Sure, to such a nice respectful boy who requests so politely, I shall send a pair of pants, even if I have to sell my own."

Thus, while dialectic humor might be represented by a "slapstick" displacement or disguise of aggression directed against others, one of the functions of dialogic humor is to contract past failure on the one hand, while contracting the perfectness of his inflated ego on the other hand, so that via mutual contraction, communication is restored.

The therapeutic implications available in Jewish humor from "Sholem Aleichem" to Woody Allen is grounded now not only in the way the strong modeling ego contracts by displaying his faults to make room for the other who may drop now his own camouflaged faults (see Rotenberg, 1983) but in the way it teaches how those very faults and failures in one's past may be contracted and put into new perspective. Put in humorous terms, oldness or old times would mean that even nostalgia is no longer what it "really used to be," because you are free to control or expand it as needed.

Consider only how the classic Jewish humorist Sholem Aleichem (1972) contracted the bitterness of becoming a poor orphan not by denying or "suppressing" this biographical event but by expanding the pleasant feelings associated with being pitied and excused through a humorous rereading of this experience:

> I sleep with mother on father's bed—the only piece of furniture left in the house. She gives me practically all of the quilt. "Cover yourself" she says

"and fall asleep, my poor orphan. There is nothing to eat." I cover myself, but I don't sleep. I repeat the *kaddish* by heart. I don't have to go to school; I don't have to study; I don't have to pray; I don't have to sing. I'm free of everything. I'm free of everything. It's grand to be an orphan! . . . How my brother Eli discovered that I go fishing—I can't imagine. He almost tore my ears off, thanks to my fishing. Luckily, Fat Persie, our neighbor, caught him at it. A mother couldn't have defended her own child as she did me. "So that's how you beat up orphans!" My brother Eli is shamed and lets go of my ear. Everyone takes my part. It's grand to be an orphan! (Pp. 22–23)

There is a story about a Russian commissar who never hesitated to increase the amount of taxes to be collected from the poor Jews even when his special adviser for Jews reported that the Jews were crying and moaning. However, when finally, his adviser reported that the Jews were laughing and joking, the commissar decided to ease the burden and reduce taxes—because if they are laughing, "things must be really bad."

Is it thus a Jewish trait to contract misery by transforming it into laughter, which phenomenologically reconstructs their reality via free attribution of meaning? If the answer is affirmative, then we must ask ourselves whether there is a difference and, if so, what it is, between the Midrashic hermeneutic dialogue in time and the existential "here and now" free attribution of meaning?

Having outlined the basic guidelines for Midrashic contraction of past failure, let me demonstrate now how the present may be used not as a hedonistic existential *end* which ends "here and now" but as a pivot for expanding the mystic future.

EXISTENTIAL HEDONISM AND THE MYSTIC WRITING OF THE FUTURE

The eighteenth-century rabbi Yechezkel Landa (the *Noda Biyehuda*) stated (1827) that the

> usurer's punishment is known: he will not rise with the dead and the reason for it seems because it is said that in the future the sun will not shine during the day and during the night the moon will not give light because God will be the eternal light. . . . And it is known that the usurer's money increases by the renewal of day and night and he awaits the changing of time; in the evening he says, I wish it would be next morning and in the morning he yearns for the evening, when will a month pass. But if times will cease, how will his money multiply . . . therefore he does not expect God's light to shine. (*Derush*, 8)

This Midrashic disapproval of usury contains, in fact, both the explicit condemnation of a rational expectation of a calculated finite future in favor of an infinite mystic-messianic anticipation of hope, as well as an implicit condemnation of sacrificing the present for an anticipated improved future.

In Albert Camus's (1955) existentialism, the absurd man also condemns the sacrifice of the present, but his hedonistic worshipping of the present moment is due to an absolute disbelief in any future and hope.

> The absurd enlightens me on this point: there is no future. Henceforth this
> is the reason for my inner freedom. . . . The absurd man thus catches sight
> of a burning and frigid, transparent and limited universe in which doing
> nothing is possible but everything is given, and beyond which all is collapse
> and nothingness. He can then decide to accept such a universe and draw
> from it his strength, his refusal to hope. . . . But what does life mean in
> such a universe? Nothing else for the moment but indifference to the future
> and a desire to use up everything that is given. (Pp. 43,44)

Thus, while Camus's "here and now" existentialism comprises a revolt against the enslavement to a predetermining teleological past that would dictate the future, its actualization possibilities must, by definition, culminate in a nihilistic exhaustion of the present, "to use up everything that is given."

Indeed, it appears that in his *The Unheard Cry for Meaning* (1982), all that Victor Frankl added to his previous books was his own personal "Cry" and plea not to identify his "logotherapy" with this nihilistic kind of existentialism. Using the sand-clock analogy, Frankl thus argued that while

> existentialism sees only the narrow passage of the present and ignores the
> upper part and the lower part; the future and the past . . . logotherapy
> would assert . . . that when we shake the sand-clock, we may mix the sand
> pebbles . . . and change the future, and in the future, when future comes, it
> is possible for us to change ourselves. (P. 122)

Thus, although Frankl's conceptualization of the past is that of a closed memory book that, as indicated previously, cannot be changed, he maintains that existentialism reflects a pessimistic present and logotherapy maintains an optimistic attitude toward the future.

In discussing the therapeutic possibility of "re-biographing" in terms of contracting past failure through the narrative art of rereading, I said that we are actually dealing with the rehabilitative feasibility of a person's paradoxic hope to have a good past. In discussing the possibility of maintaining a therapeutic dialogue with one's future, we must now refute the teleological assumption that "people's future is usually behind them." The statement that a person's "future is behind him" is popularly used to describe someone who has apparently exhausted in the past all his potential achievements, but the belief that people's future is predetermined or dictated in the apocalyptic blueprint of historical necessity might cause people to feel that their future was indeed planned *behind* their back and *before* their time. The phenomenological inpact of such a "self-fulfilling prophecy" might thus lead people to believe in the absurd possibility of being sorry to have had one or another kind of bad (miserable) future—we are thus talking about the difference between the ability to *read* or *write* the future.

But how can one write a script of one's future realistically if one has not yet been there? Here we must realize that we can understand the possibility of dialogue between one's past "I" and one's future "I" only in terms of the balance between the finite rational-material and the infinite mystic-spiritual conceptions of life that prevail in particular cultures. It is thus not only the Hegelian-Freudian material-biological conception of man, which requires an accurate predictable reading of the deterioriating human flesh, but also the apocalyptic-teleological notion of human development in general, that demands a rational reading of the finite future, because if the future was planned, written, and fixed in the past, all we can do is read and predict it accurately.

Following a Hegelian-Freudian organic conception of human development and the apocalyptic perspective, we thus have two good reasons for shunning a confrontation with the future. First, if the future is theoretically and empirically predictable because it was planned and fixed in the past, who wants to risk apocalyptic-teleological predictions that might not materialize? How devastating such finite apocalyptic predictions may be we may learn from Victor Frankl's (1982:96) description of a concentration camp prisoner who died one day after he realized that the date that, according to his dream, should have been the day of release from camp had just passed.

Second, if the future, especially for aging people, comprises only organic deterioration of the body, who would want to occupy his mind with the unavoidable decay of his own organism?

In a prophetic-Midrashic culture where the future was not dictated in the past, only the finite past, which relates to given material facts and events, must be treated and read via the rational medium of *peshat,* but the infinite future might be freely written and experienced via the spiritual Midrashic exercises of the mystic-messianic *sod,* as Albeck indicated (see Zunz, 1974).

Here again the deterministic "rational" scientist would probably feel compelled to read the future, while, paradoxically, the irrational mysticist would feel freer or to write it. In a comparative study of American and Israeli students, it was found that Americans are more deterministic than Israelis in their retrospective linear prediction in relating people's present success or failure to their past history (see Rotenberg, 1978). Baruch Fishoff (ibid.) noted similar differences between Hebrew and English speakers in regard to event perception. While the Western "scientific" type depends compulsively on biographic "causes" to explain one's subsequent success or failure, for the "mystic" type, the very belief in a prophetic-messianic future constitutes the basis for constructing a present reality of hope that may enter into a dialogue with the future.

Indeed, Aharon Wiener (1978) has shown, for example, how "the manifold and lively Aggadic representations of Elijah's [the messianic-prophet] personality and of his activity . . . maintained the firm belief of the Jewish people that, at times of spiritual need or external danger in exile, God sends a helper who will finally be the immediate precursor of the future redemption of the Jewish people and of mankind" (p. 77). Moreover, from Wiener's study it becomes evident that since the psychology of the "Elijah factor" concerns the future, the more mystic its narrativism is, the more effective it becomes. Thus, Wiener maintains that in mystic "Chasidism the Elijah hero-figure . . . becomes an inner psychic factor: the dynamic relationship between God and man. By becoming aware of his role therein, man achieves his individual redemption" (p. 197). It follows, that a mystic-*sod* orientation of typical Cabalic-Hasidism may entail, for example, the components for dealing with man's future personal redemption, because "in Chasidism the Elijah-factor leads many to psychic unity by full harmonic activation of his potential" (p. 189). But what could be the nature of such full harmonic activation of one's potential? I venture to propose here that it may refer precisely to Albeck's harmonious dialogue between one's rational *peshat*-based material past and one's mystic *sod*-anchored spiritual future. Psychologically speaking, by using the term *future* in the present intrapersonal dialogical context, we actually have in mind the state of becoming older, because it is the possibility of a dialogue between one's own factual past (youth) and one's mysterious future (oldness) that we attempt to understand.

THE FUTURE AS "OLDNESS"

One can best understand the difference between the one-dimensional material-rational and the balanced material-spiritual treatment of the relationship between reading the past and writing the future by considering how various cultures deal with "oldness" or rather with *aging*.

Myerhoff and Simic (1978) have noticed, for example, that "the anthropological literature was not explicitly very informative as to what the universal themes of aging might be. . . . A major problem was the fact that aging . . . is in reality simply part of a relatively undifferentiated biological continuum through time" (p. 18).

Attacking the unjustified claim of universality, of theorists conceptualizing aging in terms of organic deterioration, *disengagement* or *deculturation*, Myerhoff and Simic argued that

> the dominant theme is that of *alienation*, and what emerges as a common thread is the perception of aging as a personal and social problem . . . that one of the principal reasons for anthropologists' neglect of the field of aging is that they have the same aversion to the subject that characterizes American society at large. (P. 15).

Thus, conceived as a Hegelian linear biological continuum of decay characterized by increasing alienation that marks a gradual *exit* from all activities of the young society of the "fittest," "aversion" of the subject should not be too surprising.

It should not be too surprising also that in Western Darwinian societies, aging people tend to *fake* organic fitness as long as they can and that, consequently, aging is studied mostly in organic terms of longevity and continuity, that is, that oldness is predictably assessed in terms of how long one can stretch one's ability to be revered by the society of the young fittest as a rational organic competent creature.

Indeed, until Robert Butler (1963) wrote what is considered to be a revolutionary thesis about the function of reminiscence in old age, "living in the past" instead of rationally facing the approaching "future" death was viewed by Western gerontologists as the worst pathology accompanying old age. It was only after Butler's "discovery" of old people's need to review their life, that studies (see Kaminsky, 1984) began to detect an inverse relationship between old people's state of increased depression, lack of self-esteem, or ego integrity and their inability to reminisce. However, ego-adaptive mechanisms in facing their "future" and the ability to retain a more consistent sense of identity was found to be related to one's ability to reminisce (even when stories were highly exaggerated)[1] and to one's ability to contribute to societies of the aged that de-emphasize physical fitness by concentrating on spiritual activities. Consider how in the popular play, *I Am Not Rappaport*, the vitality of the old Jewish socialist enchanted the audience because of his ability to relive "many pasts."

Thus, if one conceives of "oldness" as the age of "spirituality and mysticism" that is free from all rational-material commitments that one had to be engaged in during one's younger years, the dialogue between one's rational past and one's "irrational" future may be functional and feasible.

Indeed, in societies where aging may mark an *entry* into a new spiritual or mystical role, rationality and physical fitness are not conceived of as primary prerequisites for role entry because emphasis is put on the transcendental mystic conception of "future" reality. Thus, among the Druses and in the Jewish Cabalic tradition, one is allowed to begin one's mystic religious comtemplative studies only after reaching at least the age of forty (see Idel, 1980). In general, one may even notice a trend to fake oldness in societies that leave the rational-material activities to the young, and ascribe spiritual mystic understanding of the infinite future reality to the old (sometimes only those in secret societies), because in such societies one's semiotic appearance and presentation of self as an older person might then be equated with mystic wisdom.

Here it is worth demonstrating how the dialogue between the organic youth (past) and the spiritual oldness (future) as conceived in Arabic and

Jewish philosophical and mystic traditions is, in fact, diametrically opposed to the Hegelian paradigm of organic development. Most sources prohibiting the study of philosophy and Jewish mysticism before the age of forty, cited by Idel (1980:7–8), rely on a sequential inverse correlation between organic deterioration and spiritual growing potential.

The thirteenth-century rabbi Bechye stated, for example, that "forty years for wisdom; is the time . . . when man's construction begins to decay and the power of the flesh weakens. Since the flesh weakens, the power of the mind gains strength and purity."

Similarly, the thirteenth-century cabalist Abraham Abulafia asserted that "the age of forty is a turning point in man's spiritual development because at this age the human mind is born and man is redeemed from the physical powers and he will understand one thing from another" (pp. 7, 8).

That is to say that one has to reach at least the age of forty in order to be able to understand the secrets of Cabalic mysticism (*sod*), which requires abstract, inferential thinking. If one considers oldness as a transitional *entry* phase into a new spiritual role, it should not be surprising to discover Talmudic statements positing an accumulative spiritual progression featuring scholastic activity: "Talmudic scholars the older they grow, the more wisdom is added to them, and *Amey Haaretz* (ignorants), the older they grow, stupidity is added to them" (*Shabbat*, 152:b).

Thus, while in the Hegelian mode during the third phase of organic decline, the spirit is synthesized and elevated by the organic "fitting" Oedipal son, according to Jewish philosophers and mystics, oldness may mark a spiritual victory over organic tempting powers. Thus if one considers the applicable relevance of the Cabalic tradition of teaching and practicing Jewish mysticism mostly in esoteric secret groups into which only the elders may be admitted, we have in fact a therapeutic-actualizing model for exclusive clubs for the aged that would concentrate on the infinite transcendental-mystic. Since the aged have usually done all the necessary rational-material thinking during their youth, the focus on mysticism might be quite functional for this age, during which preoccupation with the mystic approaching death is a central issue, in any event.

It is thus not only the assembly of the elders who make decisions in ancient Judaism or in contemporary Druse society, but it is the fact that the ideal norm of mystic spiritual achievements is associated with oldness that might explain why young Jewish Talmudists usually look older than their age and do not worry about it.

As a matter of interest in regard to the passage "And Abraham was old" (Gen. 24:1), the Midrash (*Tanchuma, Toldot*: 6) says that it was Abraham who asked God to arrange that the physical mark of the white beard (*zakan*) will differentiate between the young and the old (*zaken*), because up to his time, if there was a strong resemblance between father and son, as happened in the case of Abraham and Isaac, it was impossible to distinguish between them.

Thus, the Hebrew word *zakan* (beard) and *zaken* (old) are not accidentally synonymous, but reflect the famous symbolic declaration of the Talmudic sage Rabbi Elazar, the son of Azaryah. It is well-known that this assertion "I am seventy years of age" (*Berachot*, 12:b) cited by every Jew on Passover eve was made in order to stress that oldness is equated with wisdom, because Rabbi Elazar was, in fact, much younger. Naturally, the radicalism of the "Abrahams" in their attempt to reverse the contemporary Western trend by acquiring the "older look" is associated with the honor and wisdom that the title "old" bestows upon its holders. Indeed, the Talmud states that the biblical verse: "Thou shalt rise up before the hoary head, and honour the face of the Old" (Lev., 19:32) is intended to stress that "there is no old but the one that acquired wisdom" (*Kidushin*, 32:b).

To be sure, as happens in most gerontocracies, the title "old" was associated in Ancient Israel with such high positions as judges and advisers. Thus God orders Moses to "Go and gather the elders of Israel" (Exod., 3:16) and tells him that together with them he will constitute an authoritative body that will be capable of negotiating with the King of Egypt: "And thou shalt come, thou and the elders of Israel unto the King of Egypt, and ye shall say unto him" (ibid., 18).

Thus, while an organic-dialectic conception of human development forces people to fake youth, the dialogic-spiritual time perspective urges people to fake oldness, which means that the future is transposed into the present. Oldness, associated with an entry into an infinite new spiritual role associated with wisdom, that, accordingly, must not and cannot be predicted rationally, not only because of its mystic-irrational nature but because it was not preplanned in the past, must also not cause aversion but constitute the essence of the psychology of hope. Accordingly, the future may be written and rewritten as tentative scripts by individuals conceiving of it as an open branching tree of wisdom. The therapeutic dialogue in time may thus be possible through the rational or rather rationalized *rereading* of one's past and the *writing* of one's mystic future.

But how may this dialogue between the rereading of my past "I" and the writing of my future "I" facilitate the transportation of this "I" from the past into the future so that it will not remain "stuck" in the failing past?

Before we plunge into a discourse about possibilities of reading the past and writing the future, a few comments about the relationship between temporality, reading, writing, and speech are in order.

ON READING, WRITING, AND DICTATING THE FUTURE

To differentiate between a teleological reading of one's future and the possibility of writing it, let us begin by referring to Ricoeur's (1984) explication of Saint

Augustine's conception of time. On the face of it one could measure time only if it has passed, that is, after it has stopped, because one can only measure something that has a beginning and an end. However, by drawing on Augustine's classic analogy of reciting a psalm, Ricoeur demonstrated how time could be measured in a present, that is, while it is still lasting and happening.

While I am doing injustice to the very complicated theory of time presented by Ricoeur, for our limited purpose the following point seems relevant. The act of reciting (by heart?) a psalm that one knows, maintained Augustine, is divided between the two faculties of *memory* and *expectation*; the one looking backward to the past to that part that I have already recited, that is, remembered, and the other looking forward to the part that I have still to recite, that is, that I expect to recite in the very near future. Thus, while the relationship between past and future is portrayed as a measurable activity of the mind mediated through the cognitive processes of memory and expectation operating in a certain present, from our point of view, both processes involve merely the act of reading.

It is thus the difference between Augustine's expected "reciting" (reading by heart) of this part of the future "psalm" that one knows already as it was written, that was preplanned in the past, and the free narrative interpretive writing of one's future "psalm" according to personally suited meaning one derives from the psalmist's poem. Admittedly in both cases there is a "psalm" that was written in the past; nonetheless, in the first case, it is a teleological-predetermined blueprint for the future, whereas in the second case, it is only a general open outline awaiting creative narrative writing. To bring this discourse closer to the therapeutic arena in which we are interested here, let us now turn to a different famous analogy concerning the reading-writing controversy.

In a presentation of the psychoanalytic narrative as a transformational axis between writing and speech, Bellin (1984) tried to show that Freud's early positivistic notion of "psychic determinism," according to which the past determines the future, was later modified into a model of re-transcription. Bellin thus indicated that in Freud's later thinking, it was the clinical context taking place in a present that signified and reordered past events into an ever-widening hermeneutic circle that is always open for reinterpretation. Bellin asserted that without any clear distinctions between reading, writing, and speech, Freud moved "from a topographical writing metaphor of transcription and retranscription to an energetic metaphor of translation and finally to a speech metaphor since. . . . the writing metaphor . . . subsumed under speech . . . seems closer to the clinical context" (pp. 7,8).

Indeed, in his "Note upon the 'Mystic Writing-Pad'," Freud (1955) not only equated writing with speech, but also cleverly interconnected this linguistic topography with his mother discipline, neurology, from which he received his scientific status as a physician.

Thus, the psychic apparatus of perception is described as being composed of layers of neurological tissue, with the preconscious and conscious external tissues receiving their stimulation from the deeper tissue of the unconscious. However, as happens in the mystic-pad, when the writing vanishes every time the close contact between the paper that receives the stimulus and the wax slab that is to preserve the impression is broken, so we may understand, according to Freud, the preconscious and the conscious in terms of a "celluloid and wax paper cover" that operates as a protective shield against the unconscous "wax slab." The point to be stressed here is that according to Freud (pp. 230–31) it is the unconscious "wax slab" deep layer that dictates and stimulates perception and it is thus a vertical process moving from the bottom to the top layers in order "to diminish the strength of excitations" (by disconnecting the celluloid and wax paper cover) in an attempt to protect themselves against the dictations of the unconscious.

Freud thus uses the "mystic writing-pad" analogy against all logic, because it is usually the free writing on the paper from the top to the bottom wax slab that may be preserved or erased by disconnecting the top from the bottom and not the other way around. By assuming that nothing is erased from the unconscious, Freud's determinism rejects even the palimpsestic possibility of writing a new text to replace inadvertent erasure.

In Freud's analogy, there is thus only a reading of a telex that ignores the fact that on the other side of the ocean someone wrote this telex freely. Thus Freud did not really discard his positivistic determinism, he only covered it with a "wax paper" that may be temporarily disconnected. Moreover, Freud's mystic writing-pad analogy constitutes only a *restorative* model (see Scholem, 1972) in which one may read the past and its dictated fundamentalistic reconstruction in the future, whereas in the *utopian* conception of the future, which may presumably surpass whatever has ever existed before, one should be able to write one's future as often as one wishes (see Buber, 1958).

Accordingly, when a person says, "I wanted to do so many things, but life kept getting in the way . . .," he confesses, in fact, to a belief that "life" and not his free will dictates his actions. Writing your own life script means, however, activating your own free will.

It is by following Jacques Derrida's (1978) revised version of the "mystic pad" analogy, according to which writing supplements perception, that we may introduce in our final chapter the "script writing" approach to the possibility of dialogue between past and future.

NOTE

1. In a study assessing rehabilitation programs for cardiac patients (see Bar-On, 1986), it was found that an autobiographic "story" explaining why a particular patient

incurred a heart attack was crucial in determining therapeutic motivation and rehabilitation prospects. The point is that among those re-biographic stories that contributed to rehabilitation, neither accuracy of the story nor knowledge of the physical-medical facts were relevant or related to successful rehabilitation.

10 The Temporal Dialogue as "Chutzpah Therapy"

As we are not concerned here with gerontology or oldness per se but with their implications for the possiblity of dialogue between past and future, let us now consider operational possibilities for what I would venture to term a psychotherapeutic intrapersonal or temporal dialogue.

Let us begin by restating that the reason for my brief concentration on oldness was that it seems paradoxically central to the understanding of the temporal dialogue under consideration, as it relates to the past and to the future all at once and at the same time. That is to say, when we think about *other* old people, antiquity and images of the past spring to our imagination, because these old forefathers were born and were living in times past. Yet, when we think about *our* own oldness, we dream and think about the same or other images in future terms.

Oldness thus constitutes the dialogic meeting point between past memories and future dreams. Projecting memories and dreams thus become the major dialogic tools establishing dissonance or consonance between past and future. I have already indicated that while Freudian past-oriented dreaming interpretations usually prohibit prognostic projections into the future, in some Eastern cultures, such as the Senoy of Malaya (Stewart, 1969) or among Jewish mystics, people may be trained to solve dilemmas concerning their future by projecting them in their dreams.

Yoram Bilu and Henry Abramovitch (1985) have found, for example, that among Arabs and Jews from Morocco, a continuity between awakening and dreaming states prevails, and people will work out in their dreams complete dramas and dilemmas concerning their future with which they are preoccupied during the time they are awake. Ceremonial rituals during annual pilgrimages to graves of holy men are thus used as stage-setting hasteners for dreaming and also to involve the dead holy man in the psychodramatic

188

dream in order to receive advice or a hint from him that would then be used to reinforce future action. Since, therapeutically, the psychodrama may thus become the meeting point between past memories and future dreams, let us explore the temporal element in role-playing a bit further.

THE PSYCHODRAMATIZATON OF THE FUTURE

While the psychodramatic dream that is known since Talmudic times is to-day still highly popular in Eastern and mystic societies, in J. L. Moreno's (1953) therapeutic method of psychodrama, the reinterpretive projections into the past and the script-writing rehearsals of the future appear as the most suitable technique for the hermeneutic dialogue in time. Moreno (1966), the founder of psychodrama, began his time-perspective formulation by departing from Freud's organic past orientation: "Time, in the psychoanalytic doctrine, is emphasized in terms of the *past*. Freud, an exponent of genetic psychology and psychobiology, found going back and trying to find the causes of things of particular interest" (p. 146).

By introducing a variety of dramaturgic techniques, Moreno thus demonstrated how people can reenact, and thus reread and correct, their past as well as rehearse their anticipated future by stimulating interactive dramas with the help of group actors.

People may thus reenact new versions of past failures or write the script and rehearse anticipated marriage, divorce, or old age in order "to develop new techniques of living without risking serious consequences of disaster as they might in life itself" (p. 150).

The prevention of "risking disastrous consequences" is of particular interest from the present perspective because on the one hand, it permits one to act out the infinite mystic future with its irrational fears of the unknown and on the other hand, it allows one to humor and contract (minimize) past "traumas" or future anxieties[1] in a protected manner, as stated by Moreno (1953): "The humor of it may prevent and heal many potential grievances which might otherwise have led to actual conflict. . . . In actual life situations an individual often has difficulty in learning from a mistake due to the earnestness of the situation" (p. 534).

Thus, while Moreno's psychodrama might had laid the foundations for the contemporary popular simulation game technique, it should be stressed that psychodrama allows projection of mystic irrational future dreams, while simulation usually requires strict adherence to mere rational speculations.

This is not the proper place to dwell on the therapeutic techniques of psychodrama. From the present perspective, we might point out, however, that while Jacob Moreno was the creator of psychodrama, "Moseh Rabeno" (Moses, our Rabbi, in Hebrew) was probably its first Midrashic subject. A well-known and much-cited Talmudic Midrash (*Menachot*, 29:b) relates that when Moses ascended to Heaven to receive the Tablets he found God attaching many crownlets to many letters of the Torah. When Moses inquired about this peculiar activity, God is said to have answered that one man—Rabbi Akiva is his name—will, in the second century C.E., interpret mountains of laws on the basis of these crownlets. To understand the meaning of this futurist hermeneutic development, the Midrash says, God allowed Moses to skip ahead a few hundred years and visit Rabbi Akiva's Talmudic college. Nevertheless, when Moses, now participating in Rabbi Akiva's psychodramatizing group, tried to understand what Rabbi Akiva taught his disciples, he was unable to follow the lessons and he felt very aggrieved until he heard one student asking Rabbi Akiva: "How do you know that your interpretations are correct?" Rabbi Akiva's answer, that "this is the law given to Moses on Mt. Sinai," in fact epitomizes the Jewish hermeneutic dialogue in space and time, since it demonstrates how pluralism within unity and continuity, in spite of exegetic freedom, may coexist ad absurdum. Thus Moses may not understand how his own teaching is being interpreted and yet every interpretation is traceable to Moses, who received it at Mt. Sinai.

Indeed, this classic Midrash, which I say contains the essence of the hermeneutic dialogue in time, is phrased grammatically in such anachronistic terms that "the future is the present and both are also the past," as Yonah Frankel (1978:167) was able to show. More specifically, here the Midrashic dialogue between past, present, and future psychodramatizes the possibility of hermeneutic freedom of the Midrashic "I want" within the unity of the Halachic "he is being coerced" by playing with the temporal dimension of grammar and content. Frankel thus shows that Rabbi Akiva is described as existing in the present, which might mean that there will always be such sharp-minded interpreters as Rabbi Akiva, and, similarly, Moses' subsequent query: "Why was he and not Rabbi Akiva chosen to receive the Torah" is expressed in the same Midrash (ibid.) in terms of the present, which might be intended to stress that each generation might interpret the Torah according to the "Judge that shall be in those days" (Deut., 17:9). However, God's answer to Moses (ibid) "this is the thought which has emerged before Me" refers to the past (has emerged) to stress how the eternal hermeneutic unity surpasses all times.

The peculiar paradoxical compatibility and continuity between the written law of Moses and Rabbi Akiva's oral law takes us to our final concluding discursive query: Is hermeneutic therapy nothing more than a dialogue geared to balance various opposing entities in space and time?

In other words, is the presumptuous psychology of self-renewal actually a psychological device for restoring order between matter and spirit, between rationalism and mysticism, between the legal determinism of "he is being coerced" and the Midrashic free will of "he says I want"? To show how self-renewal through individual interpretation may surpass collective determinism, I shall now return to deal with the paradoxical relationship between individual repentance (*teshuvah*) and collective messianism. More poignantly, I shall attempt now to convince the reader that Midrashic therapy indeed stands for a writing conception of the future.

THE PSYCHOTELEOLOGY OF "MESSIANISM"

The imperative assertion: "Everything is expected (foreseen) and permission is given" (Fathers, 3:15) is used most frequently by Jewish philosophers to stress how the paradoxical belief in God's ability to foresee the future should not be mistaken as an unavoidable determinism counteracting people's individual freedom and their personal obligation to choose between good and evil and act accordingly.

It is also well-known that in Judaism, the messianic idea of future redemption oscilates forever between the two paradoxically related yet opposing possibilities of passive messianic determinism and active repentance. Thus, in regard to the deterministic element of redemption, Scholem stated (1972) that "the paradoxical nature of this conception . . . is in no causal sense a result of previous history" (p. 10). That is to say, that in contrast to the prophetic active view of messianism, which urges man to exercise his free will to repent and thus enact his ability and fulfill his responsibility in hastening the process of future salvation, the deterministic view maintains that the future, which is predetermined, will take place when the time is ripe and redemption has nothing to do with progress and man's efforts.

The dynamic tension between universal collective determinism and particularistic individual free will and personal responsibility, which to my mind is characteristic of the Jewish philosophy of paradoxical dialogue, is clearly reflected in Maimonides' (*Teshuvah*, 6:5) rhetorical treatment of such controversies as the predetermined slavery and torture of the Israelites in Egypt and the Egyptians' subsequent punishment:

> While it is written in the Torah (Genesis, 15:13) "and they shall serve them and they shall afflict them four hundred years" and hence He decreed-ordered the Egyptians to commit evil? . . . and why did He punish them? because He did not apply the decree to a specific known person . . . each one of the Egyptians, if he did not want to treat them [the Israelites] badly, permission is given. . . . He merely notified [Abraham] that his offsprings will eventually be enslaved in a country not of their own.

Put in modern terms, in this, as in many other passages, Maimonides reaffirms the principle of dialogic relationship that is to prevail as a rule of thumb between universal Heavenly determinism (everything is expected or foreseen) and human-individualistic freedom of choice and personal responsibility (permission is given).

While it is thus predetermined that as a collectivity the Israelites will be tortured by the Egyptians, the Egyptian individual was not preordained to commit this evil.

After introducing the Midrashic system of "deterministic free will" as a principle underlying the possibility of dialogue between past and future, let us consider whether this paradoxical double-bound system is unknown to the modern psychological thinker. I would suggest that the portrayed tension between the passive future conception of "everything is foreseen" and the prophetic active free-willed view of "permission is given" concurs, in fact, with Joseph Rychlak's (1979) teleological formulation of psychotherapy.

More specifically, while future redemption is predetermined, it is also unknown to man and thus he is free to write the script of his infinite mystic future, which retrospectively might then be conceived of as predetermined. Indeed, this is precisely the way Rychlak defines teleology:

> A free-will psychology is not inconsistent with the view of behaviour as also determined. Moving determinately toward a *predetermined* end is what will or will-power means! The question of freedom arises over whether or not it is possible to select one's ends. If we believe that it is possible, then we hold to a *teleology*. (P. 7)

Here it is of interest to note, however, that while Rychlak's definition of teleology is time-oriented, the term *tele* as used by Moreno (1964) refers to space where it takes on a different meaning

> Tele (from the Greek word far, influence into distance) is feeling of individuals into one another the cement which holds groups together. . . . Like a telephone it has two ends and facilitates two-way communication. . . . Telic relationships . . . are crucial for the therapeutic progress. (P. xi)

It is self-evident then that if we are to combine these two definitions of *telos* into one therapeutic conception of interpretation in time and in space, we might say that individual freedom of interpretation may operate diachronically within the deterministic limits of one's vertical progression possibilities in nature, and synchronistically within one's horizontal expansion possibilities in the collectivity.

Such a formulation of dialogue would then concur with a socially balancing definition of hermeneutics. In what I have termed *reciprocal-individualism* (see Rotenberg, 1978), personal interpretation would not be suppressed but enhanced via reciprocity. Indeed, Smith (1968) condemned, for example, both the collective kind of interpretation that "employs mass symbols [and] operates with an official interpreter who is not questioned, and eliminates individual interpretation and understanding" and the individualistic interpretation that "rejects what is common to all, denies the power of symbols to unite men" (p. 247).

But then again, if the hermeneutic dialogue operates merely as a force balancing opposing elements in the interpersonal sphere of space and in the intrapersonal sphere of time, in what sense does it differ from any compromising restorative system that entails no creative potential for progress? To cancel such an interpretation of the hermeneutic dialogue, we must return to differentiate between individual repentance and collective messianism. While this is not the place to dwell on the complicated phenomenological differences between passive-deterministic and active repentance-based notions of messianism, it would be useful for the present purpose to differentiate briefly between the Jewish and the Christian conceptions of messianism. It is in this messianic arena that the questions of man's ability to *read* or *write* his finite or infinite future receives its full therapeutic meaning. Jacob Neusner (1983) is probably right in arguing that in order to understand the anachronistic yet future-oriented language of salvation that characterizes the Talmud and the Midrash, one has to consider the historical-political developments that accompanied their compilation mainly during the third and fourth centuries.

Very briefly, what could be the proper and effective response to such disappointing events as the Christianization of the Roman Empire or the tantalizing postmessianic disillusion following Emperor Julian's failure in the fourth century to rebuild the Temple in Jerusalem as he had promised? It must obviously revolve around the most basic theological doctrine on which Jews and Christians disagree, and this doctrine is the messianic dogma that, according to the Christians, must be defined in terms of the *past* and that Jews must define in terms of the *future*. Thus, what could be a more concrete and effective device to rebuff the dangerous belief that perhaps Jesus was after all the Messiah, and what could be a more concrete dynamic living symbol that could substitute for the loss of the symbolic space-anchored It is, thus, the Oral Torah, which should in fact remain always "oral" and alive but which *now*, due to the rapid dissemination of Christianity (between the first and sixth centuries), must be written down so that it will be tangible, visible, and powerful enough for the symbolic inculcation of an unshakeable future-time-oriented messianic psychology of hope.

As Neusner (1983) indicated:

> The promise of salvation contained in every line of Scripture was to be kept in every deed of learning and obedience to the law effected under their auspices. To be sure, they projected backward the things they cherished in an act of . . . extraordinary anachronism. But in their eyes they carried forward, to their own time, and themselves embodied the promise of salvation for Israel contained within the written Torah of old. (P. 120)

Indeed, even Achad Ha'am (1946), one of the secular leading ideologists of the nineteenth-century Jewish Enlightenment school interpreted the meaning and purpose of studying the Talmudic oral law in precisely the messianic-futuristic terms with which we are concerned here: "Our forebearers, who transmitted to us the Torah, admitted . . . that also the Torah itself was observed by us only for the sake of the future, and without him, there would be no justified substance for observing her" (p. 148).

Achad Ha'am thus cited a Midrash from *Sifrey* confirming that "although I [God] exiled you from the Land, you [Israel] should excell in commandments so that when you return they will not be new for you." Moreover, claimed Achad Ha'am, this engagement and indulgence in Talmudic studies had a direct phenomenological impact on enhancing trust in the future:

> This philosophy about the Torah encouraged them to take the trouble to author complete tracts dealing with minor details concerning the laws of sacrifice, the priests' clothing, their work, etc., not out of love for researching antiquities . . . but because they believed full-heartedly that all these will be renewed and become once more questions of living. . . . and these tracts, with which the lads of Israel dealt generation after generation, were very effective in implanting the hope for the future deep deep in the heart of the nation, as they accustomed their students to consider the anticipated future as something real, and worthwhile of preparing for it and loosing time over it by engaging in questions, which concern it. (Ibid.)

Moreover, Achad Ha'am (1946) emphasized that the preoccupation of rationalists like Maimonides with compiling the "laws of Messiah," which he then included, in spite of major objections, among the "main religious principles," was due to his understanding that "without hope for the future, the Torah, with all its logical principles, is doomed to be forgotten" (p. 148).

Indeed, the historian Lionel Kochan (1977) has shown that the axis of Jewish survival was their messianic conception of history, in which the past was always reshaped in order to remold and transpose this past into the future. Moreover, although the influential German sociologist Max Weber (1967) portrayed the Jews as Pariah people, he admitted that in contrast to the caste status quo system,

> For the Jew the religious promise was the very opposite. The social order of the world was conceived to have been turned into the opposite of that promised for the future, but in the future, it was to be overturned. . . . The world was conceived as neither eternal nor unchangeable. . . . Its present structures were a product of man's activities, above all those of the Jews. . . . The whole attitude toward life of ancient Jewry was determined by its conception of the future. (P. 7)

Thus, if the future according to Christian theology can only be *read* in the Scripture because it must be interpreted as a reconstruction of a redemption that has already occurred in the past, then it must be finite and rational because if the events of the past have already happened, they must be known. Here, indeed, the teleological slogan "his future is behind him" may operate as a vicious-circled self-fulfilling prophecy because the person who was described by his significant others in this way may come to believe that he has indeed exhausted all his potentialities in his predetermining past. By contrast, if the Talmud and Midrash are to be studied not as a sanctified static-closed ontology but as an oral-open Messianic eschatology, then this unknown future redemption may call for a *writing* interpretation of an infinitely expanding future that may surpass what has ever existed before. Indeed, this is precisely the difference between Scholem's (1972) "restorative" and "utopian" categories of messianism. While in "restorative" messianism, promises are turned backward to reestablish and reproduce an ideal past that has once existed, in "utopian" messianism, hopes are directed to the reestablishment of an ideal past plus an ideal future that will be better and surpass anything that has ever existed before.

In my *Dialogue with Deviance* (1983), I maintained, as alluded to earlier, that Scholem's "restorative" form of future development finds its parallel in a contemporary psychological unilateral theory of personal growth such as Bandura's (1969) behavioral copying theory in which personality is explained as a unilateral process of copying or reproducing a model's behavior.

In Bandura's theory, as in most common psychological theories, there are no clear assumptions about how the son may influence or surpass the father's modeling behavior. Drawing on the Hasidic-Cabalic contraction paradigm, I have introduced the bilateral developmental model of "emulative-chutzpah" according to which man may influence God; son may influence, emulate, and surpass father by standing on his contracted soft shoulders instead of stamping on his stiff corpse. I have hence suggested that the Talmudic (*Sanhedrin*, 105:a) dictum: *"Chutzpah* toward Heaven is effective" in fact epitomizes the psychological-developmental theory of dialogic mutual contraction, because the son's permission to dare, challenge, and surpass his father does not infer the "killing" or the demolishing of this father as would presumably happen in dialectic behavior patterned after the Oedipal myth.

To extend the "emulative chutzpah" model from its *inter*personal present-based sphere in space to the *intra*personal sphere of future time, let us conclude our discourse by demonstrating how a modern Cabalic-oriented thinker such as the influential Rabbi A. I. Kook conceives the dynamic relationship between repentance and redemption as a transcending process surpassing any past paradise.

FUTURISM AND THE KOOKIAN MODEL OF "CHUTZPAH THERAPY"

Rabbi Kook (1977), who as the first Chief Rabbi of Palestine was accepted as a legal (*halachic*) authority and, in view of his writings, as a Cabalic philosopher, portrays repentance and the consequent state of redemption as an integration between two complementary forces: the collective-deterministic and the individual-volitionary process:

> Through general [collective, universal] *teshuva* [repentance] everything *returns* to the Divine, through the existence of the *teshuva* power prevailing in all the worlds, everything returns and is reconnected to the existing completeness of the Divine and through the ideas of *teshuva* . . . all thoughts, ideas and opinions, motivations and emotions are transformed . . . the general *teshuva*, which is the ascending of the world and its correction, and the private *teshuva* which concerns the individual personality of every one . . . they are together one content. (Pp. 22–23)

On the face of it, we have here a structural model according to which repentance constitutes a reconstructive-rearrangement of a paradise reality that has existed before, since "everything returns to the Divine" order. But the allusion to the "ascending of the world" already entails the notion that future redemption refers to a transcending, and not merely to an ascending, process.

Here the idea that man is a *creature* and a *creator* culminates in a very powerful and dynamic theory of what can be termed "transcendental chutz-pah therapy." Here the deterministic idea of "he is being coerced" until he "says I want," that is, until he will be able to enact his creative-corrective free will to transcend his reality, is anchored in, or rather lays the foundations of, a most basic twofold radical educational principle: On the one hand, if one's "paradise" is prepared by God or by one's parents, one will never feel the need or be motivated to exert one's personal will or transcend one's reality. On the other hand, if one lives in "hell," one will be unable to withstand the sudden explosive event of collective messianic redemption, as some determinists portray this *a*historic future of messianic salvation. Therefore, as a starving man can consume food only gradually through the concerted efforts of the "feeder" and the consumer, so the transcending into the redeemed future may be understood only in such Cabalic dynamic terms as *coercive* (deterministic) Divine contraction or *breaking* (of the vessels), which may urge man to enact gradually his "I want" to "eat" and uplift the holy sparks and to repent for the sake of corrective transcendance.

Thus, Rabbi Kook (1974) stated:

> Why did the breaking come? because the Divine gives according to his power, and the receiver is limited, so it will be a limited favor . . . because the receiver, the one who was created will not be able to receive unless he breaks entirely. And he will construct with his desire to return to his unlimited [infinite] source . . . and with this, the creature will make himself, and will reach the perfected level of a creator and he will transcend the limit of creature [one who was created]. (Vol. 2:527)

Ascending into the future is thus not merely a teleological acting out or reading of a finite plan that was dictated in the past, but a gradual transcendental process of contraction and expansion into the infinite future that may surpass all possible paradistic realities that existed in the past. It is a dynamic state of tension between reading and writing the future. Indeed, to construe the possibility of transcending into the infinite future, Rabbi Kook (1974) differentiated between two sets of terms: between the free will verb of ascending (*iluy*) and the static state of transcending (*hitalut*) and between the noun, *perfection* (*shlemut*) and the verb *perfecting* (*hishtalmut*):

> The infinity contains the negation of the possibility of addition, since what can be added to infinity, to perfection? and one must . . . construct unceasable addition which will transcend, through a deficit which prepares the addition, through contraction which facilitates expansion. (P. 528)

Thus, Rabbi Kook (1974) stated that

> the infinite, the way it is revealed to us, comprises . . . transcendentality (*hitalut*) and eternal addition . . . and although . . . there is no ascent (*iluy*) from its infinite aspect . . . still it contains this superior power of constant transcendance (*hitalut*) and this is conceived as if the absolute perfection (*hashlemut*) perfects itself (*mishtalemet*) through the act of perfecting (*hishtalmut*). (P. 530)

Future redemption thus conceived does not constitute a mere return to the primordial "paradise" that once existed; it constitutes a paradoxical "progressing backwards" because the *Chadesh Yamenu Kekedem*, "renew our days" is much more than the "Kekedem" because the word *Kekedem* paradoxically refers to the past "as old days" (*Kadum*) and to progress (*Kidma*), which refers to the future.

> The appearance, through which people come to experience the creation not as a thing that is already done and finalized, but as a matter which is constantly becoming and transcending, developing and rising, this is what lifts it from under the sun to above the sun, from a place where there is nothing new, to a place where there is nothing old, where everything is renewed. (Ibid., p. 517)

Without unduly overwhelming the reader with citations from Rabbi Kook's Cabalic poetic language, we may return to show now that man's "coerced" free will to activate his ability to transcend the infinite future reality by "progressing backwards" is, in fact, inherent in what I like to term his psychological "chutzpah power" to repent.

It is thus not only that "every thought of repentance (*teshuva*) encompasses all that has passed into the future and the future transcends itself through the ascending will of teshuvah" (see Kook, 1983:41) but that this will to transcend constitutes in essence the messianic notion of "chutzpah."

While the Talmudic (*Sota*, 49:b) assertion that "in the footsteps of the Messiah chutzpa will increase" is conventionally interpreted in derogative terms, Rabbi Kook (1982), who conceived our era as marking the beginning of messianic redemption, narrated this passage in the following radical way:

> This generation is strange, it is naughty, it is wild, but also superior and elated. . . . We will find on the one hand that "chutzpa will increase, the son is not bashful in front of the father, lads will embarrass the old," but on the other hand, feelings of charity, integrity, law and pity are overpowering, the scientific and ideal power explodes and ascends. The bulk of the young generation feels disrespect to what it was habituated to, not because its soul darkened, not because it was degraded beneath the limit on which the law and justice stands . . . but because he ascended to the point that [is relatively high in comparison] . . . according to what he was accustomed heretofore. . . . He grew and ascended at once, the troubles which washed and purified him gave him a conditioning heart and a thinking brain. . . . His spirit made him wings and in the heavens he will ascend and there his wish is not yet given to him. (P. 109)

Thus, if there is some truth in what Thomas (1928) wrote, that situations become real in their consequences if people define them as real, then teaching people to descend into their past in order to reread it so that they may ascend and plunge courageously into their infinite spiritually transcending future reality would indeed constitute the essence of "chutzpah therapy," in which one may freely write one's script for the future and not merely "recite" it verbatim, as a psalm written in the past.

In his therapeutically oriented "script analysis," Eric Berne (1961) indicated that the bulk of people seeking psychotherapeutic help suffer from a feeling that they are doomed to live out scripts that were written or rather dictated during their childhood or early adolescence.

Berne maintained further that these people believed that such tragic life scripts as "drug addiction," manic-depressive psychosis, and others operate in a teleological vicious circle of repetition compulsion, so that they are programmed to repeat the acting out of their scripts throughout their lifetime. Berne, who said that in order to break such self-fulfilling vicious circles, one has "to close down the show and put a new one on the road" contended, in fact, that therapy must teach people to *write* the scripts of their future instead of reading it as an unchangeable blueprint of life plans.

The following case reported by a colleague practicing child psychology elucidates the possibility of switching from reading to writing one's future even in the most extreme event, as in this case, when one's past has emerged from the atrocities of the Holocaust and one's present comprises a detrimental physical illness that requires one's future script for life to depend on periodic medical checkups that may only guarantee life for the next six months.

Dan (a fictitious name), whose parents were, as alluded to above, Holocaust survivors, was at the time of treatment, eleven years of age. Dan had undergone very serious surgery at the age of one month, and ever since, his "life expectancy" for the next six months depended on those periodic medical checkups mentioned earlier.

Dan, who initially refused to talk about those "checkups," conveyed, nevertheless, the feeling that for one reason or another each one of his immediate family members suffered from an injury or defect with which he was doomed to live. Put differently, Dan felt that for each of them, a tragic script had been written before their time. Thus, for a long time, all that Dan did during therapeutic sessions was to burn in a large tin can, all plastic, wooden, or other obsolete utensils that he could gather. He would then take a careful account of what "survived" the fire, which and how other items became deformed, what was turned into ashes, and so on. After sessions, Dan would forbid the therapist to clean up the ashes, which as a result of the burned plastic naturally left an almost unbearable smell in the room. When, subsequently, the therapist gave Dan a piece of clay, he made a human skeleton out of a paper clip and, after forming a human body out of the clay by molding it around the paper-clip skeleton, he used to burn this human figure and be fascinated by the way the skeleton survived the fire while the clay became all twisted and deformed.

Guided by the therapist, Dan gradually planted into this human figure various body parts, such as eyes made of pin heads, and so on, and from this point on, the therapeutic discussions began to evolve around the miraculous power of renewal inherent in seemingly deformed and broken elements. The therapist then noticed that while up to this time all that Dan did (e.g., swimming and karate lessons) was interpreted by him as means of survival, with his new surgical replanting preoccupation, he switched gradually to a constructive orientation of training and planning for the future, that is, writing his script for the future.

Accordingly, discussions employing such terms as *chimneys* (referring possibly to crematoriums), *manslaughter*, and *altars* switched gradually to consideration of the possibilities of reconstructing imperfect entities, to observing how a few raindrops bring relief and hope to the world on a hot sticky day, and the like. In a similar fashion, Dan observed how one day, out of all the arrows he used, it was only with the broken arrow that he hit the bull'seye.

Finally, in summarizing his changes and gains after an extended period of treatment, Dan stated that what still bothered him was being "ashamed of his memories, since memory is a two-edged sword." He then spoke freely for the first time about his medical checkups and, with the help of the therapist, began to plan for a future in which he saw a variety of unlimited potentials, because he realized that "everything which contains the power of survival, entails also the power of building and growing. Strength may be generated from weakness and perfection from defection." In other words, Dan finally made a full switch from reading his predetermined future to writing it. Dan's case does not expound or represent a new method or an innovative technique of a "future therapy"; rather, it is intended to illuminate the very process by which even the case of a dictating memory of an extremely fragile disillusioning finite past may turn, via present discovery of the power inherent in defection (contraction), into an expanding power to write one's infinite mystic future. Moreover, the "shame of the memories" that were perceived as a "two-edged sword" must now be understood in the sense that it is not so much the particular therapeutic method, but the change in the hermeneutic code, that granted Dan a new reading of his past, which previously he had seen as a predetermined cause of his future, and that enabled him also to move to the next step of writing his future script. Thus, while the popular ideal of "survival" may in fact connote merely the perceptual reading of the past, *chutzpah* may stand for an expansive writing of the future.

In conclusion, by using Rabbi Kook's writings as a case study to demonstrate how a Midrashic approach to a futurist kind of mysticism explicates the possibility of psychological self-renewal in terms of a psychology of hope and transcendence into the infinite future, I did not intend to claim that Rabbi Kook is representing the Midrashic school in Judaism. If likewise, I seemed to present Rabbi Kook's *vaiten Kook* (prophetic vision, in Yiddish) theosophy as a new futurist psychology or as a novel approach to surpassing the future, I haven't said much because this possibility is inherent in many philosophies, such as Bergson's (1978) theory of creative development. There couldn't be found, however, a better contemporary case study than Rabbi Kook's. The phenomenological impact of his philosophy on the future turned out to be as powerful as it did precisely because his messianic futurism was derived mainly from the long Cabalic-mystic school of *Sod*, which he integrated with the contemporizing schools of *derush*.

Thus, it is this very infinite "utopian" conception of redemption, in which universal deterministic messianism and free-willed repentance meet in a concerted dialogue, that has exerted from the time of Rabbi Kook's writing, such diversified-controversial influence on *his* future, which is *our* present, be it in the psychological, political, or religious domains. Consequently it is also Rabbi Kook's mysticism, that might serve as a useful case in point for studying how the hermeneutic dialogue between matter and spirit, between past and future, may be effectively applied to a psychology of self-renewal.

NOTE

1. I would like to cite an example of an a prioristic neutralization of a "bitter past" by humorizing it from my own family drama. When my "disorganized" daughter was about to join the Israeli army, we both anxiously anticipated the punishments that she would incur due to her unavoidable clashes with the strict army rules. When we psychodramatized and humorized such possible unpleasant experiences by role-playing how they would be recounted by her many years later, she was able to perceive them as funny adventures that happened "years ago" in the army. The irony following this exercise was that she was decorated upon finishing her basic training.

Bibliography

Achad Ha'am. *Al Parshat Derachim*. Tel Aviv: Dvir, 1946. (Hebrew)

Achi-Meir, A. *The Trial*. Tel Aviv, 1968. (Hebrew)

Alexander, I. F. "The Freud-Jung Relationship: The Other Side of Oedipus and Countertransference," *American Psychologist* 37(9): 1009–1018, 1982.

Alter, R. *The Art of Biblical Narrative*. New York: Basic Books, 1981.

Amir, E. *Tarnegol Karparot*. Tel Aviv: Am Oved, 1984.

Amsel, A. *Rational-Irrational Man*. New York: Feldhaim, 1976.

Angyal, A. *Neurosis and Treatment: A Holistic Approach*. New York: Wiley, 1965.

Arlow, J. "The Personal Myth." Unpublished paper presented at the Hebrew University of Jerusalem, 1985.

Aviad, J. *Return to Judaism*. Chicago: Chicago University Press, 1983.

Avineri, S. *The Social and Political Thought of Karl Marx*. London: Cambridge University Press, 1969.

Bakan, D. *The Duality of Human Existence*. Boston: Beacon Press, 1966.

_____. *Slaughter of the Innocents,* Boston: Beacon Press, 1972.

Bandura, A. *Principles of Behavior Modification,* New York: Holt, 1969.

Bar-On, D. *Makel Hapantomimai*. Tel Aviv: Mayrav, 1986. (Hebrew)

Bateson, G. *Steps to an Ecology of Mind*. New York: Ballantine Books, 1972.

Bauer, B. *Die Judenfrage*. Braunschweig: F. Otto, 1843.

Bauman, Z. *Hermeneutics and Social Science*. London: Hutchinson & Co., 1978.

Bellin, E. H. "The Psychoanalytic Narrative: On the Transformational Axis Between Writing and Speech," *Psychoanalysis and Contemporary Thought* 7(1):3–42, 1984.

Ben Yechezkel, M. *Sefer Hamasiyot*. Vol. 4. Tel Aviv: Dvir, 1951. (Hebrew)

Berger, P.L. *Invitation to Sociology*. Garden City, N.Y.: Anchor Books, 1963.

Bergman, S. H. *Dialogical Philosophy*. Jerusalem: Mosad Bialik, 1974.

Bergson, H. *The Developmental Creativity*. Jerusalem: Magnes, 1978. (Hebrew)

Berkowitz, E. *Not in Heaven*. New York: Ktav Publishing, 1983.

Berne, E. *Transcendental Analysis in Psychotherapy*. New York: Grove Press, 1961.

Bettelheim, B. *Freud and Man's Soul*. New York: Vintage Books, 1984.

Biale, D. *Gershom Scholem Kabbalah and Counter-History*. Cambridge: Harvard University Press, 1982.

Bilu, Y. and Abramovitch, H. "In Search of the Saddig: Visitational Dreams among Morroccans." *Psychiatry* 48(1):83–93, 1985.

Bloom, H. *The Anxiety of Influence*. New York: Oxford University Press, 1973.

Boschwitz, F. *Julius Welhausen*. Tel Aviv: Dvir, 1982.

Buber, M. *Mamre: Essays in Religion*. Melbourne: Melbourne University Press, 1946.

_____. *Moses*. New York: Harper Torchbooks, 1965.

_____. *Paths in Utopia*. Boston: Beacon Press, 1958.

_____. *Tales of the Hasidim: Early Masters*. New York: Schocken, 1978.

Butler, R. "The Life Review: An Interpretation of Reminiscence in the Aged" *Psychiatry* 26:65, 1963.

Camus, A. *The Myth of Sisyphus.* New York: Vintage Books, 1955.

Chaye Moharan. Jerusalem, 1952.

Cloward, R., and Piven, F. *The Politics of Turmoil.* New York: Vintage Books, 1974.

Cohen, H. *Dat Hatevenu Mimekorot Hayahadut.* Jerusalem: Mosad Bialik, 1971.

Collingwood, R. G. *The Idea of History.* London: Oxford University Press, 1980.

Conway, F., and Siegelman, J. *Snapping.* Philadelphia: J. B. Lippincott, 1978.

Cowgill, D. O. "A Theory of Aging in Cross-Cultural Perspective." In *D. O. Cowgill and L. D. Holmes (eds.), Aging and Modernization.* New York: Appleton-Century-Crofts, 1972.

Culler, J. *The Pursuit of Signs.* Ithaca: Cornell University Press, 1981.

Cullman, O. *Christ and Time.* London: SCN Press Ltd., 1951.

d'Aquili, E. G. "The Myth-Ritual Complex: A Biogenetic Structural Analysis." *Zygon* 18(3):247-269, 1983.

d'Aquili, E. G., and Laughlin, C. D. "The Neurobiology of Myth and Ritual." In E. G. d'Aquili et al. (Eds.), *The Spectrum of Ritual.* New York: Columbia University Press, 1979).

Davidson, J. M. "The Physiology of Meditation and Mystical States of Consciousness." *Perspectives in Biology and Medicine* 19:345-378, 1976.

Deleuze, G., and Guattari, F. *Anti-Oedipus Capitalism and Schizophrenia.* New York: Viking Press, 1972.

Derrida, J. *Writing and Difference.* Chicago: University of Chicago Press, 1978.

De Voragine, J. *The Golden Legend.* New York: Longmans, Green & Co., 1941.

Diamond, S. "Kibbutz and Shtetl: The History of an Idea." *Social Problems* 5(7):71-79, 1957.

Dillenberger, J., and Welch, C. *Protestant Christianity.* New York: Charles Scribner's Sons, 1954.

Dinnur, B. "Hakarat Heavar Betodaat Haam Uveayot Hacheker Ba." A. Segal and S. Safrai (Eds.), *Awareness of the Past,* pp. 9-24. Jerusalem: The Historical Society of Israel, 1969.

Doi, T. *The Anatomy of Dependence.* Tokyo: Kodansha International, 1973.

Eisenstadt, S. N. "Introductory Lecture." *Mizug Galuyot.* Jerusalem, Magnes Press, 1969.

_____. *The Transformation of Israeli Society.* London: Weidenfeld & Nicholson, 1985.

Eisenstein, J. D. *Otzar Midrashim.* Vol. 1. Tel Aviv: Beit Eked, 1969. (Hebrew)

Eliade, M. *The Myth of the Eternal Return.* Princeton: Princeton University Press, 1974.

Fachler, M. "Two Models of 'Return' among Israeli Women." Unpublished M.A. thesis, The Hebrew University of Jerusalem, 1986.

Fackenhaim, E. L. *God's Presence in History.* New York: Harper & Row, 1972.

_____. *The Jewish Return into History.* New York: Schocken, 1978.

Falk, A. *Moshe Dayan Haish Vehaagada.* Jerusalem: Kana Press, 1985. (Hebrew)

Falk, Z. *Hebrew Law in Biblical Times.* Jerusalem: Wahrmann, 1964.

Felman, S. "Beyond Oedipus: The Specimen Story of Psychoanalysis." In Davis R. C. (ed.), *Lacan and Narration.* Baltimore: The Johns Hopkins University Press, 1983.

Fingaratte, H. *The Self in Transformation.* New York: Basic Books, 1963.

Fishman, A. "Lehashpaat Hachasidut al Hamisna Hazoialit Harishonit shel Hapoel Hamizrachi." In *Fifth World Congress for Jewish Science*. Vol. 2, pp. 268–276. Jerusalem, 1972. (Hebrew)

Flavius, J. *Antiquities of the Jews*. Baltimore: Armstrong & Plaskitt, 1830.

Flor-Henry, P. "Psychosis, Neurosis and Epilepsy." *British Journal of Psychiatry* 124:144–150, 1974.

Frankl, V. E. *The Doctor and the Soul*. Middlesex, England: Penguin Books, 1965.

_____. *Man's Search for Meaning*. Tel Aviv: Dvir, 1982.

_____. *The Unheard Cry for Meaning*. Tel Aviv: Dvir, 1982. (Hebrew)

Frankel, Y. "Hermeneutic Problems in the Study of the Aggadic Narrative," *Tarbitz* 47(3–4):139-172, 1978. (Hebrew).

Freud, S. *Complete Psychological Works*. Vol. 4. London: Hogarth Press, 1900a.

_____. *The Interpretation of Dreams*. Vol. 4. London: Hogarth Press, 1900b.

_____. *Totem and Taboo*. Vol. 13. London: Hogarth Press, 1900c.

_____. "A Note upon the Mystic Writing Pad." *Standard Edition*. Vol. 19, pp. 226–232. London: Hogarth Press, 1955.

_____. *Civilization and Its Discontents*. New York: W. W. Norton & Co., 1961.

_____. *Moses and Monotheism*. New York: Vintage Books, 1967.

_____. *The Wolf-Man*. New York: Basic Books, 1971.

Fromm, E. *The Fear of Freedom*. London: Routledge & Kegan Paul, 1960.

Gadamer, H. G. *Truth of Method*. London: Sheed & Ward, 1975.

_____. *Hegel's Dialectic*. New Haven: Yale University Press, 1976.

Gardner, H. *The Shattered Mind*. New York: Vintage, 1975.

Garfield, S. L., and Bergin, A. E. (eds.). *Handbook of Psychotherapy and Behavior Change*. New York: Wiley, 1978.

Geschwind, N. "Disconnective Syndromes in Animals and Man," *Brain* 88, 1965.

Gesta Romanorum, London: George Bell & Sons, 1891.

Ginzberg, L. *The Legends of the Jews*. Vol.6. Philadelphia: The Jewish Publication Society, 1968.

Glanz, D., and Harrison, M. I. "Varieties of Identity Transformation: The Case of Newly Orthodox Jews." *Jewish Journal of Sociology* 20(2):129–141, 1978.

Glazer, N., and Moynihan, D. P. *Beyond the Melting Pot*. Cambridge: MIT Press, 1970.

Goffman, E. *Asylums*. Chicago: Aldine, 1956.

Graetz, H. *The Structure of Jewish History*, edited by Ismar Schorsh, New York: The Jewish Theological Seminary of America, 1975.

Greenstone, J. H. "The Pilpul System in the Talmud." In *Students Annual*. New York: The Jewish Theological Seminary of America, 1914.

Gregen, K. J., and Gregen, M. M. "Narratives of the Self." In T. R. Sarbin, and K. E. Scheibe (Eds.), *Studies in Social Identity*. New York: Praeger, 1983.

Habermas, J. *Knowledge and Human Interests*. London: Heinemann, 1972.

Hakohen, Yaacov Yosef. *Toldot Yaacov Yosef*. Jerusalem: Agudot Beit Vayelifaly, 1963.

Haley, J. *Uncommon Therapy*. New York: Norton & Co., 1973.

Handelman, S. A. *The Slayers of Moses*. Albany, N.Y.: State University of New York Press, 1982.

Harrison, M. I. "Sources of Recruitment to Catholic Pentecostalism," *Journal for the Scientific Study of Religion* 13:49–64, 1974.

Hartman, D. *A Living Covenant*. New York: Free Press, 1985.
Hegel, G. W. F. *Philosophy of History*, New York: P. F. Collier and Son, 1900.
————. *Die Vernunft in der Geschichte*. Leipzig: Felix Mainer, 1920.
————. *Early Theological Writings*. Chicago, 1948.
————. *The Phenomenology of Mind*. London: George Allen and Unwin, 1964.
————. *Phenomenology of Spirit*, Oxford: Oxford University Press, 1979.
Heidegger, M. *Being and Time*. London: SCM Press, Ltd., 1962.
Heilman, S. *The People of the Book*. Chicago: University of Chicago Press, 1983.
Heineman, Y. *Darchey Haggadah*. Jerusalem: Magnes, 1970.
Heiniman, Y. *Derashot Bezibur Bitkufat Hatalmud*. Jerusalem: Mosad Bialik, 1982.
Heirich, M. "Change of Heart: A Test of Some Widely Held Theories about Religious Conversion." *American Journal of Sociology* 83(3): 653–680, 1977.
Heschel, A. J. *Man Is Not Alone*. New York: Harper & Row, 1966.
Hodge, B., and Fowler, R. "Orwellian Linguistics." In B. Fowler, B. Hodge, G. Kress, and T. Trew (Eds.), *Language Control*. London: Routledge & Kegan Paul, 1979.
Horowitz, R. "Rosenzweig's Influence on Buber's I and Thou." In *Proceedings of the Sixth World Congress of Jewish Studies*, Jerusalem, pp. 111–120, 1977.
Husserl, E. *The Phenomenology of Internal Time-Consciousness*. Bloomington, Ind. Indiana University Press, 1964.
Idel, M. "Infinities of Torah in Kabbalah." In J. H. Hartman and S. Rudick (Eds.), *Midrash and Literature*. New Haven: Yale University Press, 1986.
Idel, M. "Letoldot Haisur lilmod Kabala lifney gil haarbaim." *American Jewish Studies Review* 5, 1980.
————. "We Have no Kabbalistic Tradition on This." In I. Twersky, (Ed.), *Rabbi Moses Nachmanides (Ramban): Exploration in His Religious and Literary Virtuosity*. Cambridge: Harvard University Press, 1983.
————. "Introduction," *Zaphnat Paaneach*; Joseph Elashkar (ms 1529), 1985. (Hebrew)
Jacobs, L. *A Tree of Life*. London: Oxford University Press, 1984.
James. W. *The Varieties of Religious Experience*. London: Fontana Library, 1971.
Japhet, S. *Emunot Vedeot Besefer Divrei Hayamim*. Jerusalem: Mosad Bialik, 1977.
Jones, E. *On the Nightmare*. London: Hogarth Press, 1931.
Jung, C. G. *Modern Man in Search of a Soul*. New York: Harcourt, 1933.
Kadushin, M. *Organic Thinking*. New York: Block Publishers, 1938.
Kafka, F. *Briefe 1902-1924*. New York: Schocken, 1958.
Kalin, M. G. *The Utopian Flight from Unhappiness*. Chicago: Nelson Hall, 1974.
Kaminsky, M. (Ed.). *The Uses of Reminiscence: New Ways of Working with Older Adults*. New York: The Haworth Press, 1984.
Kant, I. *Religion Within the Limits of Reason Alone*. New York: Harper & Row, 1960.
Kermode, F. *The Genesis of Secrecy*. Cambridge: Harvard University Press, 1980.
Kierkegaard, S. *Fear and Trembling*. Garden City, N.Y.: Doubleday, 1954.
————. *The Concept of Anxiety*. Princeton: Princeton University Press, 1980.
Kochan, L. *The Jew and His History*. New York: Schocken, 1977.
Kohut, H. *How Does Analysis Cure?* Chicago: University of Chicago Press, 1984.
Kook, A. I. *Orot Hakodesh*. Jerusalem: Mosad Harav Kook, 1974.
————. *Orot Hateshuvah*. Jerusalem: Galor Press, 1977.
————. *Adar Hayakar*. Jerusalem: Mosad Harav Kook, 1982. (Hebrew)
————. *Arfiley Tohar*. Jerusalem: Hamachon al Shem Haraya, 1983. (Hebrew)
Koyfman, Y. *Bein Netivot*. Haifa: Beit Hasefer Hareali, 1952.
Krochmal, N. *Kitvey Rabbi Nachman Krochmal*. London: Ararat, 1961. (Hebrew)

Krol, A. *Befikudecha Asicha*. Jerusalem: Levin-Epstein, 1978.

Kurtzweill, B. *Bemavak al Erkey Hayahadut*. Tel Aviv: Schocken, 1969.

Lamm, N. "Teshuvah: Thought and Action." Unpublished paper, 1986.

Landa, Y. *Ahavat Ziyon*. Vol. 1. Prague, 1827. (Hebrew)

Leavy, S. A. *The Psychoanalytic Dialogue*. New Haven: Yale University Press, 1980.

Lerner, M. *Surplus Powerlessness*. Oakland: The Institute for Labor & Mental Health, 1986.

Lev Aovot Hashalem. Jerusalem, 1970.

Levi-Strauss, C. *Structural Anthropology*. New York: Basic Books, 1963.

_____. *The Savage Mind*. Chicago: Chicago University Press, 1966.

Lifton, R. J. *Thought Reform and the Psychology of Totalism*. Middlesex, England: Penguin Books, 1967.

Lofland, J. *Doomsday Cult*. New York: Irvington, 1966.

_____. *Deviance and Identity*. Englewood Cliffs, N.J.: Prentice Hall, 1969.

Lofland, J., and Skonovd, N. "Conversion Motifs." *Journal for the Scientific Study of Religion* 20(4):373–385, 1981.

Lofland, J., and Stark, R. "Becoming a World-Saver—A Theory of Conversion to a Deviant Perspective," *American Sociological Review* 20(6):862–874, 1965.

London, P. *The Modes and Morals of Psychotherapy*. New York: Holt, 1969.

Luria, R. A. *Highly Cortical Functions in Man*. New York: Basic Books, 1966.

Maimonides, M. *Guide to the Perplexed*. London: Trabner & Co., 1885.

_____. *The Code of Maimonides*. New Haven: Yale University Press, 1949.

_____. *Moreh Nevuchim*. Jerusalem: Mosad Harav Kook, 1977. (Hebrew)

Malinowski, B. *Sex and Repression in Savage Societies*. New York: Harcourt Brace, 1927.

Mancuso, J. C., and Sarbin, T. R. "The Self-Narrative in the Enactment of Roles." In T. R. Sarbin and K. E. Scheibe (eds.), *Studies in Social Identity*. New York: Praeger, 1983.

Manuel, F. E. *Shapes of Philosophical History*. Stanford: Stanford University Press, 1967.

Marcuse, H. *Eros and Civilization*. New York: Vintage Books, 1962.

Margaliyot, E. *Hachayavim Bamikra Vezakaiim BeTalmud Ubamidrashim*. London: Ararat, 1949. (Hebrew)

Margalioth, M. *Encyclopedia of Great Men in Israel*. Tel Aviv: Yavne, 1977. (Hebrew)

Marshall, G. "Accounting for Deviance." *The International Journal of Sociology and Social Policy* 1(1):17–45, 1981.

Marx, K. *Communist Manifesto*. Chicago: Henry Regnery Co., 1949.

Matza, D. *Delinquency and Drift*. New York: Wiley, 1964.

Mead, G. H. *The Philosophy of the Present*. Chicago: The Open Court Publishing Company, 1959.

Mills, C. W. *Power, Politics and People*. London: Oxford University Press, 1974.

Montanino, F. "Protecting the Federal Witness." *American Behavioral Scientist* 27(4):501–528, 1984.

Moreno, J. L. *Who Shall Survive?* Beacon: Beacon House, 1953.

_____. *Psychodrama*. Vol. I. Beacon: Beacon House, 1964.

_____. "Psychiatry in the Twentieth Century: Function of the Unmersalia: Time, Space, Reality and Cosmos." *Group Psychotherapy* 19(3–4):146–158, 1966.

Myerhoff, B. G., and Simic, A. *Life's Career—Aging.* Beverly Hills, Calif.: Sage Publications, 1978.
Neisser, U. *Memory Observed.* San Francisco: W. H. Freeman & Co., 1982.
Neumann. E. *The Origins and History of Consciousness.* New York: Harper, 1962.
Neusner, J. *Midrash in Context.* Philadelphia: Fortress Press, 1983.
Nietzsche, F. *On the Genealogy of Morals.* New York: Vintage Books, 1969.
_____. *On the Advantage and Disadvantage of History to Life.* Indianapolis: Hackett, 1980.
Nisbet, R. A. *Social Change and History.* New York: Oxford, 1979.
Norris, C. *Deconstruction Theory and Research.* London: Methuen, 1982.
Nottingham, E. *Religion: A Sociological View.* New York: Random House, 1971.
Peli, P. H. *On Repentance.* Jerusalem: Orot, 1980.
Peres, Y. *Ethnic Relations in Israel.* Tel Aviv: Hapoalim, 1978.
Perls, F. S. *Gestalt Therapy Verbatim.* Lafayette: Real People Press, 1969.
Philo. New York: Putnam Sons, Loeb Classical Library, 1930.
Popper, K. R. *The Poverty of Historicism.* London: Routledge & Kegan Paul, 1960.
Rank, O. *Das Inzest-Motiv in Dichtung und Sage.* Leipzig: Franz Deuticke, 1912.
_____. *Will Therapy.* New York: W. W. Norton, 1978.
Rappel, D. *The Debate Over the Pilpul.* Tel Aviv: Dvir, 1979.
Rav Pealim. Warszawa: Halter and Eisenstadt Press, 1894.
Ricoeur, P. *Freud and Philosophy.* New Haven: Yale University Press, 1970.
_____. *The Conflict of Interpretation.* Evanston, Ill.: Northwestern University Press, 1981.
_____. *Hermeneutics and the Human Sciences.* London: Cambridge University Press, 1983.
_____. *Time and Narrative.* Chicago: Chicago University Press, 1984.
Rieff, P. *The Triumph of the Therapeutic.* New York: Harper & Row, 1966.
Robert, M. *From Oedipus to Moses.* New York: Anchor Books, 1976.
Roitman, B. "Sacred Language and Open Text." In G. H. Hartman and S. Budick (eds.), *Midrash and Literature.* New Haven: Yale University Press, 1986.
Rosenzweig, F. *Kochav Hageula.* Jerusalem: Mosad Bialik, 1970. (Hebrew)
_____. *The Star of Redemption.* Boston: Beacon Press, 1972.
_____. *Naharayim.* Jerusalem: Mosad Bialik, 1977.
Rossi, I. *From the Sociology of Symbols to the Sociology of Signs.* New York: Columbia University Press, 1983.
Rotenberg, M. "Conceptual and Methodological Notes on Affective and Cognitive Role-Taking (Sympathy and Empathy): An Illustrative Experiment with Delinquent-Non-Delinquent Boys." *Journal of Genetic Psychology* 125, 1974.
_____. "Cognitive Role-Taking among First and Third Year Social Work and Pharmacy Students." *International Social Work* (2):53–58, 1975.
_____. *Damnation and Deviance.* New York: The Free Press, 1978.
_____. *Dialogue with Deviance, the Hasidic Ethic and the Theory of Social Contraction.* Philadelphia: ISHI, 1983.
_____. "Imperialistic Missionarism and the Kibbutz Paradigm for Co-Existence." *Zygon: Journal of Religion and Science* 21(4), 1986.

Rotenberg, M., and Diamond, B. L. "The Biblical Conception of Psychopathy: The Law of the Stubborn and Rebellious Son." *Journal for the History of the Behavioral Sciences* 7(1), 1971.

Rotenstreich, N. *Bein Avar Lehoveh.* Jerusalem: Mosad Bialik, 1955. (Hebrew)

_____. *Judaism and Jewish Rights.* Tel Aviv: Hakibbutz Hameuhad, 1959. (Hebrew)

_____. *Tradition and Reality.* New York: Random, 1972.

_____. "On Cyclical Patterns and Their Interpretation." In F. Nicolin and O. Poggeter (Eds.), *Hegel-Studien.* Band 11. Bonn: Bouvier Verlag Herbert Grundman, 1976.

_____. *Jews and German Philosophy.* New York: Schocken Books, 1984.

Runyan, W. M. *Life Histories and Psychobiography.* New York: Oxford University Press, 1984.

Russell, B. "Philosophy and Politics." In W. Ebenstein, (Ed.), *Political Thought.* 2nd ed. New York: Holt, Reinhart & Winston, 1960.

Rychlak, J. F. *Discovering Free Will and Personal Responsibility.* New York: Oxford University Press, 1979.

Sa'adia Ga'on. *Emunot Vedeot.* Jerusalem: Mosad Harav Kook, 1970. (Hebrew)

Samuel, M. *The Professor and the Fossil.* New York: Alfred A. Knopf, 1956.

Sarbin. S. R., "Schizophrenic Thinking: A Role-Theoretical Analysis." *Journal of Personality* 37: 190–209, 1969.

Sarbin, T. R., and Adler, N. "Self-Reconstitution Processes: A Preliminary Report." *The Psychoanalytic Review* 57(4), 1970–71.

Sarbin, T. R., Taft, R., and Bailey, D. E. *Clinical Inference and Cognitive Theory.* New York: Holt, Reinhart and Winston, 1960.

Sartre, J. P. *Critique de la Raison Dialectique.* Paris: Gallimard, 1960.

_____. *Nausea.* Middlesex, England: Penguin Books, 1980.

Schafer, R. *The Analytic Attitude.* New York: Basic Books, 1983.

Schimmel, H. C. *The Oral Law.* New York: Feldheim Publishers, 1971.

Scholem, G. *Major Trends in Jewish Mysticism.* New York: Schocken Books, 1941.

_____. The Messianic Idea in Judaism. New York: Schocken Books, 1972.

_____. *Kabbalah.* Jerusalem: Keter, 1974.

_____. *Hakabala shel Sefer Hetemura Veshel Avraham Abulafia.* Jerusalem: Akademon, 1979. (Hebrew)

Schweid, E. "Herman Cohen Kemefaresh Hamikra." *Daat* 10:93-122, 1983.

Scott, M. B., and Lyman, S. M. "Accounts." *American Sociological Review* 33(1): 46–62, 1968.

Sever, M. *Michlol Hamamarim Vehapitgamim.* Vol. 1. Jerusalem: Mosad Harav Kook, 1961. (Hebrew)

Sheleff, L. *Generations Apart.* New York: McGraw-Hill, 1981.

Sheridan, A. *Michel Foucault: The Will to Truth.* London: Tavistock Publications, 1982.

Shoham, S. G. *The Tantalus Ratio.* Tel Aviv: Gome, 1977. (Hebrew)

Sholem Aleichem. *Adventures of Mottel the Cantor's Son.* New York: Collier-Macmillan, 1972.

Shpiegel, S. "Meagadot Haakeda." *Sefer Hayovel le A. Marks.* New York: The Jewish Theological Seminary, 1950. (Hebrew)

Smith, J. E. *Reason and God.* New Haven: Yale University Press, 1968.

Smooha, S. *Israel: Pluralism and Conflict*. London: Routledge & Kegan Paul, 1975.

Snow, D. A., and Phillips, C. L. "The Lofland-Stark Conversion Model: A Critical Reassessment." *Social Problems* 27(4): 430–447, 1980.

Soloveitchick, J. B. *Halakhic Man*. Philadelphia: Jewish Publication Society, 1983.

Soybelman, A. Y. *Sipurey Zadikim Hechadash*. Pieterkov, 1913. (Hebrew)

Spence, D. E. *Narrative Truth and Historical Truth*. New York: W. W. Norton, 1982.

Spero, M. "The Use of Folklore as a Developmental Phenomenon in Nouveau-Orthodox Religions." *The American Journal of Psychoanalysis* 42(2): 149–158, 1982.

Spiro, M. E. *Kibbutz Venture in Utopia*. New York: Schocken, 1971.

Steiner, G. *The Death of Tragedy*. New York: Alfred A. Knopf, 1961.

Stern, E. S. "The Mother's Homicidal Wishes to Her Child." *J. Mental Science* 94: 324–325, 1948.

Stewart, K. "Dream Theory in Malaya." In C. Tart (Ed.), *Altered States of Consciousness*. New York: Wiley, 1969.

Strack, H. L. *Introduction to the Talmud and Midrash*. New York: Temple, 1969.

Stratton, G. M. "Vision without Conversion of the Retinal Image." *Psychological Review* 4: 341–360, 1897.

Sulloway, F. J. *Freud Biologist of the Mind*. New York: Basic Books, 1983.

Sykes, G. M., and Matza, D. "Techniques of Neutralization." *American Sociological Review* 22: 667–669, 1957.

Tashma, I. "Hilcheta Kebatrai." In M. Elon (Ed.), *Shnaton Hamishpat Haivri*. Vol. 6-7, Jerusalem, 1979. (Hebrew)

Teshima, I. *Light of Life: Judaism and Makuya*. Los Angeles: Makuya, 1981.

Theunissen, M. *The Other*. Cambridge: MIT Press, 1984.

Thomas, W. I. *The Child in America*. New York: Knopf, 1928.

Tishby, I. *The Doctrine of Evil and the Kelippah in Lurianic Kabbalism*. Jerusalem: Akademon, 1975.

Todorov, T. *Symbolism and Interpretation*. Ithaca: Cornell University Press, 1982.

Toynbee, A. *A Study of History*. 8 vols. London: Oxford University Press, 1934.

Trachtenberg, J. *The Devil and the Jews*. Philadelphia: Jewish Publication Society, 1984.

Trilling, L. *Sincerity and Authenticity*. Cambridge: Harvard University Press, 1972.

Turkle, S. *Psychoanalytic Politics*. London: Burnett Books, 1978.

Turner, V. "Body, Brain and Culture." *Zygon* 18(3): 221–245, 1983.

Ullman, C. "Cognitive and Emotional Antecedents of Religious Conversion." *Journal of Personality and Social Psychology* 43(1): 183–192, 1982.

Velikovsky, I. *Oedipus and Akhnaton*. New York: Doubleday, 1960.

Vernon, T. S. "The Laius Complex." *The Humanist* 32: 27–28, 1972.

Vital, H. *Mevo Shearim,* Krakow: 1882. (Hebrew)

———. *Etz Chayim*. Jerusalem: Levy, 1890. (Hebrew)

von Wright, G. H. *Causality and Determinism*. New York: Columbia University Press, 1974.

Watzlawick, P., Weakland, J. H., and R. Fisch. *Change*. Tel Aviv: Hapoalim, 1982. (Hebrew)

Waxman, C. I. *America's Jews in Transition*. Philadelphia: Temple University Press, 1983.

Weber, M. *Ancient Judaism*. New York: Free Press, 1967.

Weil, G. *Teshuvat Harambam Bishelat Haketz HaKatzuv Lechayim.* Tel Aviv: Papyrus, Tel Aviv University, 1979.

Weiss, J. G. *Studies in Braslav Hassidism.* Jerusalem: Bialik Institute, 1974. (Hebrew)

Weiss-Rosmarin, T. *Judaism and Christianity: The Differences.* New York: Jonathan David Pub., 1972.

Wellisch, E. *Isaac and Oedipus.* London: Routledge & Kegan Paul, 1954.

Wieder, N. *The Judean Scrolls and Karaism.* London: East and West Library, 1962.

Wiener, A. *The Prophet Elijah in the Development of Judaism.* London: Routledge & Kegan Paul, 1978.

Yaker, H. M. "The Schizophrenic Perception of Time." In H. M. Yaker, H. Osmond, and F. Cheek (Eds.), *The Future of Time.* New York: Andor Books, 1972.

Yehuda, A. S. "Zigmund Freud al Moshe Vetorato." In *Ever Vearav.* New York: Shulzinger Brothers, 1946. (Hebrew)

Yerushalmi, Y. H. *Zakhor.* Seattle: Washington University Press, 1982.

Zangwill, I. *The Melting Pot.* New York: Macmillan, 1909.

Zborowski, M., and Herzog, E. *Life Is with People.* New York: International Universities Press, 1952.

Zunz, Y. L. *Haderashot Beyisrael.* Jerusalem: Bialik, 1974.

Index

absolutism, and despotism, 79
absurd man, in existentialism, 179
Achi-Meir, Abba, 68
adultery, 55-56
affective bonds, in linear conversion, 158
aging: Cabalic interpretation, 183; cross-cultural studies, 181-182; and fitness, 173; future as, 181-184; hedonism and, 180; Talmudic views, 183-184; temporal dialogue, 188
Akeda complex, 104
Aleichem, Sholem, 177-178
alienation, and aging, 181
Allen, Woody, 177
alphabet, Hebrew, 13
Alter, Robert, 140
amnesia, 52
anthropology, kibbutz study, 120
antipsychiatry, 45; Oedipalism, 44; and "straight psychiatry," 46
anxiety, of "influence," 44
apocalyptic beliefs, 75
Archaism, and Zionism, 79
Aristotle, 29-30
Art of Biblical Narrative, The (Alter, 140
assassination, 68
attribution theory, in social psychology, 1
Augustine, Saint, 75
Aviad, Janet, 154

Bauman, Zygmunt, 29
beatniks, 153
behavior: cross-cultural interpretation, 38; explaining vs. retraining, 26; "sociocultural" impacts, 73
being: Aristotelian theory, 30; and nothingness, 144-145
Beit Hamidrash, 5, 6

beliefs: in "archetypical heritages," 73; in philosophy of history, 73
Berger, Peter, 106
Berne, Eric, 198
Beyond the Melting Pot (Glazer and Moynihan), 118
Bible: Midrashic pluralism in, 11; myth vs. epic, 113
biographic interpretation, 3
biographic rehabilitation: "clean leap" approach, 49; deviance and, 50; and historical objectivity, 61-62; Midrash and, 49-71; "scientific-objective" method, 63; social reinforcement and temporal "contraction," 65-69; and story telling, 60-61; of "stubborn and rebellious son," 18-19; and useful history, 62-64
Black Muslims, 153
brain function: neurologic observations, 126-127; "snapping" phenomenon, 129-130; spatial and temporal, 126-127; survival systems, 134-135
brainwashing, 30, 130
Buber, Martin, 75
Buddhism, 151, 153

cabalic contraction dynamics, 9-10
cabalic-mystic idealism, 9
cabalic theodicy, of divine contraction, 135
cabalism, 136; and hermeneutic pluralism, 137
Camus, Albert, 179
cannibalistic legends, 103
castration complex, 96
Catholic Pentacostalism, 155
celebrities, psychiobiographies of, 168
child abuse, 96; "Isaac complex," 103
child psychology, 198-199
children, filicidal pressures, 96

child-sacrifice, 104
Christianity, and hermeneutic mission-
    arism, 32
Chosen, The (Mann), 100
chutzpah, 7, 10; "cumulative" prin-
    ciple, 86; "pipulistic," 113-117
chutzpah therapy: futurism and, 193-
    200; Kookian model of, 195-200;
    temporal dialogue as, 188-201
coercion, free will and, 196-197
cognitive attribution theory, and psy-
    chotherapy, 164
coitus, "witnessing," 36-37
collective injustice, vs. individual sin,
    114
collective sin, Golden Calf, 59-60
compassion, sternness and, 9, 14
conflict, and self-renewal, 76
concentration camps, 180
contraction dynamics, 9-10
conversion: dialectic-linear, 159-160;
    linear conceptions and progress, 153-
    154; religious, 153; research meth-
    ods, 150; root meanings, 152; social/
    psychological studies, 149-150. *See
    also* linear conversion
cosmic cyclism, 82-83; Midrashic inter-
    pretation, 82
cosmic rejuvenation, 76-77
counter culture, 108; psychedelic, 128;
    Zen Buddhist cults, 153
cults: teshuvah, 157; Zen Buddhist, 153
cyclical history, self-renewal in, 82
cyclism: cosmic vs. historic, 82; and
    re-biographing, 85-89
cyclistic history, 76-77
cyclistic teshuva: empirical differentia-
    tion, 149-171; linear conversion vs.,
    149-171; roots of accounting, 154-
    156 •

David, King, 55-56
Dayan, Moshe, 169
death penalty, 17-18
death-rebirth: analogies, 39-40; conflict-
    growth theory, 80, 84, 89

Death of Tragedy, The (Steiner),
    176
deconstruction, hermeneutic, 43-44
deculturation, aging and, 181
democracy, and philosophy of history,
    75-78
deprogramming, 130
depth hermeneutics, 39, 40
derush, Midrashic interpretation, 6
descriptive myth, vs. reflective epic,
    113
despotism, absolutism and, 79
determinism, vs. free will, 191
deviance, drastic interhomispheric
    shifting and, 128-134
deviant past, neutralization vs. ac-
    counting for, 162-164
de Voragine, Jacobus, 97
dialectic narrativism, original sin in,
    35-46
dialectic psychotherapy: constructed vs.
    reconstructive, 27; Karaite interpre-
    tation in, 37-38; narrative "mission-
    arism" in, 24-48
dialecticism, 19; hermeneutic, 28; tra-
    ditional models of, 94
dialectic tension, 105
dialogical growth, Isaac model, 103-108
dialogicalism, 3
dialogic chutzpah, 116
dialogic equilibrium, between matter
    and spirit, 142-144
dialogic narrativism, "seventy faces"
    model, 140-141
dialogic progress, pilpulistic chutzpah
    as, 113-117
dialogue, in narrative psychotherapy,
    28
Dialogue with Deviance (Rotenberg),
    21
Dickinson, Emily, 168
differential association, in yeshiva and
    kibbutz, 158
disengagement, aging and, 181
double messages, in Midrastic narra-
    tivism, 11-12

dreams: causal analysis, 81; Freudian interpretation, 35-36; Gestalt analysis, 107; interpretation of, 188; memories and, 188; psychodramatic, 189
drinking and eating habits, 15
drug addiction, 198
drunkenness, 15, 18
dynamic dialecticism, 94

early childhood, Oedipal guilt in, 36
eating, and drinking habits, 15
ecstatic prayers, 137
Eisenstadt, S. N., 119-120
Eliade, Mircea, 82
Elijah factor, psychology of, 181
encircling mind, 138
encounter groups, 108
Erickson, Milton, 166
eschatology, apocalyptic vs. prophetic, 75
evil, neo-Platonic concept, 135
exclusion, Mark's interpretive formula, 32
ex-convicts: conversion studies, 155; returning as reversed causality paradigm, 156-158; in yeshiva and kibbutz, 158-162
existential hedonism, and mystic writing of future, 178-181
existentialism, 2; absurd man in, 179
Exodus, Midrashic narrative, 50-51

Fachler, Michal, 131
fairy tales, 27
faith, in magic, 129
federal witnesses, protection program, 51
fertility, and creation, 145
fitness, aging and, 173
Flavius, Josephus, 16
form, Hasidic usage, 138
fossilized Oedipalism, and psychological growth, 78-82
Frankl, Viktor, 49, 179
free choice: and psychotherapy, 3; Midrashic interpretation, 3

freedom, moral and intellectual, 10
free will, Midrashic system of, 192
Freud, Sigmund, 4, 24, 80; on mystic writing-pad, 185-186; Oedipal complex, 95
Freud and Philosophy (Ricoer), 24
fruit-plant analogy, of death-rebirth, 39, 44
fundamentalism, 19
future: dictating, 184-186; existential hedonism and, 178-181; mystic writing of, 178-181; as "oldness," 181-184; past and, 172-187; psychodramatization of, 189-191; reading and writing of, 184-186; re-biographing possibility, 179
futurism: finite vs. infinite, 82-85; and Kookian model of chutzpah therapy, 195-200; and psychology of self-renewal, 82-85; psychotherapeutic, 86
futurist psychotherapy, 49

Ganesha, 38
genealogy, 93
genocide, psychological theories, 78-79
gerontology, 174; temporal dialogue, 188
Gestalt therapy, 107
Golden Calf, collective sin, 59-60
Golden Legend (de Voragine), 97-98
Gregory, Pope, 100
guilt, see Oedipal guilt

Ha'am, Achad, 193
haggadah, Midrashic interpretation, 174
Hakohen, Rabbi, 138
Haley, Alex, 118
Handelman, Suzan, 140, 142
Hasidic cabalism, 51, 134-137
Hasidism: rational vs. emotional women, 131-133; rational vs. irrational thought, 138; rituals, 146-147; Talmudic influence, 147
hedonism: and mystic writing of future, 178-181; existential, 178-181

Hegel, G. W. F., 39, 76
Hegelian-Marxist philosophy, 75
Hegel's aufheben, 28
hermeneutic psychology, *see* narrative psychology
hermeneutics, 1; Aristotelian and biblical origins, 29; construction and deconstruction, 43; dialecticism, 28; dialogue and interhemispheric balance, 125-148; Freudian theory, 30; Hasidic-cabalic contraction theory, 134-137; historical approach, 25; of Karaism, 29-34; of narrative "missionarism," 29-34; pluralism and interhemispheric balance, 137-140; pluralistic and fundamentalistic systems, 3; as "subjective" experience, 25
Hermeneutics and Social Sciences (Bauman), 29
holocaust, survival therapy, 198-200
historical objectivity, biographic rehabilitation, and, 61-62
history: contradictions of, 62; man and, 73; psychological theories, 78. *See also* philosophy of history
homecoming, conversion as, 154-155
humorous rereading, of past failures, 174-178
hypnotic therapy, 166

idealism, and realism, 9
ideas, of history, 73
identification, and sublimation, 105
idol worship, 56-57
immigration, dialectic-missionary phase, 119
imperialism, missionary, 31-32
incest, 54-55, 97-100; Midrashic interpretation, 100
infanticide, Midrashic interpretation, 104
infinite cyclism, and Midrashic rebiographing, 85-89
infinity: historical concepts, 83; Jewish conception of, 84; in psychological terms, 84

inner mind, 138
intelligence, wisdom vs., 135-136
interhemispheric balance: drastic shifting and deviance, 128-134; ergotropic and trophotropic systems, 127; Hasidic-cabalic contraction theory, 134-137; hermeneutic dialogue and, 125-148; hermeneutic pluralism and, 137-140; neurologic problem, 126-128
intuition, and rationality, 138-139
Isaac paradox, as dialogical growth model, 103-108
Isaac solution, Oedipal conflict and, 93-110
insight: self-blaming, 39-43; therapy, 40-41
interpretation, Aristotelian theory, 29-30
intimidation, by psychoanalyst, 37
Israel, future redemption of, 13

James, William, 40
Jewish history: vs. memory, 85; schools of interpretation, 13-14
Jewish humor, 177
Jewish psychology, 4-5
Joshua: Jewish legend, 98-99; vs. Oedipus and Judas Iscariot, 95-102
Judah, Rabbi, 16
Judaism, 4-5; ahistorical infinitism of, 83-84; derationalization of, 78-79; fossilized conception, 51, 111-112; messianic idea in, 75, 191; national revival of, 79
Judas Iscariot: Christian legend, 97-98; Joshua vs. Oedipus and, 95-102
Jung, C. G., 81

karaism: in dialectic psychotherapy, 28; vs. fundamentalism, 33; hermeneutics of, 29-34
karaite sect, 14
karma, 151
Keats, John, 45
kibbutz: anthropological study, 120; defined, 117; early development, 122;

[kibbutz]
ex-convicts in, 158-162; vs. "mizug" and material progress, 117-123; semi-collective type, 120, 122
Kock, Rabbi, 195
Kookian model of chutzpah therapy, 195-200

Lacan, Jacques, 45
Laius complex, 96
Landa, Rabbi, 178
Leavy, Stanley, 165
Levi-Strauss, Claude, 62, 102
life events, narrative forms for, 26-27
linear conversion: vs. cyclistic teshuvah, 149-171; emperical differentiation, 149-171
linguistics, and socialization, 139
living, Midrashic interpretation, 1-23
logotherapy, 179
love: and compassion, 136; inability to, 17
loving, and teaching, 137

magic, faith in, 129
Maimonides, Moses, 15, 191
man: archaic vs. historic, 82; and history, 73
manic-depressive psychosis, 198
Mann, Thomas, 100
Mao Tse-tung, 97
Marxism, 75
mass media, 27
material progress, 111; kibbutz vs. "mizug," 117-123
matter: Hasidic usage, 138; and spirit, 142-144
Mead, G. H., 157, 163
mechanistic-physical trauma, 165
meditation, rituals and, 134
melody analogy, in philosophy of history, 74
memory: confrontation vs. interpretation, 85; Jewish conception of, 85
Menashe, King, 57-59
mental-cognitive trauma, 165

Messianism: and infinite cyclism, 86; psychoteleology of, 191-195; repentance and, 193; restorative and utopian ideas of, 75, 195; Talmudic interpretation, 194
metahermeneutic code, 1; defined, 26
metahermeneutics, dialectic vs. dialogic, 28
Midrash: Aknai Oven, 7-8; and biographic rehabilitation, 49-71; and Halacha, 9; phenomenological meaning, 5; as psychological code, 13; "women's lib," 13
Midrashic interpretation, 1-23; conflict systems, 11-12; "double bind" theory, 13; dynamic power of psychology, 67; hermeneutics, 117, 125; narrative as dialogue in time, 50-52; past and future dialogue, 172-187; re-biographing, 85-89; "stubborn and rebellious son," 14-19
Midrashic pluralism, 4-14; as dialogic system, 19; ethical-moral issues, 9; Halachic interpretation, 5; "schizoid" world of, 11
Milton, John, 45
missionarism: christian, 118; defined, 31; narrative, 24-48
missionary imperialism, 31-32
mizug: defined, 117; vs. kibbutz and material progress, 117-123
morals, genealogical study of, 31
Moreno, J. L., 189, 192
Moses, Oedipalization of, 101
Moses and Monotheism (Freud), 80
multiple choice, hermeneutic code, 11
mystic rituals, 136, 137
mystic writing, of future, 178-181
mystic writing-pad, 185-186
Myth of the Eternal Return (Eliade), 82
myths, sociocultural meaning, 104

Nachman, Rabbi, 138, 146
narcissism, 105
narration, in psychology, 28
narrative insight therapy, 41-42

narrative "missionarism": in dialectic psychotherapy, 24-98; "missionarism" hermeneutics of, 29-34
narrative psychoanalysis, social reinforcement in, 65
narrative psychology, 28; controversy over, 151; "historiosophical" codes, 74-75
nepotism, 55
Neusner, Jacob, 193
neutralization: vs. accounting for deviant past, 162-164; "psychopathic," 163
"newspeak," 32-33
Nietzsche, Freidrich, 31
1984 (Orwell), 32
"non-melting pot," 111-124
nothingness, being and, 144-145
nursing homes, 108

Oedipal conflict: deconstruction and construction, 43-46; dialogic vs. dialectic concepts, 94-95; Gregory legend, 100; Hegelian concept, 106; Hegelian-Darwinian dialectics, 93-94; and Isaac solution, 93-110; Joshua vs. Judas Iscariot, 94-102; Marxian concept, 93-94; patricide vs. filicide, 96; Pawnee Indian myth, 102; thesis vs. antithesis, 93
Oedipal guilt: in dialectic psychotherapy, 27; Freudian interpretation, 35-36; fundamentalistic interpretation, 4; "original sin" and, 3
Oedipalism: and philosophy of history, 81; and psychological growth, 78-82
Oedipus: complex, 95; myth, 26
oldness: future as, 181-184; spirituality and, 182; temporal dialogue, 188. See also aging
open-mindedness, 138
oral law, 142
oral Torah, 9
original sin in dialectic narrativism, 35-46; Freudian interpretation, 35-36;

[original sin in dialectic narrativism] and Oedipal guilt, 3; psychoanalytic theory, 4
Orwell, George, 32

Palestine: colonization of, 121; Zionist conception, 118
parental authority, 16, 18
parent-child conflict, 96
parents: "neurotic" or "psychotic," 46; symbolic killing of, 27
past: and future, 172-187; hermetic, 68, 175; Jewish treatment, 51; possibility of correcting, 49; rational approach to, 174. See also sinful past
past failures: humorous rereading of, 174-178; Talmudic interpretation, 175
patricidal hermeneutics, 44
patricide: psychoanalytic concept, 80-81; in psychological theories, 78-79
perception, psychic apparatus of, 186
Perls, Fritz, 107
personal history, 83
personal myth, psychoanalytic treatment, 38
pharaoh killing, and Oedipus legend, 99
Philo, Judaeus, 17
philological rearrangement, of sinful past, 53-54
philosophy: Jewish, 52; logical realism, 9
philosophy of history, 72-92; and collective behavior, 78; Hegelian concepts, 76-77; tyranny and democracy, 75-78
Phoenix analogy, 39
pilpul, defined, 115
pilpulistic chutzpah, as dialogic progress, 113-117
platonic ideas, 3
pleasure principle, 108, 112
pluralism: hermeneutic, 137-140; and interhemispheric balance, 137-140
pluralistic narrativism, Midrash as metacode for, 4-6

poetry, "god father" in, 44-45
political rehabilitation, 50
poverty: "double message" of, 12; Midrashic interpretation, 6
praying, ritual, 137
pregnant boy, Pawnee Indian myth, 102
progress: conflict-based motion of, 76; dialogic, 113-117; spiritual vs. material, 111
prophetic eschatology, 75
prophetic revelation, 10
psychiatry: "straight," 46; subversive hermeneutic, 45
psychoanalysis: anti-self-renewal concepts, 81; Christianity and, 30; Freudian theory, 24, 80; narrative approach, 27; repressed guilt in, 106; totemic patricide in, 80-81; writing and speech in, 185
psychobiography, linear basis in, 168-169
psychodrama, 189-191
psychological change, Jewish self-renewal and, 79
psychological growth, fossilized Oedipalism and, 78-82
psychology: behavioral and psychodynamic theories, 73; narrative trend in, 26, 28; of self-renewal, 72-92
psychopathy, biblical conception, 14
psychoteleology, of Messianism, 191-195
psychotherapy, 1; cognitive attribution theory, 164; dialectic, 24-48; linear and cyclistic approaches, 164-168; Freudian influenced, 81; futurist, 49; Jewish self-renewal and, 79; Midrashic pluralism in, 19
punishment, biblical modes, 113

rabbi, Midrashic interpretation, 34
rational mind, 138
reading, of future, 184-186
re-biographing: and dialect psychotherapy, 24-48; hermeneutic dialogue and interhemispheric balance, 125-148;
[re-biographing]
infinite cyclism and, 85-89; linear conversion vs. cyclistic teshuva, 149-171; Midrashic dialogue between past and future, 172-187; Midrashic interpretation, 1-23; Midrash and rehabilitation, 49-71; narrative "missionarism," 24-48; "non-melting pot" patterns, 111-124; Oedipal guilt and Isaac solution, 93-110; and philosophy of history, 72-92; and psychology of self-renewal, 72-92; sinful past, 52-60; temporal dialogue as chutzpah theray, 188-201
rebirth, self-blaming "insight" as prerequisite for, 39-43
reciprocal individualism, 192
redemption, "utopian" conception of, 200
redundancy, 2
reframing, 2
Reich, Wilhelm, 168
religion: existentialist, 2; propagation of, 26; sociology of, 2
religious myths, 27
repentance: among Hasidic women, 131-133; Midrash and, 52, 67; rational vs. emotional, 131-133; and self-renewal, 86, 87; Talmudic interpretation, 87-88. See also teshuva
resistance: breaking initial, 42; in psychoanalysis, 37
restoration, hermeneutic, 43
returning: dialogic-cyclistic, 159-160; as reversed causality paradigm, 156-158
Reuben, incestuous sin of, 54-55
Ricoeur, Paul, 24
ritual prayers, 137
rituals: and meditation, 134; and memory, 85
root metaphors, 27
roots, searching for, 93
Roots (Haley), 118
Rosh Hashona, 8
Runyan, William, 168
Russell, Bertrand, 79
Rychlak, Joseph, 192

Sa'adia, Rabbi, 142
salvation, cabalistic concept, 136-137
Sartre, Jean-Paul, 60
"schizoanalysis," 45-46
schizophrenia, 45, 129; and amnesia, 52
script analysis, 198
secret teachings, 11
seduction, 57-59
self-blaming "insight," as prerequisite for "rebirth," 39-43
self-destruction, 39
self-knowledge, 25
self-loathing, 41
self-negation, and conflict, 77
self-renewal: genocide and, 79; Jewish concepts, 83-84; Jewish psychological concept of, 80; Midrashic system, 67; in Midrashic literature, 6; psychology of, 72-92
sex-aggression: infantile modes of, 40-41; in narrative "missionarism," 38
sexual dysfunction, "neurotic," 37
sexual intercourse, 15
shammai, 11
shtetl: material progress in, 120-121; kibbutz vs., 121-122
sinful past: "closed book" approach, 61, 63; Hasidic interpretation, 64; hermetic vs. hermeneutic approach, 64; re-biographing, 52-60
sinners, "rebiographing," 20
slapstick humor, 177
slavery, and torture, 191-192
social change: conflict-based metaphor, 78; cyclistic, linear and dialectic concepts, 76-77; strategies for, 76
social control, 31-32
socialization: causal-linear paradigm, 150; linguistics and, 139; Midrashic, 13
social progress, Oedipal conflict and, 101-102
social psychology, attribution theory, 1
social reinforcement, of biographic recounting and temporal "contraction," 65-69

sociology: and hermeneutic dialecticism, 28; Israeli immigration, 119
Solomon, King, 56-57
Soloveitchick, Rabbi, 52, 157
Spark-lifting rituals, 136, 137, 145
Spero, M. H., 167
sphinx, riddle of, 32
spiral self-renewal, 83, 89
spirit, matter and, 142-144
spiritual progress, 111; dialogic chutzpah and, 116; Freudian theory of instincts, 112
stealing, 18
Steiner, George, 176
sternness, and compassion, 9, 14, 135
story telling: biographic rehabilitation and, 60-61; Hasidic models, 66
"stubborn and rebellious son": Midrashic reinterpretation, 14-19; psychological implications, 17; Talmudic interpretation, 14-18
students, determinism of, 180
Sturm und drang, 40
sublimation: Freudian concept, 80, 105; identification and, 105
substitution, Aristotelian dialectic, 30
subversive hermeneutic psychiatry, 45
survival, and past failures, 176-177
suspicion, hermeneutics as tactic of, 43
symbolic legends, 146
symbols, in messianism, 192
synagogues, 5, 6

Talmud, 5-6; dialogic interpretation, 141; learning style, 111, 114; legal system, 8-9; "oral" connotation, 34; philosophy of history, 72
Talmudism: Hasidic influence, 146-147; and hermeneutic pluralism, 137
teaching, loving and, 137
teleology, defined, 192
telic psychotherapy, 81
temporal "contraction," social reinforcement of, 65-69
tension: dialectical, 105; psychological models, 95, 103

teshuva: conversion studies, 153; cyclistic differentiatio, 149-171; and philosophy of history, 86-88; rational and emotional styles, 131-133; rebiographing sinful past, 52-60; and roots of cyclistic accounting, 154-156; among women, 131-133
thought reform, 130
tikun: dialogic principle of, 138; rearranging and paradox, 144-148; and spiritual progress, 116
time: Augustinian conception, 185; circular and linear conceptions, 19; dialectic and dialogic perceptions, 159; "historical," 73; Midrashic narrative as dialogue in, 50-52; in Midrashic pluralism, 11
Torah, 4-5; "double messages" in, 12; mystic vs. rational interpretation, 143; myth vs. epic thought, 113; as pluralistic process, 140-141; "seventy faces" model, 140-141; written and oral, 9
totality, Sartre's concept of, 94
Toynbee, A. J., 79
tragedy, 176
transcendentalism, 3, 129
transference: manipulation during, 37; working through, 42
trauma: defined, 165; physical vs. mental, 165; in psychobiography, 168-169
Trial, The (Achi-Meir), 68
Trilling, Lionel, 24
Trobiand islanders, 107

tyranny, and philosophy of history, 75-78

Unheard Cry for Meaning, The (Frankl), 179
useful history, biographic rehabilitation and, 62-64
usury, 178-179
Utopian Flight from Unhappiness, The (Kalin), 112
utopian messianism, 75, 86

Varieties of Religious Experience (James), 40

war, and self-destruction, 77
Waxman, Chaim, 118
Weber, Max, 194
Weberian sociology, 2
whitewashing, of deviant past, 163
wisdom, vs. intelligence, 135-136
wish-fulfillments, meaning of, 36
"wishful thinking," 39
wolf-man case, 36
women: rational vs. emotional, 131-133; repentance styles, 131-133
writing, of future, 184-186

yeshiva, 117; ex-convicts in, 158-162
Yochanan, Rabbi, 111
Yom Kippur, 8
youth, adult hostility to, 96, 103

Zen Buddhism, 153
Zionism, collective farms, 117
Zionist actualization style, 111-112